Health Learning Center

Department of Nursing Development
251 E. Huron
Chicago, IL 60611

NM **Northwestern Memorial Hospital**

Enhancing Autonomy in Long-Term Care

Lucia M. Gamroth, RN, PhD, is Associate Director of the Benedictine Institute for Long Term Care in Mt. Angel, Oregon, and Assistant Professor in the School of Nursing, Oregon Health Sciences University. She served as Project Director for the National Consensus Conference on Enhancing Autonomy for Residents in Long Term Care held in September 1993. She is a former Administrator at the Benedictine Nursing Center. Dr. Gamroth holds the MPA from Portland State University and the PhD from Oregon Health Sciences University. She has published and presented widely on quality of care and ethical issues in long-term care and serves as consultant to a number of long-term care organizations.

Joyce Semradek, RN, PhD, is Director of the Benedictine Institute for Long Term Care and Professor Emeritus at the Oregon Health Sciences University School of Nursing. She holds the master's degree in nursing from Yale University. Ms. Semradek has directed a number of large-scale research and demonstration projects involving interdisciplinary and interorganizational collaboration and she was co-investigator on a recent 3-year project to facilitate restraint reduction in long-term care facilities in Oregon. Ms. Semradek has published on a variety of issues in practice-based research.

Elizabeth M. Tornquist, MA, teaches scientific writing in the School of Nursing and School of Public Health, University of North Carolina at Chapel Hill. She has a master's degree in English from the University of Chicago and is an editor and former journalist. Ms. Tornquist has authored numerous articles on scientific and technical writing and has edited a series of volumes on the utilization of research in nursing practice.

ENHANCING AUTONOMY
IN LONG-TERM CARE

Concepts and Strategies

Lucia M. Gamroth, RN, PhD

Joyce Semradek, RN, MSN

Elizabeth M. Tornquist, MA

Editors

Benedictine Institute for Long-Term Care

Springer Publishing Company

Springer Publishing Company, Inc.
536 Broadway
New York, NY 10012

97 98 99 / 5 4 3 2

Library of Congress Cataloging-in-Publication Data

Enhancing autonomy in long-term care / Lucia M. Gamroth, Joyce
   Semradek, Elizabeth M. Tornquist, editors.
      p.   cm.
   Includes bibliographical references and index.
   ISBN 0-8261-8680-7
   1. Aged—Long-term care—Moral and ethical aspects.
2. Autonomy (Psychology) in old age.   I. Gamroth, Lucia M.
II. Semradek, Joyce A.   III. Tornquist, Elizabeth M., 1933–
RC954.3.E54 1994
362.1/6—dc20   94-35281
                                                          CIP

Printed in the United States of America

Contents

v

Part II Strategies for Enhancing Autonomy

Foreword

Fear of nursing homes is universal among the elderly. Older people often speak of entering a nursing home as a situation worse than death, that is, "I'd rather die than end my life in a nursing home." Yet, the same people who so forcefully reject nursing home placement are often well aware of their infirmities, recognize their inability to live alone, and want very much not to be a burden to their families. Nevertheless, despite such realistic appraisals, older people and their families are unable to overcome their perception that entry to a nursing home inevitably results in almost total loss of autonomy over all aspects of a person's everyday life.

This volume is an important milestone for several reasons. First is the publication of ground-breaking papers that focus attention on factors affecting nursing home resident autonomy. The eminence of the authors and their international perspective underscore the cross-national nature of concerns about autonomy. Many chapters also place in perspective how far the United States has lagged behind other countries in maximizing autonomy in long-term care settings.

Perhaps the most important contribution of this volume is the second section, which spotlights the surprisingly large number of models that have been used in other countries to enhance resident autonomy. These models will go a long way toward expanding the repertoire of strategies available to practitioners and administrators in long-term care settings. The models should also help to dispel the myth of the inevitable link between long-term care and loss of autonomy. Greater concern for resident autonomy should improve our practice. It should also relieve some of the anguish experienced by increasing numbers of older persons as they anticipate their own need for nursing home services.

Mathy Mezey, EdD, FAAN

Contributors

Robert M. Arnold, is Associate Professor of Medicine and Psychiatry at the University of Pittsburgh School of Medicine. He holds an MD from the University of Missouri, Kansas City, and has been a Robert Wood Johnson Clinical Scholar at the University of Pennsylvania. He is Associate Director for Education of the University of Pittsburgh Center for Medical Ethics. His numerous publications focus on ethical issues in health care and particularly patient autonomy. He is co-author, with Charles Lidz and Lynn Fischer, of *The Erosion of Autonomy in Long Term Care.*

Barry Barkan is the founder and director of the Live Oak Institute and CEO of Regenerative Health Systems, Inc., which operates the Live Oak Living Center at Greenridge Heights, California. His work has focused on de-institutionalizing the long-term care environment by creating communities that empower the elderly and provide them meaning and connection. Mr. Barkan holds a bachelor of arts from Goddard College. He has served as a consultant in health care planning, management, and program development to numerous organizations and has spoken widely on development of autonomy for residents and staff in long term care.

Cornelia Beck, is Professor and Associate Dean for Research and Evaluation at the College of Nursing, and Associate Professor in the Department of Psychiatry and Behavioral Sciences, College of Medicine, University of Arkansas for Medical Sciences. She holds the PhD in Nursing from Texas Women's University and is currently conducting research on reducing disruptive behaviors in demented elderly, funded by the National Institute on Aging, and improving distressing behavior in cognitively impaired elderly, funded by the National Institute for Nursing Research. She has published widely on the care of the cognitively impaired elderly.

Stanley J. Brody, is Professor Emeritus of Physical Medicine and Rehabilitation in Psychiatry at the University of Pennsylvania School of Medicine. He is also Professor Emeritus of Health Care Systems in the Wharton School of Finance and Commerce, a former Professor in the School of Social Work, Chairperson Emeritus of the graduate program in Social Gerontology, and Director of the Research and Training Center for Rehabilitation of Elderly Disabled Individuals at the University of Pennsylvania. Professor Brody holds a law degree as well as a master's in social work. He has chaired the Gerontological Health Section of the American Public Health Association and was a member of the Institute of Medicine's Committees on Aging and Geriatric Medical Education and on the National Research Agenda on Aging.

Kenneth Brummel-Smith, is Associate Professor of Medicine and Family Medicine, Oregon Health Sciences University, and Director, Geriatric Evaluation and Management Program, Portland Veterans' Affairs Medical Center. He holds the MD degree from the University of Southern California. Dr. Brummel-Smith has written a text on geriatric rehabilitation and has conducted extensive research in this area; he has also published on falls among the elderly and health needs of Hispanic elderly. Dr. Brummel-Smith chaired the Consensus Panel of the National Conference on Enhancing Autonomy for Residents in Long Term Care held in September 1993.

Bart J. Collopy, is Associate for Ethical Studies at the Third Age Gerontological Center and Associate Professor in the Humanities Division, Fordham University. He holds the PhD from Yale University. Dr. Collopy serves on a number of long-term care ethics committees and has worked on various projects with the Commission on Ethics of the American Association of Homes and Services for the Aging. He writes and lectures extensively on ethical issues in long-term care of the elderly.

Pam Hayle is co-director of the Lazarus Project, a pilot program of Project Public Life, and director of the Therapeutic Programs Department at Augustana Home, Minneapolis, Minnesota.

Brian F. Hofland, is vice president of The Retirement Research Foundation, the largest private foundation in the country focusing entirely on aging. He holds the PhD in Human Development and Family Studies from Pennsylvania State University. At the Foundation, Dr. Hofland develops funding projects to respond to cutting-edge issues in aging. He is particularly well-known for a unique 5-year Foundation project on "Personal Autonomy in Long Term Care," which emphasized ethical and legal issues in autonomy and decision making for elderly with disabilities. Dr. Hofland has published widely on the topics of older adult intellectual functioning, gerontological programming, and ethical issues in long-term care.

Robert L. Kane, is a Professor and former Dean of the School of Public Health of the University of Minnesota. He currently holds the Minnesota Chair in Long Term Care and Aging at the Institute for Health Services Research in the School of Public Health, and is also Professor in the School of Medicine. Dr. Kane received his MD degree from Harvard Medical School and has done extensive research on quality and cost effectiveness issues in care of the elderly. He has published numerous articles and books and is widely known for his work on long-term care.

Rosalie Kane, is Professor in the Institute for Health Services Research, School of Public Health, and Professor in the School of Social Work of the University of Minnesota. She is also Director of the University's Long Term Care Decisions Resource Center and Faculty Associate at the Center for Biomedical Ethics. Dr. Kane holds a doctorate in social work from the University of Utah. She is currently conducting research on the effects of introducing assessment of values and preferences in long-term care, funded by the Retirement Research Foundation. Dr. Kane is widely known for her work on legal and ethical issues in long-term care.

Nancy Kari is Director of Faculty Development and Associate Professor in Occupational Therapy at the College of St. Catherine, St. Paul, Minnesota. She holds a master's degree in public health.

Ms. Kari works closely with Project Public Life, a theory building and grassroots civic education project based at the Humphrey Institute of Public Affairs at the University of Minnesota. In her work with Project Public Life, Ms. Kari co-directs the Lazarus Project, a pilot program that focuses on issues of governance in a nursing home.

Mary Lavelle is a Senior Research Assistant at the Benedictine Institute for Long Term Care and served as Nursing Home Network Coordinator of the Benedictine Institute's 3-year Restraint Reduction Project. Ms. Lavelle holds a master's degree in nursing from Oregon Health Sciences University School of Nursing. She has extensive experience in rehabilitation in both acute and long-term care.

Charles W. Lidz, is Professor of Psychiatry and Sociology in the School of Medicine, the University of Pittsburgh, and Associate Director of the University's Center for Medical Ethics. He holds the PhD in Sociology from Harvard University and has published widely on ethical issues in medical care, including coercion, informed consent, and factors in commitment decisions. Dr. Lidz's publications also include books and articles on autonomy in long-term care and the structure of nursing homes. He is co-author, with Lynn Fischer and Robert Arnold, of *The Erosion of Autonomy in Long Term Care.*

Darlene McKenzie, is Associate Professor at the Oregon Health Sciences University School of Nursing. She holds a PhD in Urban and Public Affairs from Portland State University and has had extensive experience in developing measures of functional status for long-term care residents and in working with governmental agencies on issues of policy and practice. She was coinvestigator on a recent 3-year project to facilitate restraint reduction in Oregon nursing homes.

Peg Michels is co-director of the Lazarus Project, a pilot program of Project Public Life, and director of training at the Center for Citizenship and Democracy, Humphrey Institute of Public Affairs, University of Minnesota.

Joanne Rader is a Clinical Research Fellow at the Benedictine Institute for Long Term Care and Associate Professor at the Oregon Health Sciences University School of Nursing. She holds a master's degree in nursing from Oregon Health Sciences University. She was Project Director for a 3-year grant from the Robert Wood Johnson Foundation (1991–1993) to develop a model for changing practice related to the use of physical restraints and psychoactive medications in nursing in Oregon homes. Ms. Rader has had numerous articles published addressing behavioral symptoms of the cognitively impaired such as wandering, aggression, and on individualizing care for persons with dementia. She presents frequently at conferences.

G. Janet Tulloch has been a resident of the Washington House in Washington, DC, since 1967. She notes that as a child with cerebral palsy, she always failed English because her graphite pencils kept breaking: the ball-point pen had not yet been invented, and typewriters were not given to children. Nevertheless, she became a writer and has published two books: *Happy Issue My Handicap and the Church,* and *A Home Is Not a Home,* as well as articles for the *Washingtonian Magazine,* the *Washington Post,* and *Generations.* She has been on the board of the National Citizen's Coalition for Nursing Home Reform for nine years, working on advocacy projects.

Ulla Turremark is Director of the Gråberget Nursing Home in Gothenburg, Sweden, which is widely known for its philosophy of respect and individual care and a physical environment that centers on residents' desires and tastes. Gråberget is affiliated with the Institute for Long Term Medicine and Geriatrics at Gothenburg University. Ms. Turremark holds a baccalaureate in health care administration, psychology administration, and nursing from Gothenburg University. She has spoken widely on quality of life in long-term care.

Theresa Vogelpohl is a Research Project Coordinator at the College of Nursing, University of Arkansas for Medical Sciences. She holds a Master of Nursing Science from the University of Arkansas for Medical Sciences and is a gerontological clinical nurse specialist. She is currently coordinating a study on reducing disruptive behaviors in demented elderly, funded by the National Institute on Aging, with Dr. Cornelia Beck as principal investigator.

Lis Wagner is a public health nurse and Research Fellow at the Institute of Social Medicine, the University of Copenhagen, Denmark. A former director of a nursing home, she directed several projects in recent years in which nursing homes were transformed into private housing for residents and health care centers for entire rural communities. She holds a Doctor of Public Health degree from Portland State University School of Public Health and serves as consultant to municipalities on projects in primary health care, aging, self-care and health promotion among the elderly.

Keren Brown Wilson, is President of Concepts in Community Living, Inc., in Portland, and Sterling Management Company in Wichita, which specialize in the development and management of assisted living projects. She is also Associate Professor at the Institute on Aging of Portland State University and holds a PhD degree. She designed, developed, and managed Oregon's first assisted living facility and in part as a result of her work, Oregon is considered a national leader in assisted living. She serves on the Board of the Assisted Living Facilities Association of America and is President of Oregon's Assisted Living Facilities Association. She is a past President of The Oregon Gerontological Association and past Treasurer of The American Society in Aging.

Introduction: Setting the Stage for Change

Lucia Gamroth

The most pressing issue in long-term care today—apart from how to pay for care—is how to create an individualized, resident-centered model of care in institutional settings, such as nursing homes and residential care facilities. There is general agreement that some long-term care residents can and should be agents of their own care, but there is uncertainty about other residents' ability to function in this way. This uncertainty stems from a lack of clarity about the way and degree to which physical and cognitive disability influences autonomy. Even when residents are able to function independently, the role of professional and nonprofessional care givers, the structure and financing of the long-term care system, the legal system and the regulatory system may interfere.

The literature to date on autonomy in long-term care has focused on conceptual issues and the complexity of decision making related to resident characteristics, interactions between staff and family and institutional barriers. There are few articles that report interventions to increase resident autonomy and self-determination.

In September 1993, the Benedictine Institute for Long Term Care, in cooperation with the Benedictine Nursing Center and the Oregon Health Sciences University School of Nursing, convened a Consensus Conference to establish guidelines for program and policy development that systematically address the current barriers to autonomy of residents in long-term care facilities. Long-term care facilities were considered to include nursing homes, residential care, and assisted living facilities that are large enough to have certain components, such as congregate meals, organized activities, routinized care, or other factors that may constrain autonomy.

The specific objectives of the conference were the following: (a) to reach a common understanding of what autonomy and self-determination mean for residents; (b) to identify the factors that facilitate and hinder residents' self-determination and autonomy; (c) to identify strategies to overcoming barriers to self-determination and autonomy; (d) to determine what structural, economic, practice, and policy changes are required to institute a model of care that enhances resident autonomy and self-determination; and (e) to formulate a research agenda for long-term care that addresses changes in practice designed to enhance autonomy and self-determination of residents. This volume is a collection of papers from the conference, and represents some of the best thinking to date on the subject.

In the first chapter, Bart Collopy explores the many facets of autonomy and the dilemmas inherent in its application to practice settings. In the next chapter Brian Hofland provides an overview of the research that has been conducted on autonomy and the lessons learned from that research, and makes suggestions for further work. Resident characteristics in and of themselves may not limit a resident's capability for autonomous living but they may influence the level or kind of autonomy that a resident exerts. Kenneth Brummel-Smith discusses physical disabilities and Cornelia Beck discusses cognitive disabilities and their effects on the decision-making capacity of long-term care residents. Sometimes it is not disability itself, but staff and family perceptions of disability that influence a resident's ability to exert autonomy. Janet Tulloch describes her experience of living with disability, others' perceptions of her disability, and nursing home policies and procedures that inhibit or support autonomy. Charles Lidz addresses the limitations of institutions and compares the approach to individual needs and preferences in two different long-term care environments.

Although individual, staff, and facility characteristics influence a resident's ability to live autonomously, the systems of regulating and financing long-term care facilities further complicate the issues of autonomous living. Rosalie Kane examines the ways in which regulations help and hinder autonomy, and makes suggestions for change. Robert Kane discusses the structure of the Medicaid system, the financing of long-term care, and the limitations of the current reimbursement system.

The concluding chapters focus on models and strategies for care in the United States and in other countries that are designed to enhance resident autonomy. Keren Wilson describes the philosophy and values that serve as the foundation for assisted living. Lis Wagner has implemented a model in Denmark in which a nursing home was converted into a community health center serving the health needs of an entire rural community on a 24-hour basis. Ulla Turremark, administrator of the Gråberget Nursing Home in Sweden, has transformed a medically oriented rehabilitation facility into a home-like environment, the core of which is individualized care. Barry Barkan describes a regenerative community in which self-esteem and connection to others are fostered. Nan Kari describes the Lazarus Project, a program that encourages residents to become involved in the activities and decisions that affect their daily lives in the nursing home. Joanne Rader describes the Oregon Restraint Reduction Project, which has developed a collaborative model involving consumers, providers, and regulators for the development of new practice guidelines.

The 12-member Consensus Panel represented residents, family members, professional and nonprofessional providers, regulators, and payers. The panel was convened at the end of the conference to formulate responses to the following questions:

1. What are the factors that hinder autonomy and self-determination of residents in long-term care facilities?
2. What are the characteristics of models in the U.S. and abroad that facilitate autonomy and self-determination of residents in long-term care facilities?
3. What are the constraints to instituting a model of care that supports resident autonomy and self-determination?
4. What changes in policy and practice are required to enhance resident autonomy?
5. What are the priorities for future research to enhance resident autonomy and self-determination?

The panel's responses provided the basis for the final Consensus Statement, which appears in the Appendix.

The most important aspect of the conference from which the book was derived was its collaborative nature. It brought together the people who provide and receive the care, the families and other advocates of quality care, and those who write and interpret policy around the provision of care. Too often the efforts of these groups take place in isolation from one another. Consequently, proposed standards of quality are sometimes unrealistic for the population currently residing in institutions, or the best approaches to enhancing autonomy never get to the right people—the residents and staff who can make a difference in care for the future. The strengths of this conference, and we hope this book, lay in its connections to practice and the everyday reality of residents, and in the change in attitudes and approaches it inspired from a diverse group of participants.

We see three primary outcomes from the conference and from this book: (1) enhanced autonomy for persons living within long-term care institutional settings; (2) change in the way that staff relate to the needs of residents; and (3) a series of demonstration projects to test and evaluate the recommendations made. The hope of the editors is that this volume will encourage readers to question the way they have always done things or the way they have interpreted or failed to challenge regulations that do not support resident life. We hope it will inspire creative thinking, encourage residents and providers to try new approaches, and to think in new ways. When that happens, environments will emerge that support meaningful living for residents in nursing homes.

Acknowledgments

This volume is the result of contributions of many diverse groups of individuals. As noted in the Introduction, participants were strategically invited to represent differing perspectives on the issues of resident autonomy. A special thanks to Carol Lindeman, Dean of the Oregon Health Sciences University School of Nursing and President of the National League for Nursing, for facilitating the consensus development process. Her skill and good humor kept the presentations on time and provided focus and involvement from all participants.

Because of the diversity of the participants and the tireless efforts of the consensus panel, the consensus statement reflects the connections between research, practice, and the everyday reality of residents. Members of the panel included Jackie Coombs, resident, Meredith Cote, Ombudsperson, Maggie Donius, Gerontological Clinical Specialist, Walt Friesen, family member, Steven Helgerson, Health Care Financing Administration, Region X, Lana Huiras, Certified Nursing Assistant, Darlene McKenzie, Associate Professor, Maurice Reece, Administrator, Marion Sodergren, Director of Nursing, Carter Catlett Williams, Social Work Consultant on Aging, and James Wilson, Senior and Disabled Services Division, State of Oregon. The panel was chaired by Kenneth Brummel-Smith, MD, whose leadership and time was invaluable in writing and presenting the statement for feedback from the conference participants.

Thanks are due Luanne Crawford-Richey, conference coordinator and her assistant, Gloria Garcia for their painstaking efforts at conference arrangements and materials and arranging for all the last-minute requests of the participants. Luanne coordinated the preparation and editing of all the manuscripts for publication. Mary Lavelle and Catherine VanSon provided assistance to the staff and participants during the conference.

The planning advisory committee met numerous times to advise staff on the content and organization of the conference. The planning committee members included Kenneth Brummel-Smith, Leonard Cain, Joyce Colling, Maggie Donius, Bev Hoeffer, John Hogan, Joanne Rader, Shirley Saries, Vicki Schmall, Joyce Semradek, and Joy Smith. In addition to committee meetings, Bev Hoeffer, Shirley Saries, and Vicki Schmall facilitated the panel work groups at the conference.

And, finally, and most importantly, the Meyer Memorial Trust and the Collins Foundation of Portland, Oregon, provided the financial support that made this conference possible. Without the help of these two foundations, the work of the conference and this publication would not have been possible.

Part I

Factors Affecting Resident Autonomy

Chapter One

Power, Paternalism, and the Ambiguities of Autonomy

Bart J. Collopy

For the last 20 years, the autonomy of patients has been a central concept in biomedical ethics and a driving force behind an ever-lengthening list of changes in health care practice. The primacy of autonomy does not, however, stir unalloyed enthusiasm on the part of ethicists and health care practitioners. Some do, indeed, see autonomy as a kind of conceptual adrenaline, a value that has effectively awakened health care from the long doze of medical paternalism. Others view autonomy as a value gone hyperactive, a rallying cry for narrow individualism, for a consumer ethic that sees patients and care providers as strangers warily circling each other. Between these polar views are wide stretches of ambivalence, where autonomy is clearly seen as an elemental right of the individual, but one that, too single-mindedly pursued, can work against communal values and wall us off within our various combative self-interests.

Rather than argue that any one of these evaluations is the single correct one, I want to suggest that all of them offer defensible and illuminating readings of autonomy. By its very nature autonomy is a highly "geological" concept, marked by multiple layers of meaning, ideological deposits from varied sources, and all sorts of sub-surface tensions and slidings. On the legal and statutory surfaces of health care, autonomy may come down to a signed consent form or advance directive; however, in its conceptual and empirical reaches, autonomy stirs a complex mix of moral perceptions and values—a flow of contradictory, sometimes combustible viewpoints and commitments.

Defining Autonomy

This complexity shows itself quickly enough even on the level of definition (Christman, 1989; Dworkin, 1988). The primary etymological meaning of autonomy is "self-rule," but in common discourse the term conveys a multitude of connected and overlapping notions: liberty of thought and action; the inviolability of the self; the freedom of individuals to choose from among a plurality of beliefs and values; and the right to be singular, idiosyncratic, even eccentric, and to live on one's own moral recognizance.

As its working synonym, "self-determination," implies, autonomy focuses our attention on the ideal of moral agents free from coercion, control, and interference; and the ideal of individuals making *their own* lives, for better or worse—and doing so, even when frail, disabled, sick, debilitated, or dying. We cannot proceed very far along the path of "*self*-rule" or "*self*-determination," however, without coming on the rule and determinations of others. The individual moral agent lives among a multitude of potential facilitators and cooperators, coercers, and coopters. However intensely autonomy makes us focus on self-rule, it also brings us face to face with the encircling agency of others. An individual's choice or action occurs in a context swarming with others who are also choosing and acting, who shape the universe of possibilities and outcomes, who *powerfully* shape it. Thus, thinking about autonomy leads us to reflect on questions of power as well as the others who can support or suppress autonomy, and bring it resources or restraints.

Autonomy: Political and Marketplace Models

The link between questions of autonomy and questions of power is obvious in the way contemporary bioethical discussion of autonomy traces one of its main lines of descent from political theory and practice—where the individual's autonomy must be protected against the collective will of the state or the dominant culture

(Young, 1986). A classical locus for the discussion has been John Stuart Mill's (1977) unswerving rejection of state or cultural paternalism:

> The only purpose for which power can be rightly exercised over any member of a civilized community, against his will, is to prevent harm to others. His own good, either physical or moral, is not a sufficient warrant. (p. 223)

Mill defends the autonomy of the lone individual against the power of the larger collective, specifically against the power of the beneficent collective that would intrude on individuals for their own good. Mill's focus on *beneficence* and *power* identifies the twin entry points where political models of autonomy are relevant to health care. The power of the health care system is not unlike the power of the state. It easily encloses and envelops the individual, and creates a professional and institutional culture that sets its own powerful, frequently unreflective, expectations about human values and choices. Thus, like the state, the health care system has to be made sensitive to the claims of personal autonomy. Political understandings of autonomy are not, however, the only ones that echo into health care. Marketplace notions of autonomy also add an adversarial element to the patient–care provider relationship. To the extent that health care involves a marketplace exchange, patients are customers, and providers are an industry selling goods and services. Within this framework, *caveat emptor,* "buyer beware," becomes a primary rule for patients who want to pursue their own goals, set their own outcomes, and follow their own values. They cannot assume that their goals, values, and desired outcomes are the same as those of providers.

As in any marketplace, then, customer choice and decision making must be protected against the power of a controlling industry. Moreover, in the arena of long-term care, protection of the consumer and regulation of the provider must be pursued with special urgency because care reaches into the most private and essential precincts of life, and because the "consumer" is often a frail and dependent elder, more vulnerable and resourceless than any customer eyeing a used-car sticker or the repair bill for a quirky transmission.

Questions of collective power and individual autonomy in the health care arena are not the same as those in the state or the marketplace, but there are clear resemblances, echoes, or common resonances. Indeed one ethicist Nancy Dubler (1992) has suggested that the pursuit of bioethical issues inevitably leads us to widen our definition of who is "vulnerable" in our society. She suggests that every one of us entering the health care system becomes vulnerable before a larger power. The system she says, is too intimidating, distant, and foreign to give the average patient or family member a fair chance at understanding options and affecting medical outcomes.

If bioethics has the task of drawing out the adversarial dimensions of autonomy, however, it also has the task of asking how political and economic assumptions can distort the issue of autonomy. Is it true, for example, that patients and care providers are moral strangers dealing with each other from behind barricades of unshared goals and values (McCullough & Wear, 1985)? Are providers so instinctively paternalistic that they cannot see their own stake in the autonomy of patients (Whitbeck, 1985)? In what sense are long-term care residents certainly *not* customers or consumers? In what sense is long-term care not simply an industry offering goods or services? How can the theoretical discussion and practical advancement of residents' autonomy be kept free of unwarranted adversarial bite?

Power and Paternalism

In bioethics much of the critique of medical power has focused on its paternalistic forms (Childress, 1982; Sartorius, 1983). This critique was historically pivotal, given the challenges that had to be mounted against the persistent forms of paternalism embedded in health care practice. With the success of many of these challenges, however, might it be possible now to hold the line firmly against paternalism and yet give more sympathetic attention to the moral ambiguities of care providers who feel paternalism as a distinctly *moral* pull, a concern about the good of patients?

To put the question another way, is it time for bioethics to explore more fully the ways that respecting patients' autonomy can leave providers with some sharp moral ambiguities? What does it mean, for example, when providers respect a patient's autonomy and yet find themselves morally torn, because from their vantage point the patient's choice seems mistaken, unwise, damaging, destructive, even tragic?

Ambiguities of Autonomy

To examine the pull of this ambiguity, it might be helpful to leave the context of contemporary health care for a moment and recall how ancient is the view that autonomy is itself deeply problematic, that it generates moral dark as well as light. A text of Sophocles or the early chapters of Genesis serve as quick enough reminders here. Recalling Genesis, we know that for the *full* human story to be told, the garden of primal beauty and bliss must be lost. Otherwise the tale of Eden would not be our human tale. Similarly, we know there *must* be a great hero brought out on stage in the last act, his eyes bloody in self-inflicted blindness because of what he has chosen to hear and not hear, what he has chosen to do and not do. In short, the history of autonomy is not a story of unabated good, of unbroken wisdom and fulfillment, of human potential realized stunningly and steadfastly. We know from our personal experience and from the common experience of humankind that autonomy means we can choose against ourselves, against our well-being, against our best interests. Freedom is morally ironic. Being free, we can make risky choices, self-limiting and self-diminishing choices, destructive, even tragic choices.

And *these* choices, above all others, are the testing ground for autonomy. If our autonomy is respected only when we choose and behave well, wisely, rightly, responsibly, prudently, and productively—then how do we know it is our autonomy that is being respected and not simply the will of the collective that we replicate obediently in our lives? If only "compliant" autonomy is respected, have we yet gotten to the heart of the matter? Would real respect for autonomy be strong enough to permit and protect the outlier, the one who pulls against the current, who cuts against the grain, who veers from our common and concerted wisdom?

But *then*, respecting autonomy does not always bring providers into the bright light of moral certitude and comfort. Instead, they will often feel moral qualm and reluctance. And the reluctance might not be the product of paternalism or providers' fierce fix on their own values and interests. It may come from a real commitment to patients' interests, a valuing of their freedom, an accompanying realization that autonomous patients make harmful choices, that allowing freedom means dealing with the wreckage of these choices, bearing the dark side of patients' autonomy.

In this interpretation, ambivalence about autonomy can stem from moral sensibility, from a recognition that autonomy is a value fraught with ambiguities. Thus, the task of conceptualizing autonomy means playing out its ambiguities, challenging overly neat and one-sided definitions of autonomy. This is a particularly crucial task for long-term care because it must struggle with definitions of autonomy imported from acute care, ones that suit the hospital, but do not fit the nursing home or home care agency.

Atomistic and Rationalistic Descriptions of Autonomy

In acute care, autonomy is often described in atomistic and rationalistic fashion. The autonomous patient is depicted as a resolutely individualistic, self-contained, singular self, an independent agent who makes decisions by carefully weighing benefits and burdens in the light of consistent, well-defined values and goals. Within this model, autonomy requires that the decision maker be protected against all "intervening others" who could be potentially coercive or controlling.

The problem with this model of autonomy is that it is especially out of touch with long-term care, where decision making often occurs in the context of family relationships and shared decision making that is supportive, autonomy enhancing, and deeply valued by the elderly person (Agich, 1990, 1993). In addition, a highly rationalistic model of autonomy does not reflect the nonlinear, trial-and-error cluttered way we muddle out our autonomy in practice. Thus, in facing progressive frailty any one of us might recalculate our interests and goals, and renegotiate the debt of disability we are willing or unwilling to bear. I might, for example, opt for immediate autonomy over long-term autonomy in one area of life rather than another. Thus, I might choose to live in my apartment with a minimum level of formal care, even though this will leave me increasingly immobile and isolated. My care providers, concerned about my shrinking options and even greater loss of self-determination in the future, may find this unreasonable. And our resulting conflict will revolve around different notions of autonomy—their concern for its many dimensions and its long-term prospects, my concern simply to be, for the present, autonomous about where and how privately I live.

The rationalistic model of autonomy poorly fits long-term care for another reason. It tends to find the normative expression of autonomy in decisions about medical treatment. Although such decisions may map out much of acute care, they provide a limited picture of long-term care, in which the "everyday ethics" of autonomy often revolves around the basic, constantly repeated, semiautomatic activities of daily life (Kane & Caplan, 1990). These activities do not present the kind of discrete, clearly bound "decisional events" that define medical decision making. They are not well suited to an "informed consent" exchange between providers and residents, but require various sorts of negotiation and accommodation, a recognition that autonomy can be embedded in the daily rhythms of lifestyle; in the eccentricities of personality; in the habitual schedules, logistics, and relational patterns of an individual's life (Collopy, Dubler, & Zuckerman, 1990; Moody, 1988).

Because long-term care constantly deals with these other dimensions of autonomy, it must recognize self-determination that flows from an individual's affective metabolism, and expresses itself not in atomistic decision making, but through intensive sharing and interchange with family members and care providers. The principle of respect for autonomy should warn care providers not to submerge the elderly individual in the family, not to make the family the primary arbiter of an elderly person's care and lifestyle (Blustein, 1993). But the principle also calls for recognizing the complex ways in which individuals compose their autonomy from their relationships.

Autonomous Doing/Autonomous Deciding

In long-term care, atomistic definitions of autonomy can be especially misleading because they stress self-assertiveness and self-sufficiency, the ability to *carry out* decisions as well as to make them. This leads to a definition of autonomy that prizes independence and sees autonomy in the active capacities with which it bristles. Here autonomy is "autonomy of execution," the ability to implement, act on, and operationalize one's choices.

Autonomy, however, can also be defined on the level of "decisional autonomy," where self-determination consists in the capacity to make decisions, to have personal preferences and values, *even though* one might not be able to act on them independently or accomplish them without assistance (Collopy, 1988). Thus, the elderly in long-term care are often intellectually and volitionally autonomous but unable to carry out this autonomy in independent fashion. For them it is crucial that autonomy be defined in terms of the ability to choose and decide, in terms of autonomy's bedrock: the presence of personal goals, and purposes and values.

If autonomy is recognized only when the individual can carry out these purposes, many of the elderly will be seen as nonautonomous, even though they are still *decisionally* autonomous. Thus, the nursing home resident who cannot dress herself may be granted little voice about when she is dressed, or how, or by whom. Because she cannot dress herself, because she cannot independently carry out her inner autonomy, her care providers may never wait to hear what she wants to wear on a particular day—what dress, or shoes, or underwear even.

These are not small decisions when they are taken from us. In fact, as the range of our independent doing shrinks, the inner ability to decide may become increasingly important to us. Loss of executional ability may only make it more imperative that we preserve our decisional autonomy.

Autonomy, Reasonableness, and Authenticity

Often this decisional autonomy will have to face the test of competency or "reasonableness." This is especially true when the elderly make decisions that run against the judgments of family members, their care providers, the institutional aspects of the health care system, or the culture at large. The test of reasonableness, however, should not use as its measure the reasonableness of care providers or family members or the so-called person in the street.

To be reasonable, the choices of the elderly should coherently reflect *their own* values, goals, and expectations. So understood, reasonableness is tied closely to the notion of authenticity. Authentic choice or behavior reflects the moral history, past character, and persistent values of a person. Conversely, inauthentic decisions and behavior are those that are seriously out of character—discontinuous with the individual's personal history and values.

Imagine, for example, two residents who have all but stopped eating. One, a long time resident in the home, has grown progressively weaker, removed, and noncommunicative. She is neither hostile nor confused, simply distanced, disconnected, more and more internalized. Her daughter encourages her to eat, even raises the prospect of tube feeding. But the woman responds, "No need, no need." She tells her daughter that she feels her death is at hand, that she does not want to prolong things. "It's not worth the struggle. But don't worry. I'm willing to face the end." Her daughter grieves over what is happening, but she feels that this decision clearly bespeaks her mother. She decides that she will not agree to tube feeding.

But another resident's refusal to eat might be far from authentic; it might stem from depression rooted in her fierce resentment at nursing home placement. This woman's daughter might rightly feel that the refusal to eat is not authentic, that her mother must be fed, if need be by tube, until she is once again her true self.

In both of these cases, the issue of authenticity provides crucial personal context, directs attention beyond the abstract *reasonableness* of a decision to the personal reasons for the decision, the way it reflects the logic and cohesiveness of an individual's life. Authenticity might add to the complexities of autonomy, but it adds a complexity that can help care providers sift true from dubious autonomy.

Responding to Autonomy: Noninterference Versus Enhancement

Respect for autonomy is often defined in terms of *not interfering* with a patient's choice or behavior. This is a particularly crucial definition in long-term care. It provides a first line of defense for autonomy, challenging the assumption that care of the frail elderly means constant and aggressive intervention, surrogate action and decision making at every turn. As a first response to the autonomy of the frail elderly, "do not interfere" checks the instinct to intervene. It highlights the likelihood that any one of us who becomes elderly and frail might want our caregivers to keep their distance, might want them to follow *our* lead, to recognize that we still have authority over our lives—our medical care, our pain, our willingness to take risks, to be socially odd, to live eccentrically, and so on.

Although the principle of noninterference is a first line of defense for autonomy, it is not a full-fledged response to the intricacies of autonomy. In fact, defining respect for autonomy mainly in negative terms can have an erosive effect on the caregiving relationship. It can suggest that autonomy calls on care providers *only* to step back, *only* to leave the elderly alone. At its worst this view can produce a kind of "hands-off" approach that would let the elderly stew in their rights, that would simply let them sit in whatever harm they choose, whatever lessening of their lives they seem bent on pursuing.

But negative rights, rights against interference, ought to be counterbalanced by the positive rights that are so crucial to autonomy, rights that oblige others not to leave us alone but to step forward with assistance, to provide resources, to offer instrumental means to our ends.

Thus, in terms of current issues, the Patient Self-Determination Act defends a patient's negative right to refuse treatment. If advance directives are to be effective, however, many of the elderly will need a positive, enhancing, empowering response from care providers who supply information, clarify options, explain what treatment or nontreatment will mean. If they are to tell others when finally not to interfere, many elderly will need a good deal of intermediate assistance in thinking about end-of-life care, formulating directives, and discussing their wishes with surrogates who might pull back from such talk. They may even need assistance in broaching this topic with their physicians. In short, noninterference in this area might leave many elderly with an information packet about advance directive but no real help in shaping truly autonomous decisions about end-of-life care.

Who Should Be Conceptualizing About Autonomy?

I want to end by asking some *strategic* questions about autonomy as a concept. Who should be conceptualizing about autonomy in long-term care? To put it more bluntly and politically, who should be setting the conceptual agenda here? Is most of the conceptualizing about autonomy now carried on by advocates, researchers, bioethicists, even regulators? Are care providers unduly passive in this area? As a result, do they find that some (a good deal of?) thinking about autonomy is wide of the mark—too abstract and academic, too unrealistic and unaware of the complexities of providing care? Does some of the dominant conceptualizing about autonomy encourage an overly adversarial stance toward providers?

My response to these last four questions is a worried "yes." The discussion of autonomy in long-term care—in fact, the public, policy-level discussion of most ethical issues—has been shaped primarily by the ethicists, researchers, and others mentioned earlier, with care providers left in a reactive, frequently defensive position. The implication of this for the future of long-term care is disheartening. It suggests a continuing adversarial climate around ethical issues, a situation in which providers will be largely managed by regulation when it comes to the moral dimensions of care. This will restrict the moral discretion of providers, dismiss their moral insights, and fail to engage their moral passions.

Faced with such a grim prospect, care providers should not leave it to others to shape thinking about autonomy, while they struggle to translate this thinking into practice—or worse, struggle against this thinking as an unwanted and unwarranted intrusion into health care practice. A reactive and protectionist strategy of this sort is not liable to work. The conceptual agenda will inevitably shape the agendas of practice, legislation, regulation, even funding. Conceptualizing about autonomy is no "merely" philosophical enterprise, then. It is a pivotal task for providers. In the end, the autonomy agenda is not only about the self-determination of the elderly. It is also very much about the moral agency, the autonomy, of care providers.

References

Agich, G. J. (1990). Reassessing autonomy in long-term care. *Hastings Center Report, 20,* 12–17.

Agich, G. J. (1993). *Autonomy and long-term care.* New York: Oxford University Press.

Blustein, J. (1993). The family in medical decisionmaking. *Hastings Center Report, 23,* 6–13.

Childress, J. (1982). *Who should decide? Paternalism in health care.* New York: Oxford University Press.

Christman, J. (Ed.). (1989). *The inner citadel: Essays on individual autonomy.* New York: Oxford University Press.

Collopy, B. J. (1988). Autonomy in long term care: Some crucial distinctions. *The Gerontologist, 28*(Suppl.), 10–17.

Collopy, B., Dubler, N., & Zuckerman, C. (1990). The ethics of home care: Autonomy and accommodation. *Hastings Center Report, 20*(Suppl.), 1–16.

Dubler, N. N. (1992). *Ethics on call.* New York: Harmony Books.

Dworkin, G. (1988). *The theory and practice of autonomy.* New York: Cambridge University Press.

Kane, R. A., & Caplan, A. L. (Eds.). (1990). *Everyday ethics: Resolving dilemmas in nursing home life.* New York: Springer.

McCullough, L., & Wear, S. (1985). Respect for autonomy and medical paternalism reconsidered. *Theoretical Medicine, 6,* 295–308.

Mill, J. S. (1977). *On liberty. Collected works of John Stuart Mill* (Vol. 18). Toronto: University of Toronto Press.

Moody, H. R. (1988). From informed consent to negotiated consent. *The Gerontologist, 28*(Suppl.), 64–70.

Sartorius, R. (Ed.). (1983). *Paternalism.* Minneapolis: University of Minnesota Press.

Whitbeck, C. (1985). Why the attention to paternalism in medical ethics? *Journal of Health Care Politics, Policy, and Law, 10,* 181–187.

Young, R. (1986). *Personal autonomy: Beyond negative and positive liberty.* New York: St. Martin's Press.

Chapter Two

Resident Autonomy in Long-Term Care: Paradoxes and Challenges

Brian F. Hofland

P ersonal autonomy is a central value of our society. In long-term care institutions, professionals influence the exercise of autonomy by older adults who have physical or cognitive disabilities (Hofland, 1990). Autonomy can be either enhanced or diminished through professional practices and actions. Although most professionals would agree that older residents are entitled to maximum possible self-determination and dignity, they all too easily can begin or hasten an erosion of personal autonomy for these residents. The following brief case examples illustrate these points.

Mrs. A., a 93-year-old widow, is moving from a one-bedroom senior-building apartment to a nearby nursing home because of increasing frailty. When she initially moved into the senior building from her home of 58 years, it was difficult to choose which pieces of furniture to keep and which to give to her five children. Mrs. A. realizes that she will once again have to downsize her belongings drastically; she chooses a cherished dresser that she and her late husband bought shortly after they were married, an easy chair, and a wall-hung wooden case in which she displays a variety of mementos, souvenirs, and small gifts collected over the years. She is dismayed when the nursing home's administrative staff informs her children that strict rules will allow her only to bring the easy chair. "The move is bad enough," says Mrs. A., "but to give up all my treasures—my life is over."

Mrs. S., an 87-year-old cognitively intact woman residing in a nursing home, needs assistance getting dressed in the morning. At first the nursing assistant allows Mrs. S. to choose what she wants to put on each morning, but in the rush to get through her heavy workload, the assistant finds it easier and quicker simply to pull some items from Mrs. S.'s closet and put them on her. Although a seemingly small matter, in Mrs. S.'s severely constrained world she has lost control over an important dimension of choice that allows her to define and communicate who she is.

Mrs. D., a widow, has lived at the Valley View nursing home for several years and is largely confined to a wheelchair. Mr. E., a widower who can no longer live independently, has recently become a resident. They sit next to each other at dinner and strike up a lively conversation, finding that they have many common interests. Both are lonely and have few visitors, and soon they begin to spend much time together. They are often seen in the hallways, Mr. E. pushing Mrs. D.'s wheelchair, or sitting together chatting quietly. One day, a nursing assistant discovers the two in Mrs. D.'s bed, caressing, with Mrs. D. partially unclothed. The director of nursing is informed, and she confronts the two, saying, "I won't allow this kind of behavior in my nursing home!" Mr. E. retorts angrily, "Who put you in charge of our sex lives?"

Why Is Autonomy in Long-Term Care Important?

Autonomy is one of several competing values in long-term care; others include justice (including, but not limited to, issues of resource allocation), beneficence (doing good), and nonmaleficence (doing no harm). Autonomy is an important (though overlooked) value in long-term care institutions, but it is not a supreme value that trumps all others.

If autonomy is not a supreme value in long-term care, but one of several competing values, why single it out for special attention and discourse, and the development of strategies and guidelines for practitioners to overcome barriers to it? The answer to that question comes from several perspectives.

From a legal perspective, autonomy in long-term care is important because of basic civil rights issues. The due-process and equal-rights protections of institutionalized older adults are often compromised and violated in the policies, procedures, and low goals of long-term care institutions. As with so many other vulnerable groups whose civil rights have been violated, the violation has usually occurred in the name of protection for individuals deemed to be biologically inferior. Younger adults with disabilities, flush from their victory with the Americans with Disabilities Act, now look with dismay at the paternalistic and restrictive nature of facilities and programs designed for older adults. Indeed, Thomasma (1985, p. 225) maintains that "the next great civil rights issue in the United States may well be that of persons in long term care." The limited autonomy goals for impaired elders held by society, professionals, and the elderly themselves should become the focal point for the same powerful analysis that brought about such remarkable changes in the law and social understanding for other groups such as African Americans, women, the disabled, and the mentally retarded. Just as we now are shocked at the way mentally retarded individuals were treated 30 years ago and at the low goals for them, so 30 years from now will we be shocked at today's low goals for and treatment of older adults with disabilities in residential facilities.

From the perspective of medical ethics, patient autonomy has been emphasized recently in the form of informed consent, but the dominant framework of moral responsibility within the Hippocratic tradition remains the beneficence model. The physician promotes and protects the best interests of the patient by seeking the greater balance of good over harm in treatment and care. In an acute care setting, problems are usually well defined, making reliable assessment of the benefits and burdens of various therapies relatively straightforward. This is less true of a long-term care setting. Because the basic ills of chronic care clients are not curable, what is in their best interests is less clear than in acute settings. Choices are murkier and more subjective, and often they depend on differing values. For example, a care plan would be constructed differently for an older resident who has difficulty walking if she placed a priority on security and not falling than if she valued maintaining independence. There is no objective standard for weighting the good of security more heavily than the good of maintaining independence. The client's preferences are centrally important.

From a psychosocial perspective, a body of research focusing on autonomy among institutionalized older adults, often under the rubrics of "control," "iatrogenic dependency," and "learned helplessness," has shown an impressive convergence of findings, despite a variety of measures and conditions. The enhancement of autonomy and control has positive effects on the emotional, physical, and behavioral well-being of nursing home residents. The benefits of often simple interventions include increased happiness and alertness, greater time spent in social activities, improved health, and even decreased mortality. In reviewing the research on control and aging, Rowe and Kahn (1987, p. 146) concluded that "the extent to which autonomy and control are encouraged or denied may be a major determinant of whether aging is usual or successful on a number of physiologic and behavioral dimensions." It is also significant that surveys of nursing home residents themselves (Kane, Caplan, Freeman, Aroskar, & Urv-Wong, 1990a; National Citizens Coalition for Nursing Home Reform, 1985) identified respect from staff for resident independence and the ability to make choices as key issues.

Autonomy Paradoxes

Given the importance of respect for autonomy in long-term care institutions, the enhancement of autonomy for long-term care residents might seem a fairly straightforward mandate, easily achieved. However, it is complex and made more complex by the multiplicity of interpersonal relationships that can exist in long-term care facilities. The resident's needs tend to be multiple, and they involve social as well as physical and psychological dimensions. Care often must be interdisciplinary, and caregivers usually include a wide range of professionals, such as nurses, nursing assistants, social workers, physical therapists, rehabilitation therapists, physicians, and others. Communication between and among the different professionals and the resident can be difficult. Each brings his or her own set of values and legitimate agenda to the situation. The complexity of enhancing resident autonomy is perhaps heightened most, however, by a set of fundamental paradoxes associated with autonomy.

Paradox 1: Autonomy Is Played Out Within a Social Context

Agich (1993) maintains that the atomistic view of autonomous persons as independent, self-ruled entities who make decisions solely for their own reasons, free from all external influence, is simply wrong-headed and sociologically naive. All humans live within a historical, social, and cultural context. People do not autonomously choose many critical aspects of their lives including their genetic background, their parents, or the society and culture into which they are born. As Lidz and Arnold (1990) have argued, autonomy should not be equated with absolute independence, but must recognize individuals within a historical and social context, within some kind of institutional structures. Rather than assume that, because to be fully autonomous one must be left alone, all institutional structures (including all long-term care institutions) are by definition an interference with autonomy, one must instead ask how these structures affect one's actions. Likewise, rather than assuming that influences by others on a person's choice inhibit autonomy, the appropriate question is whether these influences corrupt that person's control, reasoning, or identification with his or her actions.

Both Agich (1993) and Lidz, Fischer, and Arnold (1992) suggest that, from this perspective, it is useful to think of autonomous activity as that which is consistent with a person's long-term goals, present commitments, and past activities rather than as individual, isolated decisions or actions. Thus, long-term care institutional characteristics and policies that enable residents to develop and fulfill their freely chosen life plans and commitments, to be themselves, are autonomy promoting. Those that do the opposite are autonomy impeding (Lidz & Arnold, 1990). For example, as Tulloch (1990) has suggested, a facility that finds creative and comfortable ways to help residents keep up such normal interactions between friends as sending Christmas cards is enhancing autonomy.

Paradox 2: Older Persons in Long-Term Care Often Are Dependent on Others to Implement or Assist in the Implementation of Decisions

This paradox is essentially a corollary of the first. Too often, autonomy is thought of only in physical, functional, and concrete terms related to freedom of mobility and physical independence. The inability of an older person to implement decisions is perceived by caregivers as an inability to make decisions. Autonomy is thought of as an either-or phenomenon. If one requires assistance to execute decisions, then, de facto, one lacks autonomy. However, a long-term care resident could be paralyzed from a stroke and largely immobile, yet have considerable personal autonomy by making an array of major decisions that are carried out by others. Conversely, an older resident with no mobility restrictions could have a very low level of personal autonomy if she had few opportunities to make significant decisions. One of the implications of this distinction, termed by Collopy (1988, p. 11) as "decisional autonomy" versus "autonomy of execution," is that direct caregivers who execute resident decisions are not automatically autonomy impeders. Rather, they have the potential to be key autonomy enhancers.

Paradox 3: True Autonomy Implies Both Rights and Responsibilities

Responsibilities of residents constitute a significant but largely overlooked aspect of autonomy (Jameton, 1988). They are both a part of and a limit to autonomy. Responsibility implies a relationship of integrity and dignity with others, a relationship that is reciprocal and an expression of membership in a community. How persons carry out their responsibilities helps to define the kind of persons they are (Agich, 1993).

Resident responsibilities in nursing homes are complex and can involve both other residents and staff. Jameton (1988) noted that such responsibilities can include several kinds: (a) responsibility for performing specific tasks, such as pushing other residents' wheelchairs, sewing for others, making beds, assisting with meals, and so on; (b) responsibilities to caregivers, such as feeling gratitude (perhaps expressed through small gifts or tips to the caregivers) and complaining appropriately to staff so as to not overburden them, and basic responsibilities not to hit, insult, or abuse staff; (c) responsibilities to follow institutional rules and customs; (d) responsibilities to other residents, such as helping others gain access to care, giving advice, and assisting others in activities of daily living; (e) personal responsibilities for self-care and grooming; and (f) responsibilities to others outside the facility, such as maintaining contacts with relatives and friends, observing birthdays, and giving advice.

To counter the commonly found "residents' bill of rights" that implies that autonomy is a one-way street, Ackermann (1990) developed a "bill of resident responsibilities," arguing that for both residents and staff, rights and responsibilities go together. Perhaps the most important responsibilities of the resident are involvement in the development of his or her care plan and participation in residents councils. Lidz and Arnold (1990) have pointed out that autonomy in its fullest sense makes each resident responsible for shaping and fulfilling his or her life according to freely chosen principles, commitments, and plans.

Paradox 4: Autonomous Choice for Some Older Residents Is to Choose Not to Be Autonomous

Older adults residing in long-term care institutions differ from each other in many ways including their preferences concerning care and the degree to which they want direct or indirect control over care decisions. It would be ironic if practitioners were to put themselves in the ridiculous situation of commanding, "You must be autonomous!" Practitioners need to make an effort to learn resident preferences in all aspects of care including control. It is likely that future cohorts of residents, such as individuals from the baby-boom generation, will demand greater direct involvement in the formulation and execution of their care plans. Nevertheless, some people may choose not to be involved.

Lessons From the Personal Autonomy in Long-Term Care Initiative

Beginning in 1986, the Retirement Research Foundation sponsored the Personal Autonomy in Long Term Care Initiative, a 5-year, 28-project grant program that emphasized key ethical and legal issues in autonomy and decision making for older adults with disabilities (see special issues of *The Gerontologist, 28,* 1988, and of *Generations, 14,* 1990 for a fuller description of the initiative and articles based on many of the initiative projects). The major lessons regarding autonomy and its enhancement in long-term care facilities that can be drawn from this initiative have been summarized by Hofland and David (1990).

The first major lesson is that personal autonomy is seriously and unduly restricted in many long-term care facilities. Most nursing home residents report that they value autonomy highly and want more control over everyday aspects of their lives and care including their personal space, room, and day-to-day lifestyle. Both professional and paraprofessional staff members agree that it is important for residents to exercise control over everyday matters, but staff members sometimes doubt that it is possible in the present regulatory and reimbursement environment.

Kane and her colleagues (1990a) concluded that, from an ethical perspective, it is clear that long-term care for older adults should be arranged in a way that is much more respectful of their personal autonomy. However, there are necessary limits to that autonomy, and autonomous living inevitably entails negotiation, compromise, and accommodation. Also, respect for autonomy is not a panacea. Nevertheless, there can be no moral justification for the extent to which residents' lives and fundamental rights are constricted and compromised. For example, residents do not control such basic features of everyday life as what to wear and eat, when to get up and go to bed, and who their roommates are.

A second major conclusion is that there is often a substantial mismatch between resident and staff perceptions. Long-term care facility staff members often make paternalistic statements, such as, "I know what my residents like and want," but actually they often do not know. Wetle, Levkoff, Cwikel, and Rosen (1988) found that nurses overestimated the amount and adequacy of health care decision-making information that residents received in nursing homes. Kane and her colleagues (1990b) found that nurses' aides and residents differed considerably in how each group ranked which aspects of day-to-day life were most important for residents to control. The two items rated highly by most residents were trips out of the facility and use of the telephone, whereas nursing assistants most frequently rated organized facility activities, such as bingo and arts and crafts, as important and least frequently rated using the telephone as important. The lesson here is that if facility staff would like or need to know what the preferences or values of residents are, they need to ask the residents.

Third, procedures to assess decisional capacity are seriously flawed and often biased against the elderly. Decisional capacity is frequently treated as a global, all-or-nothing phenomenon rather than as specific to a particular decision. Capacity can fluctuate because of such factors as the time of day, illness, reaction to drugs, anxiety, depression, grief, or a short-term confusional state. What a professional may perceive as irreversible declining capacity may, in fact, be the result of a reversible condition. A finding of incapacity must be supported by evidence of decisional impairment over time and should be accompanied by a thorough physical and psychological assessment. Also, as Collopy (1990) points out, seemingly irrational decisions can often be understood as reasonable in the context of the person's values history. Too often, assumptions of incapacity and actual legal determinations of incompetence result from the mere presence of advanced age, frailty, poor health, eccentricities, or a medical diagnosis, such as Alzheimer's disease or a related dementia. Moreover, once an older person is labeled as incapacitated or a guardianship has been instated, staff often wrongly assumes that the person is incapable of making any choices or decisions.

A fourth lesson is that the environment should be changed to meet the needs and preferences of older residents rather than expecting older residents to adapt to the environment. The physical, programmatic, and policy environments of residential facilities often seriously inhibit autonomy because of their inflexibility. A classic example is the inappropriate use of physical restraints. Older adults sometimes are tied up to avoid falls and injury, in one of the grossest affronts to autonomy rather than using alternatives, such as lowering beds, positioning residents in chairs with pillows, employing half side rails, or softening the environment by removing sharp edges and eliminating hard floors. Similarly, the use of staff-imposed, rigid toileting schedules that do not conform to the longstanding toileting habits of the residents can sometimes result in resident incontinence, and the use of catheters or diapers.

A fifth lesson learned is that although nursing assistants provide the bulk of direct care in facilities and are critical for support of resident autonomy, their task-oriented work approach reduces that autonomy. Aides usually see their work as implementing routines for such tasks as lifting, turning, dressing, feeding, waking, putting to bed, and toileting residents. This functional approach does not foster good communication between aides and residents. If aides perceive residents as objects on whom "bed and body" work is performed, then it is difficult for aides to perceive residents as persons with values, preferences, and life goals and plans. Instead, residents become almost interchangeable work units that need to be processed as quickly and efficiently as possible.

Kane and her colleagues (1990b) suggested several solutions to this dehumanizing situation. Initial and continuing education and training for aides that includes discussions of enhancement of resident autonomy in their everyday work would be a good starting point. Also important are the involvement of aides in the development of care plans, modeling of appropriate behavior by senior and professional staff, and assignment of aides to specific residents so that the aides come to know, care about, and feel responsible for these residents. Most important, autonomy must become a central goal of care, and autonomy-enhancing efforts must be rewarded through regulatory and reimbursement mechanisms.

The last lesson learned is that the medical model prevalent in long-term care facilities causes enormous problems in autonomy enhancement. Aging is often perceived as a medical problem, and the medicalization of long-term care is one manifestation of this perspective (Estes & Binney, 1989). This worldview has many negative implications for the personal autonomy of residents. For example, the medical model structures role relationships such that patients do what health care staff tells them. Patients are expected to follow orders, not act independently. As Tulloch (1990) argues so eloquently, helping relationships need to become more symmetrical. Long-term care staff should see themselves as consultants and assistants who help older adults gain access to, organize, and use resources to support their goals, plans, and preferences.

The medical model also creates an environment in which medical expenses are reimbursed, but not personal assistance, psychosocial support, and other social services that older adults with disabilities may need and want. Other kinds of facilities and community-based service programs that can serve as autonomy-enhancing alternatives to nursing homes may struggle for financial survival or not even exist because of the current reimbursement mechanisms.

Kapp (1990) noted that there are three different kinds of long-term care services: (a) health care, (b) personal care, and (c) housekeeping services. Institutional facilities often are not good at providing the last two kinds of services. The three kinds of services need to be separated. For example, nursing homes could learn a lot from the hotel industry about providing rooms, meals, and other amenities. Personal care and housekeeping services could be placed largely under consumer direction, as many of the rapidly growing numbers of assisted living facilities in the country are doing. Similarly, some of the new assisted living facilities are providing housing services but subcontracting out home health and personal care services to an independent agency.

The language used in the long-term care field is heavily influenced by the medical model. "Patient," "resident," "consumer," and "customer" carry different connotations about services and personal autonomy. Kane and Kane (1990) noted the sad truth that the older adult is often not perceived as the customer; rather the customer is the state or the family that pays the long-term care bills. In the case of the state, it controls what it wants to buy with public funds through regulation and reimbursement policies.

Challenges for the Future

Much progress has been made in the arena of autonomy enhancement in long-term care in the last 5 years. First, considerable consciousness raising has occurred. Long-term care professionals may not yet have all the solutions, but at least they realize that there are problems with the goals for and the practices toward facility residents regarding their autonomy. Second, the assisted living movement is a rapidly growing and encouraging trend. A recent U.S. Department of Health and Human Services study reported that 30,000 assisted living arrangements now serve up to 1 million people. Kane and Wilson (1993) have highlighted the autonomy-enhancing features that assisted living settings can provide to allow residents to live a normal life, such as lockable doors, single-occupancy units, flexible visiting hours, and a respect for privacy by staff. Third, the recent passage and implementation of the Patient Self-Determination Act offers considerable potential for control by residents over end-of-life decision making through the increased use of advance directives.

Given this progress and the lessons that have been learned about personal autonomy in long-term care institutions, what are the challenges for the future?

How Does Autonomy Vary Across Groups?

Is the whole notion of autonomy enhancement in long-term care institutions essentially a white middle-class concept? Most of the studies to date have used mainly white middle-class samples, so our knowledge base is limited and may be rather skewed. We need information about how autonomy and preferences vary according to ethnicity, culture, gender, age, class, cohort, and setting. Some of our current thoughts about and strategies for autonomy enhancement may be overly simplistic or misguided. For example, practitioners who are trying to implement the Patient Self-Determination Act report that the whole concept of advance directives is foreign and even inappropriate for some ethnic groups. In this and other attempts to support autonomy for residents, we need to build our approaches on a much richer and more diverse empirical base to assure appropriately targeted efforts.

Importance of Meaning in Enhancing Autonomy

For autonomy to be enhanced in long-term-care institutions, it is not enough that residents have opportunities to make a variety of choices. The choices must be meaningful for them, and allow them to express and develop their own individuality as persons (Agich, 1993). It would be a mistake to try to correct the current situation of autonomy diminishment and compromise in many long-term facilities by introducing measures that are superficial and trivial, or what one gerontologist (Gatz, 1989, personal communication) has termed "autonomy therapy." Gatz's fear is that nursing home residents will be wheeled into the activities room and asked to choose among white and colored socks. After choosing a color, the residents will be informed, "It's wonderful that you made the choice that you did. Unfortunately, the laundry service that we use will only allow white socks."

Lidz and his colleagues (1992), in discussing autonomy as "consistency," caution against an exclusive focus on autonomy as discrete, isolated acts or decisions. Just as the sentences and paragraphs in a novel cannot be fully understood by analyzing individual words and phrases and their relationships in isolation from other sentences and paragraphs, the assessment of whether a particular decision by a resident is truly autonomous requires that it be examined within the fuller and more integrated context of the resident's life. From this perspective, enhancing autonomy would mean nothing less than enabling the resident to continue to live his or her own life. Staff would have to pay attention to who the resident has been and also provide support for continuing and new interests, goals, and plans. As Cohen (1990) put it, "Services should enable, encourage, and support the ability of the elderly person with disabilities to flourish—to engage in roles as parent, grand-parent, neighbor, citizen, communicant, friend, and colleague, as appropriate" (p. 13). Examples, according to Cohen, include trans-portation to enable visits to grandchildren and other family mem-bers, voting, participation in community activities, and attendance at community church services. This vision does not imply some modest tinkering with our long-term care system, but the challenge of a radical overhaul.

What Is Autonomy for Persons with Dementia?

There is an encouraging trend in the U.S. toward rapid prolifera-tion of alternative residential settings for older adults who require supports primarily for activities of daily living rather than for medical care. One nursing home industry leader (Goldberg, 1993, personal communication) speculates that within 10 years at least half of the current profile of individuals residing in nursing homes will instead be living in assisted living facilities, other alternative facilities, or in their own homes with community-based supports. The future of nursing homes will be as specialized care facilities for individuals in moderate to advanced stages of dementia, for in-dividuals with heavy medical care needs because of subacute con-ditions, or for older individuals with intensive mental health needs. If realized, this projection probably will mean significant advances in the enhancement of autonomy for those older individuals with primarily personal assistance needs. Those individuals with in-tensive subacute medical needs and those with serious mental health needs will be in facilities more closely resembling hospitals. But what about those older individuals with serious dementia? Is autonomy and its enhancement possible for them?

Lidz and his colleagues (1992) argue that it is not, that autonomy is an irrelevant value for these individuals. Autonomy requires the cognitive capacity and skills for effective decision making and for maintaining enduring goals and desires over time; persons with advanced dementia often lack this capacity. To attempt to promote these individuals' autonomy would be a mistake, Lidz and his colleagues maintain, because it would be unfair to hold them responsible for their actions. Promotion of their autonomy also could result in neglect, and cruel and potentially harmful abandonment of them because of noninterference in decisions and acts that are seen as autonomous but are actually nondeliberative and inconsistent.

Cohen (1988, 1990) offers a different perspective, arguing that persons with dementia simply become the frontline victims of the "elderly mystique," stigmatized because of their biological inferiority. Notions of autonomy, from his view, are relevant for this group but would need to be broadened and reconceptualized to include the idea of the "right to flourish." Translation of this idea into practice and policy would include activities for persons with dementia that reflect remaining capacities and former histories instead of the children's activities so often provided to these individuals, and training for direct caregivers so that they communicate with demented persons in a respectful, patient, caring way rather than in a paternalistic and condescending manner. Similarly, Cohen and Weisman (1990) offer specific environmental design principles to maximize autonomy for older adults with cognitive impairments. Much more creative thought needs to be given to autonomy enhancement for persons with dementia in terms of what it means in concept and practice.

Involvement of the Family

Family members are a significant part of the social context for autonomy of many older adults and the major support network through which a long-term care plan is implemented in the community. Also, the family often plays, or expects to play, a role in institutional decision making. For the practitioner, the dilemmas are: Who is the client? What are the stakes and possible conflicts of interest of the family members? We need more information about how families are involved in decision making for older residents, how the perceptions and preferences of family members differ from those of older residents, and how conflicts can effectively be resolved.

If autonomy is thought of as "consistency," then it would be wrong to categorically exclude the family from decision making, yet it would also be wrong to allow the preferences and values of the family to automatically trump those of the resident. A key point of information would be the extent to which the resident wants the family involved in his or her affairs. If the family is paying part or all of the bill, the situation is further complicated. We need to develop concepts of "family autonomy" as well as individual autonomy, as both High (1988) and Cicirelli (1992) have suggested.

Just as the dimension of meaning is critical to a true or full conceptualization of personal autonomy, meaning may also be important to family autonomy. Professionals in long-term care facilities need to do a better job of including family members in the care of older residents and creating meaningful roles for them so that they can feel they are fulfilling their filial duties. For example, some new assisted living facilities unbundle services so that family members can either do the personal laundry of residents or include this in a package of purchased services. What does it mean to be a good spouse or good son/daughter of a person with cognitive or physical impairments living in a long-term care facility? This is a question that long-term care professionals need to ask, and then structure the answers in policy and practice.

Rethinking Design and Design Codes/Regulation

A significant but often overlooked dimension in the enhancement of the autonomy of older adults residing in institutions is the physical environment in which they live. Cohen and Weisman (1990, 1991), who examined environments for older adults with cognitive impairments, maintain that the physical environment can be a therapeutic resource to support autonomy. For example, the opportunity for a resident to personalize his or her room may make it more distinctive and memorable, and thereby improve the resident's degree of spatial orientation and ability to walk around independently. Similarly, the elimination of environmental barriers, such as threshholds and difficult-to-operate door handles can promote both independence and control. Wandering can be viewed not as a problem but as an opportunity for residents to engage in activities that occur along well-defined, safe, and interesting paths. Cohen and Day (1993) have offered a casebook that presents and analyzes several facilities outstanding in the degree to which they embody the design principles and guidelines developed by Cohen and his colleagues. Similarly, Regnier and his colleagues (1991) have addressed best practices and innovations in the design of assisted living facilities.

The work of Mark Rakatansky, an architect at the University of Illinois–Chicago, is also creative and noteworthy. Rakatansky is working on environmental design features for community-based and institutional long-term-care settings that respond to the critical question, "How can design go beyond a functional purpose to provide a setting of meaning for the long-term-care client?" He developed a handrail in an adult day care center, for example, that included armatures with clips that hold pictures of the center clients from their earlier lives. Clients and staff are both engaged by the pictorial display, and gain a sense of the personal histories of the individuals shown.

The efforts of these architects are laudable, but the possibilities of using design elements to support autonomy is a surface that has barely been scratched. Much more attention needs to be paid to this arena. One of the inhibiting factors has been the stultifying effect of state and federal design codes and regulations for nursing homes, which often are borrowed unthinkingly from hospitals and for the most part are not based on any empirical justification. The American Association of Homes for the Aging has played a leadership role in examining, publicizing, and reforming these outdated design codes and regulations through the creation of a National Clearinghouse on Aging and Environmental Design Codes and a congressional symposium on the topic held in Washington, DC, in March 1993.

Linking Research, Ethics, and Practice

Good practice should be grounded in conceptual and empirical research so that it builds on the best thinking and information available. In long-term care, facts cannot settle value questions (including those involving autonomy issues) for practitioners, but empirical research can help frame the analysis of difficult questions. In the ethical analysis of any situation, the first step is always to establish the facts about the situation, what ethicists refer to as the "is."

Good practice also should be a function both of what professionals know ought to be done and of the minimum that must be done. Laws, and the regulations that operationalize them, set minimal standards of what practitioners must do. Ethical standards are higher and prescribe what practitioners ought to do. For example, almost every long-term care professional knows of a nursing home that is administered to meet the letter of the law and does not receive regulatory citations, but still provides shoddy care. Laws and rules are based in the "ought" articulations of moral codes, but their power is limited. They are effective at stopping the worst offenses of bad practice, but they do not provide a vision for nor motivate practitioners toward what is possible in terms of good practice. Often, they only frustrate good practitioners. Laws are a necessary, but insufficient, condition to assure good practice. They must be accompanied by an active and conscious effort to elevate the moral stance underpinning the legal requirements. Rather than be reactive to the minimal standards of the law, practitioners should be proactive in setting higher ethical standards for themselves.

This book and the consensus conference on which it is based have used a process that is an important exemplar of such a proactive quest for higher ethical standards. The chapters in this book formulate the "is" by summarizing much of the best thinking and research information available on the topic of enhancing resident autonomy. A panel of practitioners, consumers, family members, regulators, and policy makers have developed the "ought" by building on this base through analysis of the knowledge available and, grounded in the realities of the long-term care setting, by developing strategies to overcome barriers to autonomy enhancement in institutions. These strategies have been initially tested by the critical review of conference participants and later will be tested by actual field demonstration. It is an ambitious and worthy agenda with considerable potential to improve practice and enhance the quality of life for residents.

References

Ackermann, J. (1990). A bill of responsibilities for nursing home residents. *Generations, 14*(Suppl.), 81–82.

Agich, G. J. (1993). *Autonomy and long-term care.* New York: Oxford University Press.

Cicirelli, V. G. (1992). *Family caregiving.* Newbury Park: Sage Publications.

Cohen, E. S. (1988). The elderly mystique: Constraints on the autonomy of the elderly with disabilities. *The Gerontologist, 28*(Suppl.), 24–31.

Cohen, E. S. (1990). The elderly mystique: Impediment to advocacy and empowerment. *Generations, 14*(Suppl.), 13–16.

Cohen, U., & Day, K. (1993). *Contemporary environments for people with dementia.* Baltimore: The Johns Hopkins University Press.

Cohen, U., & Weisman, G. D. (1990). Environmental design to maximize autonomy for older adults with cognitive impairments. *Generations, 14*(Suppl.), 75–78.

Cohen, U., & Weisman, G. D. (1991). *Holding on to home: Designing environments for people with dementia.* Baltimore: The Johns Hopkins University Press.

Collopy, B. J. (1988). Autonomy in long term care: Some crucial distinctions. *The Gerontologist, 28*(Suppl.), 10–17.

Collopy, B. J. (1990). Ethical dimensions of autonomy in long-term care. *Generations, 14*(Suppl.), 9–12.

Estes, C. L., & Binney, E. A. (1989). The biomedicalization of aging: Dangers and dilemmas. *The Gerontologist, 29,* 587–96.

High, D. M. (1988). All in the family: Extended autonomy and expectations in surrogate health care decision-making. *The Gerontologist, 28*(Suppl.), 46–51.

Hofland, B. F. (1990). Autonomy and long-term-care practice: Introduction. *Generations, 14*(Suppl.), 5–8.

Hofland, B. F., & David, D. (1990). Autonomy and long-term-care practice: Conclusions and next steps. *Generations, 14*(Suppl.), 91–94.

Jameton, A. (1988). In the borderlands of autonomy: Responsibility in long term care facilities. *The Gerontologist, 28*(Suppl.), 18–23.

Kane, R. L., & Kane, R. A. (1990). The impact of long-term-care financing on personal autonomy. *Generations, 14*(Suppl.), 86–89.

Kane, R. A., Caplan, A. L., Freeman, I. C., Aroskar, M. A., & Urv-Wong, E. K. (1990a). Avenues to appropriate autonomy: What next? In R. A. Kane & A. L. Caplan (Eds.), *Everyday ethics: Resolving dilemmas in nursing home life.* New York: Springer.

Kane, R. A., Freeman, I. C., Caplan, A. L., Aroskar, M. A., & Urv-Wong, E. K. (1990b). Everyday autonomy in nursing homes. *Generations, 14*(Suppl.), 69–71.

Kane, R. A., & Wilson, K. B. (1993). *Assisted living in the United States: A new paradigm for residential care for frail older persons?* Washington, DC: American Association of Retired Persons.

Kapp, M. B. (1990). Home care client-centered systems: Consumer choice vs. protection. *Generations, 14*(Suppl.), 33–35.

Lidz, C. W., & Arnold, R. M. (1990). Institutional constraints on autonomy. *Generations, 14*(Suppl.), 65–68.

Lidz, C. W., Fischer, L., & Arnold, R. M. (1992). *The erosion of autonomy in long-term care.* New York: Oxford University Press.

National Citizens Coalition for Nursing Home Reform. (1985). *A consumer perspective on quality care: The residents' point of view.* Washington, DC: National Citizens Coalition.

Regnier, V., Hamilton, J., & Yatabe, S. (1991). *Best practices in assisted living: Innovations in design, management and financing.* Los Angeles: Andrus Gerontology Center.

Rowe, J. W., & Kahn, R. L. (1987). Human aging: Usual and successful. *Science, 237,* 143–149.

Thomasma, D. C. (1985). Personal autonomy of the elderly in long-term care settings. *Journal of the American Geriatrics Society, 33,* 225.

Tulloch, G. J. (1990). From inside a nursing home: A resident writes about autonomy. *Generations, 14*(Suppl.), 83–85.

Wetle, T., Levkoff, S., Cwikel, J., & Rosen, A. (1988). Nursing home resident participation in medical decisions: Perceptions and preferences. *The Gerontologist, 28*(Suppl.), 32–38.

Chapter Three

The Nursing Home Population

Kenneth Brummel-Smith and Stanley J. Brody

The population is aging, and the number of persons requiring long-term institutional care is rising. Patients are being discharged to nursing homes sooner after acute illnesses, are more disabled and, typically, are sicker than those cared for in the past. The population is also not static, with patients entering from acute hospitals, Veterans' Affairs programs, rehabilitation facilities, mental health institutions, and the home. Residents leave the nursing home by being discharged back to these same facilities and by dying (Densen, 1991). Transfers to and from various institutional settings may occur often in a resident's life (see Figures 3.1 & 3.2). These factors have important implications for the role of autonomy in long-term care.

In 1985, it was estimated that 1.3 million persons were in nursing homes (Hing, 1987). The number in the other forms of institutions is probably double that. However, figures regarding the population living in other forms of institutional settings, such as board and care homes, assisted living centers, and foster homes are more difficult to come by. Today, only about 5% of those older than age 65 are in a nursing home. Among those who are in nursing homes, there is a clear preponderance of the "old-old," that is, those older than age 75. About 16% of nursing home residents are ages 65 to 74, 39% are ages 75 to 84, and 45% are older than age 85 (National Center for Health Statistics, 1984). Of the total population older than age 65, 1% of those ages 65 to 74 and 22% of those older than age 85 are in nursing homes. The lifetime risk for

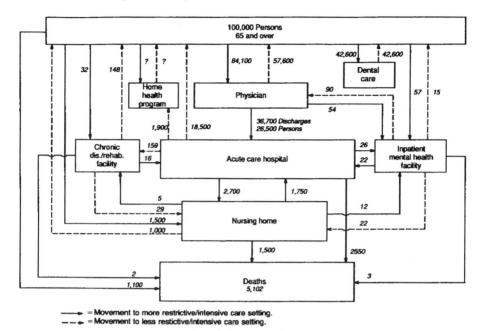

FIGURE 3.1 Annual movement of persons 65 and over through the health care system.

Used with permission from P. M. Densen, (1987). The elderly and the health care system: Another perspective. *The Milbank Quarterly,* 65, 614, 638.

institutionalization is estimated at 52% for women at age 65 and 30% for men (Cohen, Tell, & Wallack, 1986). Since the advent of Medicare in 1966, the rate of nursing home use has almost doubled.

The major pathway to nursing home admission is the acute hospital (Densen, 1987). In 1986, about 26% of the elderly population were admitted to an acute hospital. About 10% of those discharged from an acute hospital went to a nursing home. This is an increase of about 3% from 1983 when the prospective payment system went into effect (Gornick & Hall, 1988). A smaller percentage are directly admitted to the nursing home from the community, though the number of such admissions is growing rapidly (see Table 3.1). In the old-old population, the number discharged from the acute hospital to the nursing home approaches 16% (see Table 3.2). Therefore, though families and informal care systems continue to provide the bulk of care to even very old persons, the number of

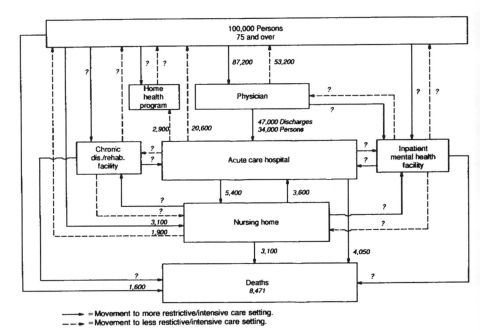

FIGURE 3.2   Annual movement of persons 75 and over through the health care system.

Used with permission from P. M. Densen, (1987). The elderly and the health care system: Another perspective. *The Milbank Quarterly, 65*, 614, 638.

elderly residents in nursing homes can be expected to continue to rise as the general population ages. In total, about two thirds of all patients admitted to a nursing home come from an acute hospital, and one third comes from the community.

There are two populations of nursing home residents: those who stay for a short time (defined as less than 90 days) and those who stay for longer than 180 days. The characteristics of these two groups are different and may influence the role that autonomy plays in their daily lives. Short stayers are typically those receiving rehabilitation, hospice patients, and those recuperating from acute illness. Long stayers are those with end-stage dementia, or cardiac, pulmonary, or neurological diseases.

More than one third of those persons older than age 65 admitted to a nursing home dies there. A significant portion (42%) reenters an acute care facility each year, and this percentage does not vary much by age (see Table 3.3). About 24% are discharged to the

TABLE 3.1 Utilization of the Major Parts of the Health Care System in 1986 by a Hypothetical Cohort of 100,000 Elderly 65 and over and Changes since Early 1980s

Measure of utilization[a]	1986	Early 1980s		Percentage of change
		Number	Year	
Saw doctor	84,100	80,000	1980–81	+5.1
Saw dentist	42,600	39,600	1983	+7.6
Admitted to acute-care hospital from home	26,500	31,000	1983	−14.5
Admitted to nursing home from all sources	4,376	2,727	1983	+60.5
from acute-care hospital	2,700	2,150	1983	+25.6
from home	1,500	500	1983	+200.0
Used a community service	30,000	22,000	1984	+36.4
Used a home health service Medicare beneficiaries)	5,000	3,400	1984	+47.0

[a]Persons who used service at least once during year.

TABLE 3.2 Percentage of Elderly Hospitalized Persons Discharged Home and Percentage Discharged to a Nursing Home by Age; 1986[a]

Discharge destination	Age		
	65 and over	65–74	75 and over
Home	77.5	85.7	69.2
Informal care	70.2	80.0	60.7
Home care program	7.3	5.7	8.5
Nursing home	10.2	3.9	15.9

[a]Includes those discharged with and without referrals to a home care program.

TABLE 3.3 Discharge Destination of Persons Discharged from Nursing Homes Expressed as a Percentage of Persons Admitted, by Age; 1986

Age group	Persons admitted[a]	Persons discharged to			Discharges as percent of persons admitted[b]		
		Community	Acute-care hospitals	Death	Community	Acute-care hospitals	Death
65 and over	4,100	1,000	1,800	1,500	24.4	43.9	36.6
65–74	1,250	400	600	300	32.0	48.0	24.0
75 and over	8,500	1,900	3,600	3,100	22.4	42.4	36.5

[a]From a population of 100,000 exclusive of persons admitted from rehabilitation and mental health facilities.
[b]Percentages differ from 100 percent because of rounding and because of footnote 1.

community. Five percent of whites older than the age of 65 were in nursing homes in 1985, whereas African Americans accounted for about 3% and other races made up 2% of the nursing home population (Hing, 1987).

In the future, one can expect that the trend toward shorter length of stay in acute care facilities will continue and even increase. Under managed care systems hospital admission rates are generally lower, and stays are usually shorter. It is likely, then, that more patients will require at least short-term placement in nursing homes. Alternatives to nursing homes, such as foster homes and alternative living institutions (already well established in Oregon) are also developing. Patients discharged from acute care facilities are likely to be both sicker and older.

Characteristics of Nursing Home Residents

Seventy-five percent of nursing home residents are women. Most are white (93%), whereas 6% are African American, and 1% are other races. Almost two thirds are widowed, 16% are married, and nearly 14% were never married. Six percent are divorced or separated (*Aging America,* 1988).

Rates of Disability

A striking feature of the nursing home population is the significant degree of dependency. Nearly all residents require assistance in bathing, three quarters need help in dressing, and two thirds need someone to help them use the toilet. Even getting in or out of bed or transferring to a chair is difficult for most, with 63% requiring the assistance of another. Fully 40% must be helped to eat. When the population is segmented into decades, clearly the old-old have even greater rates of deficits in activities of daily living (ADLs) than the preceding figures. For instance, 82% of those older than age 85 need help dressing. Nearly 55% have difficulty with bowel and bladder control (*Aging America,* 1988).

Despite these high figures, they still do not accurately reflect the immense degree of disability of nursing home residents. This is because most residents have more than one ADL deficit. Fifty-one percent of nursing home residents have more than five ADL deficits, 23% have three or four deficits, and only 12% have lost the ability to do only one or two activities. In the community only 5% of the elderly population have deficits in five to six ADLs. The percentage of community-dwelling elders who are unable to perform one or two ADLs is much closer to the percentage in nursing homes, at 8% (*Aging America,* 1988).

Therefore, independently performing ADL may not be physically possible for most nursing home residents. This fact has significant implications for those attempting to enhance the free choices of nursing home residents. Although a resident may want to choose the particular outfit of clothing she wears, it is likely that someone must assist her in donning it. It is unknown what role "learned helplessness" may play in the limitation of physical functioning that is so prevalent among nursing home residents. Time must pass before any significant change in functional performance might be seen because of the greater emphasis on maintenance or enhancement of function brought on by the regulations related to the Omnibus Budget Reconciliation Act (OBRA) of 1987.

Changes in Mental Function

Nursing home residents also have a high prevalence of cognitive disturbances. Sixty-three percent have some form of disorientation or memory impairment. The diagnoses of "senile dementia" or "chronic organic brain syndrome" are applied to 47% to 87% of residents. Many residents may have lesser degrees of dementia that have not been recognized or evaluated (Barnes & Raskind, 1981). Those with delirium (an acute change in mental functioning caused by problems outside the central nervous system, such as drugs or infections) may not be evaluated because their problem is mistakenly attributed to degenerative dementia.

The high prevalence of mental impairments undoubtably has major effects on residents' ability to act autonomously. Furthermore, impairments may fluctuate over time, even with Alzheimer's disease. Intercurrent illnesses, drug effects, and the trauma of being transferred to a different facility or even a different room all can temporarily affect cognitive performance and, therefore, decision making.

Finally, the type of dementia may also affect the resident's ability to make autonomous decisions or act on them. For instance, Alzheimer's disease and strokes that predominately affect the left hemisphere may be associated with a high prevalence of depression that could adversely affect decisions. The progressive nature of Alzheimer's disease affects memory and language functions early, while preserving basic values until later. Early in the course of the disease a resident may not clearly express his independent desires, although he may have some knowledge of those wants.

Depression

Depression is also very common in nursing home residents. It has been estimated that the rates range from 30% to 68% (Phan & Reifler, 1988). Many symptoms of depression experienced by older persons can adversely affect autonomy. In a review by Kupfer (1983), 100% of patients reported decreased interests, 98% decreased energy, 95% difficulty concentrating, and 90% feelings of hopelessness or helplessness; 80% showed evidence of psychomotor retardation. It seems likely that any of these symptoms would adversely affect a resident's ability to make autonomous decisions or act on them.

"Sicker and Quicker"

Another important feature of nursing home residents that may affect the ability of the person to think or act autonomously is the "toxicity of hospitalization." Since the advent of the Prospective Payment System in 1983, patients are being discharged from acute facilities to nursing homes sooner and often while still in the throes of their illness. Those discharged from acute facilities are often still affected by medications or anesthetic responses, though some drugs may have been discontinued many days before the admission to the long-term-care facility. Iatrogenic complications, such as adverse drug effects, have been shown to be common in acute facilities. Such changes, even if recognized and treated promptly, may take months to resolve completely. Meanwhile, alterations in thinking, emotional reactions, and judgment may be significant.

Effects of Resident Characteristics on Autonomy

The effects of various resident characteristics on the resident's ability to express decisions and act autonomously can be viewed in terms of those related to the system and those referable to the resident. The system effects are compounded by the dual nature of the population. Short-term stayers are entering and leaving the institution quickly, placing a burden on the staff's ability to determine what autonomous wishes the resident may have. Such patients are also more likely to have continuing effects of hospital treatments (such as pain and limited mobility) or adverse outcomes (such as drug or anesthetic reactions causing confusion, apathy, or depression). Staff members, when treating rehabilitation patients, may feel pressure to ensure participation of the resident in therapies while the resident "just wants to rest."

Residents who stay for long periods may have different problems affecting their ability to exert autonomy. Physical disabilities may limit what actions a resident can perform. Cognitive disabilities may bring into question the competence to make such decisions. Mental health problems, particularly depression, may be unrecognized or inadequately treated. Even when it is recognized, the depressed person may express little interest in making his or her own decisions. Many older persons suffer from a lack of motivation that hinders personal desire to act autonomously.

Social characteristics also play a role in how autonomous the resident may act. Long-term stayers have usually spent down their savings and have few additional resources to purchase items they may choose or arrange for alternative care. A history of social isolation before admission may have left the resident ill equipped to make independent decisions and may even promote a belief in a "right to dependency." Finally, by the time the family chooses placement, they may believe that the person is so disabled that he must be protected "at all costs." For instance, attitudinal studies of restraint use in nursing homes have shown that families are often the party most desirous of their use (Wanlass, 1993).

Summary

The nursing home population is composed of persons who are mostly women, quite old, usually widowed, and very disabled. The prevalence of cognitive and affective problems is high. There are increasing numbers of residents who are still sick and recovering from serious illness for which they had received treatment in the acute hospital. These factors will have a significant impact on any attempt to promote residents' autonomy in nursing homes.

References

Barnes, R. F., & Raskind, M. A. (1981). DSM III criteria and the clinical diagnosis of dementia: A nursing home study. *Journal of Gerontology, 36,* 20–27.

Cohen, M., Tell, E. J., & Wallack, S. S. (1986). The lifetime risks and costs of nursing home use among the elderly. *Medical Care, 24,* 12.

Densen, P. M. (1987). The elderly and health care system: Another perspective. *Milbank Quarterly, 65,* 614–638.

Densen, P. M. (1991, January). *Tracing the elderly through the health care system: An update* (AHCPR Monograph No. 91-11). Washington, DC: U.S. Department of Health and Human Services.

Gornick, M., & Hall, M. J. (1988). Trends in Medicare utilization of skilled nursing facility, home health agency, and inpatient hospital rehabilitation services. *Health Care Financing Review* (Suppl.).

Hing E. (1987, May). *Use of nursing homes by the elderly: Preliminary data from the 1985 national nursing home survey* (Advance Data No. 135). National Center for Health Statistics, Bethesda, MD.

Kupfer, D. J. (1983). Toward a unified view of affective disorder. In M. R. Zales (Ed.), *Affective schizophrenic disorders: New approaches to diagnosis and treatment* (pp. 225–264). New York: Brunner/Mazel.

National Center for Health Statistics (1984). Data from the National Health Interview Survey: Supplement on Aging and the National Nursing Home Survey. *Advance Data, 115, 121, 133,* and *135.*

Phan, T. T., & Reifler, B. V. (1988). Psychiatric disorders among nursing home residents. *Clinical Geriatric Medicine, 4,* 601–611.

Trends and projections. (1988). *Aging America* (1987–88) (USDHHS, LR 3377, D 12198).

U.S. Senate Special Committee on Aging, 1988. *Aging Americans: Trends and Projections,* 1987–88 Edition, Washington, D.C.

Wanlass, W. (1993, November). *Attitudes of residents, staff and family toward restraint use.* (Abstract presentation). Annual meeting of the American Geriatric Society, New Orleans.

Chapter Four

Cognitive Impairment and Autonomy

Cornelia K. Beck and Theresa S. Vogelpohl

C ognitively impaired elders make up approximately 75% of the residents in long-term-care facilities. Supporting autonomy for these residents presents many challenges and conflicts. Although OBRA mandates that we respect the rights and autonomy of residents, OBRA regulations provide few clues to resolving the dilemmas that arise when this mandate is applied to cognitively impaired individuals.

Admission to a long-term-care facility usually results from radical alterations in an older adult's self-care capabilities. For the cognitively impaired elder, functional dependence often accompanies the cognitive impairment. Following admission, this dependence is exacerbated by the regimentation, loss of privacy, and diminished independent decision making inherent in a conjugate living arrangement. Cognitively impaired residents' limited words, gestures, and facial expressions, along with their unique terminology and minimal eye contact, inhibit communication (Elander, Drechsler, & Persson, 1993) and promote slow adaptation to the new environment. Receptive aphasias and memory deficits further compromise their capacity to adapt to a new environment. These limitations make it difficult to discern the cognitively impaired resident's decision-making capacity and judgment.

There is little information available on what constitutes autonomy for cognitively impaired elders, or what interventions are effective in maintaining independence and involvement for this group. Lacking information on what promotes autonomy for cognitively impaired residents of long-term-care facilities, we must rely on intuition and personal perceptions to accomplish this goal.

Although most discussions of autonomy for cognitively impaired residents focus on use of expensive, death-delaying technology and treatments, in this chapter we focus on the day-to-day exercise of autonomy that is an essential ingredient in an individual's self-concept and perception of worth. We look briefly at the following issues: (a) impediments to autonomy, (b) complicating issues and factors that affect autonomy for cognitively impaired residents, (c) consequences of allowing or disallowing autonomy, and (d) strategies for promoting autonomy in this group. We use case examples from our research to illustrate the positive outcomes that are achievable when cognitively impaired residents are given a measure of autonomy, no matter how small.

Impediments to Autonomy

There are many psychological, educational, organizational, and societal barriers to autonomy for cognitively impaired nursing home residents. Psychological barriers are among the most insidious. One such obstacle to autonomy is low goal formulation for cognitively impaired elders. People often assume that a cognitively impaired elder cannot regain a self-care function once it has been lost. Further, they assume that elders who are impaired in one cognitive ability are impaired in all abilities including the ability to express their own needs and wishes. Finally, people may not recognize that skills learned over a lifetime, such as dressing, can be regained if appropriate supportive interventions are employed. Such perceptions of disability and concomitant low-goal formulation contribute to excess disability in cognitively impaired elders by imposing dependence in a wider range of functions than is warranted.

The approach to care of cognitively impaired elders based on assumptions of disability and low-goal formulation contrasts sharply with health care providers' approach to a young, head-injured patient. When caring for a head-injured patient, providers thoroughly assess specific injuries sustained, identify remaining abilities, formulate goals that promote maximum independence, and pursue an aggressive multidisciplinary treatment plan to maximize the functional independence and autonomy of the young patient.

Learned attitudes toward authority and authority figures pose another psychological impediment to autonomy for cognitively impaired elders. Older adults tend to relinquish autonomy more readily than younger individuals might because older adults were brought up with a stronger belief in the absolute power of authority figures (Cohen, 1988; Elander et al., 1993), and they tend to be fearful of opposing authority. This acquiescence to authority may be exhibited as passivity and may lead to the assumption that cognitively impaired elders lack the capacity for continued meaningful engagement. Cognitively impaired elders may be perceived as inferior to younger, cognitively intact individuals. As a result, caregivers may view cognitively impaired residents as incompetent and deprive them of self-determination. In one nursing home, a nurse was heard to say, "When patients arrive they usually want to keep their habits, but after a while they adjust to routines, which makes it easier for the nurses" (Elander et al., 1993, p. 96).

Educational impediments further inhibit autonomy for cognitively impaired elders. Educational obstacles include caregivers' lack of understanding of dementia and their lack of skills needed for effective communication with cognitively impaired residents. Much of the day-to-day care for cognitively impaired residents in nursing homes is provided by nursing assistants and nurses who may have had limited exposure to information on cognitive impairment. In one study, nursing assistants felt justified in making decisions for the cognitively impaired residents because they believed that the residents were not aware of opportunities for decision making. Some nursing assistants believed that they did not need to talk with demented residents because of the residents' impaired communication abilities (Elander et al., 1993).

Without adequate knowledge of dementia, caregivers may not recognize the heterogeneity of cognitively impaired elders and may assume that all of them have the same cognitive deficits. Thus, caregivers may not recognize that one cognitively impaired resident is able to make good judgments despite little memory capacity, whereas another may have more memory capacity but be unable to make good judgments. Without adequate knowledge, care becomes mechanical and depersonalizing for both residents and staff.

Organizational impediments to resident autonomy include institutional regimentation codified in regulations, policies, and practices; resource constraints; and staff turnover. Most long-term-care settings provide care according to a depersonalized medical model rather than supporting the self-care efforts of autonomous individuals with defined deficits. (We could learn much about respecting personhood from countries such as China where long-term-care residents' rooms are decorated with memorabilia of accomplishments from their younger years.) Further, resource constraints inhibit the search for alternative modes of care, and staff turnover confounds efforts to improve the situation through education and continuity. There is also a subtle reimbursement bias against providing care to cognitively impaired residents.

Societal issues also contribute to the lack of autonomy-enhancing care for cognitively impaired elders. Most dementias are progressively degenerating diseases requiring long term care, but health care money is tight. Because of limited financial resources, policy makers have begun to raise questions about the extent of treatment to be provided persons with terminal illnesses or in so-called hopeless situations. Economic goals can perhaps be better met by providing care that protects the dignity of cognitively impaired residents and maintains their engagement in the environment as long as possible rather than merely extending the number of years of breathing. Interventions that extend life tend to be costly and may, in fact, have a negative effect on a resident's autonomy, whereas interventions that promote quality of life are less costly and can significantly enhance autonomy.

Additional societal issues have to do with the current structure of our health care system, which values dependence rather than autonomy, compliance rather than commitment, and youthful vigor rather than the decline of old age. Is nonmaleficence or the removal of impediments to autonomy sufficient, or are we impelled to take positive action to support autonomy? What constitutes extraordinary care for cognitively impaired residents? If we err in our decisions, should we err on the side of liberty and autonomy or on the side of safety and beneficence (Fitting, 1980). These are volatile issues, to be sure, yet we must address them if we are to develop an agenda for promoting autonomy for cognitively impaired residents.

Related Issues

When developing plans and evaluating outcomes of interventions to promote autonomy for cognitively impaired nursing home residents, we cannot make decisions based on the usual outcome measures of morbidity and mortality. Instead, we must develop new outcome measures, such as quality of life, psychological integration, and sense of dignity. However, it may be difficult, if not impossible, to state with certainty that a cognitively impaired resident has experienced autonomy because the person may be incapable of verifying that. It is likewise difficult to determine whether a cognitively impaired elder perceives an opportunity for greater autonomy as beneficial. Individuals with a lifetime of passivity and care receiving may prefer to continue their dependence rather than participate in a program that promotes independence. The case example of Sophia R., a 73-year-old widow from Mobile, Alabama, illustrates this point.

> Sophia, the only child of a Baptist minister, was carefully supervised in all of her childhood activities to ensure that she did nothing to embarrass the family. She remained single until her father died. At age 35 she married an older man with four grown children. Her new husband was protective of his younger wife, and she seldom went anywhere without him. His sudden death left her unprepared to assume responsibility for herself. After 3 years of widowhood, she was placed in a nursing home because of moderate cognitive impairment. While a subject in one of our studies, Sophia was sweet and cooperated with our psychosocial interventions. However, she steadfastly refused to participate in bathing and dressing herself, preferring instead for staff to perform these activities.

Health care workers generally espouse the view that nursing home residents have the right to high-quality care, but who decides what that means? What parties have a legitimate right to set standards for the long-term care of cognitively impaired residents? Currently, educated, powerful professionals make these decisions. Who else should participate, and to what extent? Society generally measures quality of care in long-term-care settings by standards derived from the acute care "cure" model. Because most cognitively impaired residents have chronic conditions not amenable to cure, we must redefine quality care in terms of the life perspective of older adults. This may mean providing opportunities for cognitively impaired residents to continue meaningful activities and to participate in decision making on proposed treatments.

The cognitively impaired resident often makes seemingly irrational decisions, and caregivers feel the need to "protect" the person from the unpleasant effects of such decisions. However, even competent, cognitively intact individuals make irrational decisions that may not seem to be in their best interest, yet we allow them to go forward with such decisions despite evident negative consequences. Does a resident lose this right because of cognitive impairment?

As we protect the rights of the individual resident, another issue arises: To what extent should an institution be required to commit resources to meet the needs and demands of cognitively impaired residents? If a resident refuses to cooperate with efforts to maintain/promote autonomy, how far must the staff go in efforts to rehabilitate (Collopy, 1988)? Intrinsic and extrinsic rewards exist for the cognitively impaired resident who opts for dependence rather than autonomy. Do we accept this decision? Are there limitations to entitlements (Collopy, 1988)? Inherent in any effort to grant more rights to one group is the danger of violating the rights of another group. We run the risk of damaging the collective good of all nursing home residents by granting more autonomy to cognitively impaired elders unless we plan carefully. For example, granting a cognitively impaired resident the right to wander may encroach on the right to privacy of other residents when the wanderer enters their rooms. The cognitively impaired resident who "collects" things can cause great distress to fellow residents and staff, who consider that individual a thief. How can we simultaneously protect the interests of all residents and staff? Are special care units required?

Family members also have rights and values that deserve attention when considering greater autonomy for cognitively impaired residents. Unfortunately, interests and goals of cognitively impaired residents and their families are often in conflict. In our research to promote functional independence in dressing, one daughter gave consent for her mother to participate in our behavioral intervention. However, another daughter believed that her mother should not be "bothered" with our intervention. At the beginning of our study, a nursing assistant completely dressed this almost nonverbal resident. By the end of our study, the resident was actively participating in her dressing and was so excited about being able to put on her blouse that she exclaimed, "I did it, I did it," and hugged the nursing assistant. Despite this improvement in the resident's functional independence, the second daughter remained discontent with our intervention, believing that her mother should be "left alone."

Families faced with multiple obligations and commitments may have trouble recognizing that the cognitively impaired resident's wishes differ from their own. One family refused to give consent for their father to participate in our study, fearing that his functional level would improve, and he would be discharged from the nursing home. Decision making in this emotionally charged climate is difficult. We must find ways to facilitate the decision-making process for all concerned.

We must also recognize that autonomy is multifaceted, and we may need to restrict one aspect of autonomy to facilitate another. For example, it is sometimes necessary to persuade a resident strongly to participate in a program that promotes dressing independence so the individual may exercise greater autonomy in dressing in the future. To illustrate, Mrs. B., an 84-year-old widow, refused to come out of her room for meals or other facility activities. She also refused to interact with her family. When initially enrolled in our study, she vigorously resisted the efforts of our nursing assistant to engage her in study activities, even chasing the nursing assistant from her room with a cane. After a month in the study, however, Mrs. B. voluntarily left her room and sought opportunities to be involved in facility activities. Her family was even able to take her on a trip to visit relatives in another state.

Inner autonomy may be promoted by limiting outer autonomy. In our study, we offered a cognitively impaired resident only two choices of dresses to wear, and she was able to point to one. In contrast, placing her in front of the closet and asking her to choose from a larger selection overwhelmed her decision-making capacity.

Definite actions to promote independence are likely to achieve greater results than merely removing impediments to autonomy (Collopy, 1988). For example, Mrs. K., a 93-year-old wheelchair-bound subject in our study, ate her meals alone in her room. The project nursing assistant encouraged engagement by taking Mrs. K. to the dining room and reinforcing her socialization during the meal. By the end of the study, Mrs. K. was wheeling herself to the dining room and interacting with others at the table.

Usually we perceive autonomy and paternalism as opposite ends of the spectrum of care. However, we may need to embrace a philosophy of autonomy-promoting paternalism, in which the caregiver allows maximum independence while protecting the cognitively impaired resident from harm (Hegeman & Tobin, 1988). This approach is likely to achieve better results than beneficence, which encourages staff to perform ADLs for the cognitively impaired resident.

Consequences of Allowing or Disallowing Autonomy

The consequences of allowing more autonomy for cognitively impaired residents include better physical and psychological health for the cognitively impaired resident, better staff morale, and more cost-effective care. In our current study of disruptive behavior, we have found that intervention subjects, who were permitted greater autonomy than usual in a nursing home setting, appeared more relaxed and interacted with their environment more. Staff appeared more relaxed as well. One nursing attendant even cheered when a resident put on his own pants with only verbal prompting. Minutes earlier two attendants had been struggling to dress the unbendable, uncooperative man.

The consequences of not allowing autonomy for cognitively impaired residents include excess disability and an increased probability of disruptive behavior. Residents often develop a taut, drawn visage reminiscent of those seen in unrelenting, high-anxiety situations. They alternately withdraw into their own shell of rigidity, or strike out physically and verbally at their environment. The staff members are likewise affected; they may experience low morale and burnout from constant dilemmas and internal conflicts. With care prescribed by institutional regimentation, staff members become frustrated by their inability to give special care to meet the needs of a particular resident. Some have stated that they feel like robots, going through routines with no consideration for the personhood of their care recipients (Ekman & Norberg, 1988). Faced with these circumstances on a daily basis, hopelessness becomes endemic.

Strategies for Promoting Autonomy

As noted earlier, cognitive impairment does not signal total incompetence mandating loss of autonomy and total dependence. Through a variety of means, including legal and social, we must try to determine the extent of mental incompetence accompanying cognitive impairment. We can then support the remaining decision-making capability by activities that involve a continuum of support. The continuum begins with advocacy and progresses to empowerment, persuasion, and surrogate decision making (Moody, 1988). Mental capacity fluctuates unpredictably, leaving the cognitively impaired resident lucid and rational at times and impaired at others (Fitting, 1980). Thus, the cognitively impaired resident may have complete capacity to make some decisions and total incapacity to make others. By employing advocacy, empowerment, and persuasion, caregivers can maximize and honor the cognitively impaired resident's mental capacity while not exacerbating areas of incompetence. Cognitive impairment does not always lead to significant behavioral abnormalities if caregivers provide support in activities that cognitively impaired residents are not able to perform independently (Rabins & Mace, 1986).

Inferences about competence must rest on an understanding of the effects of dementia on behavior and judgment, not on the fact that dementia is present (Rabins & Mace, 1986). Rarely is decisional incapacity absolute (Fitting, 1980); thus, we must protect the cognitively impaired resident's right to choose as much as possible. Protecting the right to choose in day-to-day activities is especially important, given the heterogeneity of cognitive loss and the daily fluctuations of cognition.

As we plan programs for promoting the autonomy of cognitively impaired residents, we must also consider all facets of each individual in our care. We can do this by taking steps to preserve and respect the personhood of each resident. To illustrate, Mr. W. has a 70-year history of going to bed at midnight and sleeping until 8:00 A.M.; should this suddenly change when he becomes a nursing home resident? If Mr. W. resists efforts to promote an earlier bedtime and watches television until midnight, what harm is caused? We are better able to understand the behaviors of our cognitively impaired elders if we take the time to learn about their past values, habits, and decisions.

In the preceding example, we might respond that Mr. W.'s best interests would be served by imposing a more reasonable bedtime. He is less likely to experience delusions precipitated by nighttime lighting and sound levels. But who decides what constitutes "best interests"? The individual is best suited to make such a determination if the person is competent.

Ideally, the cognitively impaired elder appoints a proxy early in the dementing illness and makes general treatment choices and decisions before competence becomes an issue (Pratt, Schmall, & Wright, 1987; Veatch, 1984). These decisions should be put in writing to encourage future adherence to choices. In the absence of such foresight, caregivers can facilitate autonomy for the cognitively impaired resident by attempting to learn about personal preferences, habits, and care routines. We act in the best interests of the cognitively impaired resident when we consider that person's lived history and imagine outcomes of a particular course of action in the light of that person's decision-making pattern. In other words, we establish a plan based on what that person would do if capable of making the decision. In doing so, we must recognize that acting in the "best interests" does not always entail technological interventions (Rabins & Mace, 1986; Veatch, 1984).

In making decisions affecting the autonomy of cognitively impaired residents, we must consider the needs and values of all persons involved. The team providing care to the cognitively impaired resident brings to this not only their particular educational and professional preparation, but also their unique histories, interests, and values. Although this diversity provides rich resources to promote quality care, it may also serve as a source of conflict concerning autonomy for cognitively impaired residents. For example, nursing staff members often spend more time with residents than the family or other care team members, and they may develop a considerable attachment to the residents. We have witnessed this to such an extent that nursing staff members sometimes consider themselves to be surrogate family. They then become reluctant to carry out the wishes of the legally recognized family when they perceive those wishes to be in conflict with actions nursing staff members deem appropriate. The inability of cognitively impaired residents to clearly articulate their own wishes further complicates the situation.

Health team members may sometimes make decisions based on their own personal biases. Nursing home staff members are not immune to the effects of ageism and selfishness. Some care patterns are established for staff convenience, and others reflect the preferences of staff rather than residents.

How to weigh the needs and wishes of team members is but one of the dilemmas of enhancing autonomy for cognitively impaired residents. Surrogate decision making regarding care and treatments poses another dilimma. There is currently no way to avoid situations requiring a surrogate decision maker for the cognitively impaired elder; however, we can maintain some degree of autonomy for the resident by careful planning. If the cognitively impaired elder does not designate a proxie, we must be careful to choose the right decision maker when questions about care arise. The right decision maker is not necessarily a member of the immediate family; therefore, we must find ways to identify the person(s) who can best represent the wishes of the cognitively impaired resident. The first choice would be an individual with close emotional ties to the cognitively impaired resident (Fitting, 1980). The next choice would be a family member who is knowledgeable of the values and wishes of the resident. The family history gives important clues to the choice of an appropriate surrogate decision maker.

Open, ongoing communication among team members is particularly important in promoting autonomy for the cognitively impaired residents. The team should include nursing staff, social worker, physician, and other facility staff as well as the family and cognitively impaired resident. Communication between family and staff should aim at a deeper understanding of the history, values, interests, and preferences of the resident. Family members can bring in or help develop a scrapbook of pictures and letters that emphasize the personhood of the cognitively impaired elder. Staff also should explore the family's understanding of the dementing illness as well as the coping levels of various family members.

Communication among staff members should focus on ways to establish effective communication with cognitively impaired residents. All staff, including dietary and housekeeping personnel, should be involved in identifying the meaning of specific cues or behaviors from the resident. They should share with each other specific techniques that are successful in engaging the cognitively impaired resident in exercising autonomy. In addition, staff can assist each other by serving as "safety valves" for coworkers. When the tension and frustration of ongoing dealings with cognitively impaired residents become too intense, hearing "take 10" from a coworker (a suggestion to take a ten minute break) helps ease the strain. "Take 10" alerts the caregiver that the strain present in the interaction is having negative consequences, and the caregiver needs to use some stress reduction techniques for herself.

Communicating with cognitively impaired residents is essential for promoting their autonomy. Development of skills in communicating with cognitively impaired residents should be part of ongoing staff development programs, with specific training in active listening and keen observation. Faced with interrupted thought processes, unique ways of expressing needs and wishes, and decreased attention spans, staff interacting with cognitively impaired residents face daily challenges akin to those of communicating with a visitor from another country. Communication techniques that have proven effective with cognitively impaired elders include short, simple sentences; lots of smiles; displays of respect, and appropriate use of touch. Frequent reinforcement from supervisors and each other will help staff members increase their sensitivity to cues from the cognitively impaired resident.

Ongoing staff development is an important element. Caregivers can more effectively promote autonomy and independence when they are educated to the variability in cognitive deficits and remaining assets of cognitively impaired elders. In addition to communication skills, topics for continuing education should include on a rotating basis dementia education, stress reduction techniques, and care strategies that promote functional independence and dignity. Staff development might also involve experiential training in which a staff member "lives" the life of a resident for a day, and then shares feelings and experiences with fellow employees. Staff training should emphasize giving respect, care, and assistance without expecting responses or gratitude from the cognitively impaired resident, who may not be able to reciprocate (Binstock, Post, & Whitehouse, 1992).

Staffing patterns can also be used to promote autonomy. Supervisors should consider assigning consistent caregivers to cognitively impaired residents so that both caregiver and care recipient can become familiar with each other. Facilities might consider using specialized staff for dementia care.

There are many other policies and practices that facilities can adopt to promote autonomy for cognitively impaired residents. Protective environments are one option. Current data indicate that special care units give more freedom and functional independence to cognitively impaired elders. Other protective environments include a home-like therapeutic milieu (similar to the milieu created for the mentally retarded) and wander-proof lounges provide daytime respite for other residents and staff when behaviors of the cognitively impaired residents are particularly disruptive (Hegeman & Tobin, 1988).

In addition, a facility can implement special programs to enhance autonomy and independence for cognitively impaired residents including reminiscence, validation therapy, sensory stimulation, and psychosocial activities. We have used psychosocial activities successfully to decrease the disruptive behavior of cognitively impaired residents. These activities include reminiscence, physical activity, crafts, letter writing, and validation.

To promote the cognitively impaired resident's functional performance, we have developed a continuum of interventions that we call levels of assistance. These capacity-appropriate interventions begin with stimulus control, which entails minimizing interruptions, controlling noise levels, and maximizing use of visual cues. Visual cues include placing clothing on a sharply contrasting background, stacking clothing in the order of dressing, and placing an item, such as a shoe, next to the appropriate extremity.

Verbal prompting is the second level of assistance. The caregiver uses a one-step command to remind the cognitively impaired resident of the next action needed to complete a process. Gestures and modeling, the third level of assistance, provide visual cues to persons with receptive aphasia. In the fourth level of assistance, physical prompting, the caregiver touches the extremity that the resident is to move next. This helps orient residents with apraxias. The caregiver uses physical guidance, the fifth level, to initiate an action that the cognitively impaired elder completes either independently or with verbal prompting. The final level, complete assistance, employs reverse chaining as follows: On day 1, the caregiver completes the entire process for the resident while using verbal and physical prompting to encourage resident participation. On subsequent days, the caregiver gradually decreases the amount of assistance provided while continuing to use other levels of assistance to promote task completion.

Implementing these various strategies will change patterns of care and bring us back to the vision set forth by Virginia Henderson in 1966: "The nurse assists the individual . . . to perform activities . . . that the individual would perform unaided if he had necessary strength, will, or knowledge" (Henderson, 1966, p. 15). To fulfill this vision, we must move our care philosophy for cognitively impaired elders from caregiver to supportive proxie, from enforced dependence to supported independence (Collopy, 1988).

References

Binstock, R. H., Post, S. G., & Whitehouse, P. J. (Eds.). (1992). *Dementia and aging. Ethics, values, and policy choices.* Baltimore: The Johns Hopkins University Press.

Cohen, E. S. (1988). The elderly mystique: Constraints of the autonomy of the elderly with disabilities. *The Gerontologist, 28,* 24–31.

Collopy, B. J. (1988). Autonomy in long term care: Some crucial distinctions. *The Gerontologist, 28,* 10–17.

Ekman, S. L., & Norberg, A. (1988). The autonomy of demented patients: Interviews with caregivers. *Journal of Medical Ethics, 14,* 184–187.

Elander, G., Drechsler, K., & Persson, K. W. (1993). Ethical dilemmas in long-term care settings: Interviews with nurses in Sweden and England. *International Journal of Nursing Studies, 30,* 91–97.

Fitting, M. D. (1980). Professional and ethical responsibilities for psychologists working with the elderly. *The Counseling Psychologist, 12,* 69–78.

Hegeman, C., & Tobin, S. (1988). Enhancing the autonomy of mentally impaired nursing home residents. *The Gerontologist, 28,* 71–75.

Henderson, V. A. (1966). *The nature of nursing.* New York: Macmillan.

Moody, H. R. (1988). From informed consent to negotiated consent. *The Gerontologist, 28,* 64–70.

Pratt, C., Schmall, V., & Wright, S. (1987). Ethical concerns of family caregivers to dementia patients. *The Gerontologist, 27,* 632–638.

Rabins, P. V., & Mace, N. L. (1986). Some ethical issues in dementia care. In *Clinical Gerontologist* (pp. 503–512). The Haworth Press.

Veatch, R. M. (1984). An ethical framework for terminal care decisions: A new classification of patients. *Journal of the American Geriatrics Society, 32,* 665–669.

Chapter Five

The Impact of Long-Term-Care Financing on Personal Autonomy

Robert L. Kane

A mericans can be characterized by two prominent traits that shape their approach to long-term care. Since the founding of this country, great weight has been placed on the importance of individualism and the responsibility that goes with the choices afforded. A second dominant belief is related to the first one. Great faith is placed in the marketplace. Competition is relied on heavily as a leveler of playing fields. Indeed, democracy, with its support of individual rights (and responsibilities), is often paired with capitalism. One might say that America then is the land of both the Bill of Rights and the right to bill.

Economic forces play a strong role in shaping behaviors, especially when the money involved is public. Private money may be spent according to marketplace ethics, but public funds will inevitably lead to a regulatory response, especially when the funds are disbursed to proprietary providers.

Formal services in America are thus greatly influenced by two types of regulatory forces: the more obvious quality regulation, and the less overt but equally potent policies around public payments. Payment affects both who and what are covered, and, hence, what types of services are provided to whom. One could hardly propose a more direct intrusion on personal autonomy.

The issue is, thus, less a question of the existence of an impact than of the extent of that impact. In a country like the United States, where much of long-term care is financed with public dollars paid to private, often proprietary, providers, payment controls become an important tool of policy. In accepting public money, both the provider and the client must submit to the dictates of others.

Eligibility

Policies around eligibility for public support establish limits on what kinds of people will be helped and what kinds of help are deemed appropriate. Because most of the public funding for long-term care is linked to the Medicaid program, coverage comes at the cost of penury, which, in turn, is linked to a loss of the resources that might permit subsequent restoration of autonomy. The modern reports of changing behavior among middle-class persons, with active pursuit of strategies to become eligible for Medicaid assistance by divesting themselves of assets, suggest that the view of Medicaid may be shifting toward an entitlement. Nonetheless, becoming eligible for such a service places a person in a fundamentally dependent position.

One must establish need in terms of both disability and poverty. The criteria for both vary from state to state. The criteria for the former are usually based on some form of judgment about the need for care at the nursing home level. This requirement may extend so far as to require that the applicant actually apply for admission to a nursing home, as a means of establishing eligibility from community-based care. Because the assessment of disability relies heavily on requiring the assistance of others, those persons who are receiving help are most likely to qualify. Persons who are struggling to maintain their autonomy are less likely to be judged in need.

The decision about disability eligibility is generally conducted on an all-or-nothing basis. Persons deemed to have crossed an arbitrary threshold are judged eligible for the full array of benefits possible. Those that do not get nothing. There is no provision for modest services to those with only modest needs. Financial eligibility is more complicated. A minority of persons are eligible on the basis of being in a categorical welfare program such as Old Age Assistance. Most older persons receiving Medicaid support get it on the basis of being medically needy; that is, their medical costs exceed an established proportion of their income. Of course, to achieve eligibility in this manner, one must first have incurred the costs. In many cases, this produces a catch-22. Many older people are hesitant to spend themselves into poverty. Hence, the benefits of Medicaid are heavily tilted toward those whose disabilities require major investments and those for whom the extent of the costs can be easily established in advance, namely, those in nursing homes.

Choice of Services and Providers

Not everything is covered. The disbursement of public funds appears as too important a task to be left to the clients. Clients dependent on public funds are limited in the options available to meet their needs. They may be constrained in terms of the types of services for which they are eligible and the agencies that can provide those services. Benefit packages may be limited by professional beliefs about what works, or by concerns about not covering too broad and expensive a repertoire of services. Providers of covered services must often be certified as qualified, further limiting choice.

Professional beliefs about orthodoxy may also restrict the types of care available. Despite a dearth of hard data about what sorts of services are effective in maintaining function, there is a strong propensity to work with existing forms of care and to resist innovations. Pressures associated, at least in part, with fear of being judged neglectful push agencies to support established approaches rather than to innovate. Often the safety of an environment, especially its physical accoutrements and the professional credentials of the staff, may play a stronger role in establishing its legitimacy than its programs. Issues, such as its attention to the preferences of individual clients, will be less appreciated and may even be considered a breach if they involve unorthodox activities.

Institutions are inherently restrictive. Institutions that must follow rigid regulations to be eligible for reimbursement are likely to be even more restrictive.

Biases in Approaches to Payment

The way care is paid for will influence what sort of care is given and perhaps indirectly what happens as a result. Under the pressure of the Boren amendment, governments have been obliged to pay nursing homes an amount that is supposed to represent the costs of adequate care. This requirement has created a strong interest in case-mix approaches to funding. However, ironically, a case-mix strategy may threaten the autonomy some saw it as improving. The underlying premise of a case-mix approach is that the greater a client's needs, the larger the payment. Hence, the system provides a real, if subtle, incentive to see clients become more, rather than less, dependent. When the case-mix technique is applied to other types of long-term care, such as home care, the situation is exacerbated.

Although case mix addresses a long-existing problem—namely, the propensity of nursing homes to avoid heavy care cases—there is reason to be concerned that case mix may not be sensitive to the full range of clients treated in nursing homes today. The pressure for earlier discharge from hospitals has created new pressures on long-term care to treat more acutely ill patients. The case-mix approach focuses on more chronic dependence and associated care needs and may not detect changes in medical needs as readily. As a result, patients may not get the attention they need, and their problems may be treated as chronic when in fact the problems are remediable.

The case-mix approach is based on modeling the care that is presently delivered, not necessarily the appropriate care. Often elaborate techniques are employed to associate the personnel effort devoted to clients with the characteristics of those clients to deduce the amount of care needed for clients with varying traits. However, redistributing the current level of effort is different from providing the sort of care that may yield a better result. One grievous example may suffice. In terms of expedition, it is often much faster to feed someone who requires considerable assistance than to work with that individual to encourage her to perform the tasks as much as possible on her own. However, fostering independence is a major goal of chronic care. Thus, this pseudoefficiency becomes the enemy of autonomy.

The case-mix payment system may also discourage some providers from doing more than they need to. Although there is good reason to believe that many acute exacerbations of chronic problems can be effectively treated in a nursing home, it may be difficult to get such an institution to take on the added work and the responsibility associated with that care, especially when there

is no commensurate payment for it. It is much easier to transfer the
patient into the acute care sector, and leave the work and the
burden to others. A single case-mix rate is not flexible enough to
cope with this different approach to defining needs for care.

Home Care

Most people dependent on public support have only limited access
to home care programs. Although home health care is a benefit
under Medicaid for those deemed eligible, basic support with
chronic problems is available on an uneven basis at state option. A
few states have elected to develop an extensive system of community care, but most offer only rudimentary services that affect a small
minority of the long-term care population.

When it is available, home care presents some special problems.
Payment for home care is often organized into minimum blocks of
time. That is, a home visit must last at least a certain time to write
off the costs of transportation against the charges for the direct
services. Such practices guarantee a more profitable business, but
make each visit more expensive and, hence, may limit the number
of visits made because of budgetary constraints. Clients at home
need regular services, but they often need them for only small
aliquots of time; moreover, the specific timing is essential to maintaining autonomy. For example, a person who needs assistance
with transferring will require someone to come to the home in the
morning to help him get out of bed and again in the evening to get
him back in bed. Each visit can be brief, but it is not efficient to
combine the time expended in the two trips into a single visit.
Payment for home care must thus provide a flexible set of services.

Relying on public funding for home care means allowing public
representatives into your home. This invasion of privacy can be
threatening to some older persons' autonomy. Once the sanctity of
the threshold is breached, the older person's living situation comes
under scrutiny. Professionals may find some homes too dangerous
or unsanitary for their professional standards. As a consequence,
older clients may be pressured to move into an institution where
they can live more sanitarily, if not necessarily more happily.

Thus, allowing government agents into the home may mean
making an older person a ward of the state. Receiving assistance
implies a level of frailty that marks the older person as a vulner-

able adult. Plans of care are established to protect the older person from possible harms. These plans can frequently lead to institutionalization in the name of safety.

Finally, home care recipients are often case managed. Case management is viewed as an effective method to assure that public funds are spent prudently, but few people—given a choice—would opt to have someone else make decisions about the care they will receive.

Nursing Homes

The nursing home is largely a creation of Medicaid. Although they were established before the passage of Title XIX of the Social Security Act in 1965, nursing homes grew enormously in the unanticipated wake of that provision. Indeed, the original regulations called for a level of care that could not be provided by existing institutions. A new category of nursing home, the so-called intermediate care facility (presumably intermediate between skilled care and something much less), had to be created. The nursing home has since emerged as the touchstone of long-term care. Ironically, it was first seen as the most expensive form of long-term care and eventually was viewed as the best buy. More than a decade of demonstration programs and research projects were devoted to finding less expensive community alternatives without success.

As a medium for covering the costs of both room and board and services, the nursing home is a frugal purchase. Unfortunately, it may not buy much. On average, Medicaid-supported nursing home stays provide little service (less than an hour a day of all types of direct nursing care) and nothing that resembles a home-like atmosphere. Persons supported by public funds have only a few options, of which the nursing home is by far the most common. Other approaches to meeting their housing and service needs are not available except under special demonstration project situations.

Payment Options

The approach to paying for care most conducive to enhancing autonomy would be to provide each disabled person with a sum of money, and allow her to purchase whatever care she thinks she needs and wants. This strategy is essentially what organizations of younger disabled adults have lobbied for. However, there are several reasons why such an approach has not been, and is not likely to be, adopted.

Providing unconstrained cash offers the greatest amount of freedom and control. It is, therefore, the most attractive. Were disability the trigger for cash payments, it is reasonable to expect that many more people would make claims and, thus, greatly increase the cost of long-term care. Cash payments provide no controls over how the money is spent. Unlike private insurance companies, which often offer indemnity policies that, in essence, put a fixed price on various unfortunate events, governments may find themselves in a double bind. As the place of last resort, they are less able to negotiate a closed-ended deal with a client. A client who takes the cash payment and squanders it may still come back to the government to demand care. It is politically difficult to turn away such a petitioner on the grounds of previous profligacy. Indeed, this question of individual responsibility raises the whole issue of blaming the victim: To what extent should society assume responsibility for problems that a person brings on himself or herself (e.g., self-inflicted injury, disease caused by poor health behavior, or unwise use of resources)?

It is, therefore, to the government's advantage not to allow unrestricted use of public resources. A parallel argument can be made from the perspective of beneficence, namely, that these sorts of decisions are simply too complex to be totally given over to laypersons. Obtaining the often complicated array of services needed taxes even experienced professionals, let alone amateurs doing it for the first time.

The bottom line is that unrestricted funding is an unlikely option, certainly for a group that is defined by frailty, including mental frailty. One might argue that many frail older people have hearty relatives and friends who could act as their agents and advocates, but this line of reasoning would create two classes of people: those with social support and those without. There are many reasons why a two-class approach is not desirable.[1]

The next step along the way to decreasing levels of autonomy would be some form of voucher. In this case, a person who needs assistance would not get money but, rather, some form of limited use coverage. The voucher could be used with any vendor who would accept it (as with food stamps), but it could only be legitimately used for specified types of services. (The potential for a black market, as with food stamps, would exist, however.) A voucher approach allows the government to exert greater levels of control. A professional can determine what types of services are needed and, in effect, write a prepaid prescription. However, the client retains a wide latitude of control over who supplies the needed service.

Critics of the voucher approach again worry about the potential for misuse. The clients are still left largely on their own to find providers, although the case managers or service prescribers could suggest potential sources of care. Nevertheless, critics envision clients falling into the hands of cadres of manipulative providers who will take their vouchers but provide little tangible assistance. To the degree that the vouchers can be cashed, they approximate the (discounted) dangers of abuse noted with cash payments.

One might envision a system in which the vouchers could only be redeemed at authorized locations, where authorization would effectively constitute the certification and licensure in use today. This step would substantially reduce the distance between vouchers and the present system of direct payment. Even within the current method of direct payment to providers, there are some options to at least enhance client autonomy. With the voucher system, clients could be given greater choice about who the provider would be, in terms of both generic type and specific provider within a type of care. Clients could be allowed to change providers if they were dissatisfied.

However, both of these consumer autonomy protections are difficult to operationalize, especially once the client is institutionalized. It is practically difficult for a client to express dissatisfaction safely with the people who control her daily environment, and the client may become inured to the situation to the point that she accepts such treatment as inevitable. These problems should not justify rejecting efforts to elicit client satisfaction. Rather, they should form the basis for recognizing the need for strong external forces to enhance client autonomy.

One method to enhance client autonomy in the context of direct payment is to alter the basis for the payment. If the payment can be used to reward improvements (or even maintenance) of autonomous function and other outcomes that include client satisfaction, the providers of care will at least be more motivated to develop approaches to care and service that are conducive to these ends. It is possible to measure a variety of outcomes that reflect aspects of function and autonomy including the following:

- Physiological
- Pain/discomfort
- Functional
- Cognitive
- Affective
- Social interaction
- Social participation
- Satisfaction with care
- Satisfaction with environment

Each of these items can be measured (Kane, Bell, Riegler, Wilson, & Kane, 1983). It is further possible to create equations that will permit one to predict a client's future status and to contrast the actual outcomes with those expected (Kane, Bell, Riegler, Wilson, & Keeler, 1983). It is also possible to develop weights for each domain based on the preferences of clients and other interested parties (Kane, Bell, & Riegler, 1986), which permit the creation of

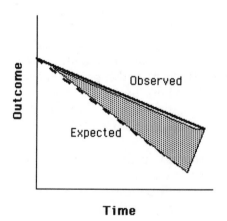

Time

Figure 5.1 Slowing the rate of decline.

single composite measures of outcomes. Because many long-term-care clients are frail and are likely to become more frail, preserving autonomy is best viewed as slowing the rate of decline. This concept is illustrated in Figure 5.1. Effective care is reflected in the size of the area between what would be the expected course and what actually occurs. It is feasible to incorporate such an approach into the payment methods for long-term care, at least to the extent that rewards are provided for those whose clients do consistently well and penalties assessed when clients do consistently poorly. Other techniques, such as publicity about good and bad care, may be even more effective and more easily implemented. If this were combined with greater consumer choice, it would provide a strong incentive for providers to want to achieve better outcomes and, hence, to enhance client autonomy. Such a circumstance would provide more of a win-win situation in which better care was associated with greater rewards for the caregiver and the payers were more confident that they were buying better results.

Note

1. One need only think about the problems of using the availability of social support as the basis for determining eligibility for public support or allocating such assistance to appreciate the mine fields such an approach would create.

References

Kane R. L., Bell R., Riegler S., Wilson A., & Kane, R. A. (1983). Assessing the outcomes of nursing home patients. *Journal of Gerontology, 38,* 385–393.

Kane R. L., Bell R. M., & Riegler S. Z. (1986). Value preferences for nursing-home outcomes. *The Gerontologist, 26,* 303–308.

Kane R. L., Bell R. M., Riegler S. Z., Wilson A., & Keeler, E. (1983). Predicting the outcomes of nursing-home patients. *The Gerontologist, 23,* 200–206.

Chapter Six

Autonomy and Regulation in Long-Term Care: An Odd Couple, An Ambiguous Relationship

Rosalie A. Kane

Long-Term Care Is Highly Regulated

Long-term care, particularly in nursing homes, is known to be highly regulated. Some have even compared it to nuclear power plants in the detail and care with which operating procedures are spelled out. Many reasons, historical and contextual, account for this. First, in the United States, governments are heavily involved in paying for nursing home care but not in providing it directly. Therefore, to get their money's worth, governments interest themselves in the details of what they are buying. Distrust is increased by the fact that so many of the care providers run for-profit businesses. Second, since the 1960s, the history of the nursing home industry has been punctuated by periodic dramatic lapses in the quality of care provided by some facilities; the typical response to each lapse is further regulation. Third, the inherent vulnerability of the population needing long-term care fosters a protective attitude, be it ever so paternalistic. Although regulatory reform in nursing homes has been almost a constant for the last 30 years, the overall result, including the landmark 1987 reforms (Institute of Medicine, 1986), has been to change but not appreciably lessen the requirements that nursing homes must meet.

Although nursing home staff and residents bear the brunt, regulations have also mounted in other long-term-care sectors, such as home care and board and care. Moreover, there is a constant appetite for further regulations. Whenever care or safety problems are found, a common reaction is "there should be a law against it."

Regulations that govern professional practitioners, such as nurses or pharmacists who work in long-term-care settings, also must be considered as part of the total volume of regulations affecting long-term care. As this chapter argues, however, the motivation for such regulation is as much to protect the practice scope of professionals as to enhance safety for clients.

Autonomy in Long-Term Care Tends to Be Lacking

Nursing homes and other long-term-care settings are easy targets for those on the prowl for autonomy-robbing social institutions. Whether respect for autonomy is defined negatively as freedom from interference with people's choices or decisions, or more positively as creation of an environment where real choice is feasible, few critics give nursing homes high marks (Collopy, Jennings, & Boyle, 1992; Kane & Caplan, 1990; Lidz, 1992). Arguing along the lines of George Agich (1993), one could construe respect for autonomy in long-term care to include helping residents maintain continuity with their past lifestyles and values. Here, again, the homogenized routines, settings, and activities; the difficulty in getting out of the nursing home; and the lack of privacy within it all militate against a resident's efforts to maintain such continuity. Sheldon Tobin (1991) refers to the struggle to maintain one's own identity or "personhood," given the ravages of disability and the impersonality of caregiving institutions, as one of the most difficult tasks for long-term-care clients. As many anthropologists and social scientists (e.g., Kaufman, 1986; Schmidt, 1990; Shield, 1988) have testified, the physical setting and social organization of the nursing home render this task even more difficult.

Residents tend to enter nursing homes with two strikes against them in the autonomy department. First, they tend not to have chosen nursing home care, and they tend not to have participated in the search to find the particular facility. Exerting one's right to act autonomously is difficult when one is transported perhaps against one's will, perhaps even without one's knowledge, into an alien environment.

Connection Between Regulation and Autonomy

The regulations that are prevalent in long-term care have a connection to the lack of personal autonomy, which for long-term-care clients seems the rule rather than the exception. It would be absurd, however, to blame regulations for all erosion of autonomy. Residents who are cognitively impaired; who have major sensory impairments that affect vision, hearing, and communication; or who are extremely ill, debilitated, or immobile will, by definition, have difficulty exerting autonomy. These difficulties limit the capacity to act and the scope of action.

Furthermore, it would be nihilistic to suggest that all regulations that infringe on a resident's autonomy should be abandoned. Regulations that promote safety are all around us, affecting the physical environment, the highways we drive on, and the food and clothing we buy. Regulations, many of them imperceptible to the general citizenry, are integral to our social communities. Although technically they restrict the freedom of those being protected, arguably regulations serve an important social good and enjoy the collective consent of the citizenry. The question is whether regulations have gone too far or taken off in the wrong direction in long-term care, in a way that improperly affects the autonomy of those most involved—the consumers of care. Another question is whether the regulations affecting the lives of those in nursing homes and long-term-care settings really do reflect the consent of the governed, in the same manner as, say, regulations that ensure the purity of food manufacture or the safety of bridges. Few consumers would argue that their rights are infringed by the regulations described previously, yet many nursing home residents do believe that their basic rights are violated by many nursing home rules. Nursing home rules, in turn, are often justified by regulation.

As we consider the complex relationship between regulation and autonomy, several questions about each regulation are useful: To what extent does this regulation alter the behavior of the person being protected? To what extent does the regulation result from the concerns of those being protected, as opposed to third-party advocacy? When applicable, to what extent does this regulation have a social purpose that should override the consent of those being protected?

First, this chapter briefly looks at different kinds of regulations in long-term care. It then considers the following four propositions: regulations in long-term care have reached the stage where they unfairly restrict the very clientele they were designed to protect; regulations in long-term care can be used to enhance client autonomy as well as to restrict it (recent regulatory reform concerning physical restraints is a prime example); it is easier to design regulations to restrict autonomy than to enhance it; regulations are sometimes used as scapegoats for other problems that restrict autonomy. The chapter concludes with thoughts about how to make long-term-care regulation more compatible with personal autonomy.

Types of Regulations Affecting Long-Term Care

Regulations in long-term care come in many forms, affect many different areas of practice, and are promulgated and monitored by a great variety of agencies at different governmental levels. All converge to shape the lives of the clientele.

Standards for Certification and Licensure

Nursing homes and home health agencies must be certified before they can participate as vendors in Medicare and Medicaid. The federal government cedes the inspections to the states, which also license nursing homes and, usually, home health agencies. State licensure requirements must conform with but may go beyond federal certification requirements. Even with perennial reforms geared to simplifying and directing regulations in ways that are important to the residents' care and life, the details are complex. Those who would comply with and those who would enforce the regulations must study thick volumes of regulations, rules, and interpretive guidelines. Nursing homes also are subject to other state and local ordinances affecting zoning, fire safety, and building costs.

Regulation in other long-term-care settings, such as board and care (Hawes, Wildfire, & Lux, 1993) and home care (Harrington &

Grant, 1990), differs from state to state more than regulation of nursing homes because less standardization tied to payment occurs at the federal level. But they, too, must meet varying state and local standards. In the emerging arena of assisted living, for example, states have established licensure standards that affect the physical environment, staffing, services, and clientele that may be admitted and retained (Kane & Wilson, 1993).

Standards are typically divided into three types: structure, process, and outcome. Most regulations affecting long-term care are "structural," referring, for example, to the interior and exterior of the building itself; the equipment in it; the types, numbers, and training of staff; the system for residents' records; and various governance and committee arrangements that must be in place. Such structural standards pertain to the program as a whole; all clientele, regardless of particular needs, are potentially benefited or affected by, say, the fire walls and sprinklers, presence of a qualified nurse, staffing ratios, safe storage of medications, staff development program, and quality-of-care committee.

Regulations geared toward "process" govern the care processes required for particular clients with particular conditions. Based on professional consensus about good practice, such regulations might assert the steps needed (including the observations made) to care for a bedsore, identify and treat urinary tract infections, or manage a wound in a person with diabetes. Such standards can be almost infinite in number and must evolve with rapidly changing professional knowledge; they do not lend themselves well to governmental regulation. Thus, process standards tend to be vague in the law (e.g., a nursing home must provide all nursing and rehabilitative care necessary). Long-term-care providers, however, can be held to account by regulatory bodies and potentially by private legal action, if their care falls short of professional norms. Long-term care poses particular difficulties in setting process standards, however, as one moves away from technical procedures to personal care assistance and daily living assistance: At some point, one must ask whether professional orthodoxy on matters, such as bathing, housekeeping, and ambulation assistance, should give way to the personal preferences of clients.

An "outcome" standards is, as it sounds, a standard that specifies acceptable outcomes for the long-term-care program. Outcome standards must be used to describe a group rather than an individual and must consider the person's characteristics on admission. Standards about acceptable death rates, for example, must consider the proportion of persons with terminal illness entering the program. It is feasible to set standards governing outcomes, such as adverse health conditions related to care (e.g., percentage of bedsores, falls, or urinary tract infections), about functional status of residents (e.g., percentage of residents who do not feed themselves or percentage who are bedbound), and about psychological and social outcomes (percentage who are depressed or percentage who have visitors). Some beginning efforts have been made to use outcomes in nursing home regulation. For example, surveyors (i.e., inspectors) are expected to look for adverse outcomes and, if they are present, conduct a more detailed inspection geared to structure and process.

Providers raise the perennial question of whether they should be held responsible for outcomes, particularly in situations, such as home care or outpatient care, in which the interventions are intermittent and care providers cannot control the entire process (Kane, Illston, Eustis, & Kane, 1991). In nursing homes and residential care settings for frail elderly people, it is feasible for care providers to control processes (e.g., restrict what the resident eats, dispense all medications, maintain a sterile environment by restricting items brought in), but this probably infringes inappropriately on the client's autonomy. At issue is whether a residential long-term-care setting should be regarded as a total therapeutic environment, like a hospital, or considered more analogous to home care: that is, the resident lives in the setting and receives care there, but retains autonomous control over a wide range of activities that may have some bearing on his or her health.

Reimbursement Rules

Regulations related to payment affect clients' autonomy in subtle ways. For the most part, rate setting is a matter of state regulation. More than a dozen states reimburse nursing homes according to case-mix–adjusted formulas whereby the disability level and needs for specialized services of the client dictate the amount the facility is paid. Such rules may affect the amount the facility is paid. Such rules may affect the client's access to services, and his or her literal accommodation while in the nursing home. For example, residents may be moved to parts of the facility with staffing levels that correspond to their "case-mix" designation. Obviously, the amounts set for reimbursement place constraints on the services; these "bottom lines" combined with regulatory requirements may lead programs to provide care in ways that residents perceive as antithetical to their autonomy.

Regulation of Supply/Certificate of Need

Some regulation is designed to limit and rationalize the supply of long-term-care programs. The perverse workings of demand and supply in health care operate so that the demand for care rises to meet the supply. Therefore, if nursing home beds exist, they are likely to be filled. It follows that public resources may not be available to pay for home-based services unless the growth of the expensive institutional sector is curbed. Rules limiting the supply of programs, however, also limit access and choice for potential clients.

Regulation of Professional Practice

State law governs the licensure of various professional and occupational groups. Thus, the scope of practice is regulated for nurses, pharmacists, social workers, physical therapists, and others who work in long-term care. Regarding nursing, the dominant discipline in long-term care, nurse practice acts define what must be done directly by or under the supervision of a licensed nurse. Although we tend not to think of professional practice acts as part of the regulations that constrain long-term-care providers and perhaps limit the autonomy of long-term-care clientele, in fact, the ability of clients to purchase particular services at particular prices is a direct function of nurse-practice provisions. For example, in most states, only a licensed nurse may dispense oral or injectable medications, care for catheters and ostomies, perform wound care, and so on. Although family members typically provide such care to their relatives, if no family member is available, the care must be done by a nurse. This, in turn, leads to higher prices, which prevent public programs from purchasing care at home for people who need intermittent nursing services for an indefinite period and render the care exorbitantly expensive to purchase privately. Several states have developed nurse delegation provisions that enable non-nurses to perform nursing procedures in home care and residential care (other than nursing homes, where federal law overrides the state law); in these instances, regulatory change has provided clients with more choice in their locus of care.

Little analysis has been done on how the bulk of professional practice provisions protect and restrict long-term-care clients. It would be useful to distinguish, as much as possible, those provisions that serve largely to protect the vested interests of professions in preserving their markets from those that genuinely protect that client.

Contractual Rules

Much long-term care provided by other than nursing homes is financed under state-funded programs or Medicaid-waiver programs. These programs typically employ case managers at the local level to determine client eligibility and arrange services. Often services must be purchased from organizations that have contracts with the long-term-care program. Often, too, quality-control elements are inserted into the contracts. Some contracts contain structural requirements for staff qualifications and ratio of staff to clients. Some programs use the contract process to establish additional qualitative criteria (e.g., policies for home care agencies to deal with no-shows, policies for meeting needs of non–English-speaking clients). The nature of the requirements built into contracts may foster or detract from client autonomy, just as the number of contracts made will increase or decrease client choice. Program rules also establish whether nonagency vendors may be reimbursed, and may even establish admission and retention criteria (e.g., there could be a rule saying payment of care for clients in adult foster care can only be made if the clients are ambulatory and able to transfer).

Adult Abuse Protection Laws and Regulations

Another kind of accountability for long-term-care providers stems from adult protection statutes. Such provisions are not directed at nursing homes and other long-term-care providers specifically, yet they apply to long-term-care clients and help shape the atmosphere in which personal autonomy may give way to beneficently intended coercion to promote safety. Most states have enacted some provisions to report, prevent, treat, and punish neglect or abuse of elders or of dependent adults in general. The emphasis is not only on abuse through acts of commission but also on neglect through acts of omission. Nursing homes and their staff may be judged neglectful not only if they fail to provide adequate standards of comfort, cleanliness, and food, but also if they fail to administer what is considered an adequate standard of protection and care. Many states further muddy the waters by including "self-neglect" as a form of abuse, neglect, or exploitation; this leaves only the possibility that clients' choices to behave in ways considered injurious to their health, well-being, or safety will be judged to be reportable instances of "self-neglect."

Minnesota's Vulnerable Adults Act contains one of the most sweeping provisions for protection of long-term-care clients. It provides that all those caring for vulnerable adults must put into place a "vulnerable adult's protection plan." Moreover, all those in nursing homes are, by definition, defined as vulnerable adults, as are all adults who, because of disabilities of various kinds, are judged unable to get help if they are abused or neglected (Kane, 1990). Thus, Minnesota nursing homes need to document for each resident precisely how they intend to provide protection and supervision to reduce risks associated with their particular condition. No countervailing requirement exists for a "vulnerable adult's autonomy enhancement plan." Closely related to adult protection statutes and associated regulations are the state laws and regulations that govern guardianship and conservatorship. Becoming a ward restricts autonomy, and the way in which petitions are adjudicated as well as the provisions for review, monitoring, and reversal also affect autonomy.

Four Propositions on Regulation and Autonomy

Regulations Restrict Autonomy

Most regulations have a dual edge, protecting but also restricting those who are protected. In nursing homes, regulations govern the way furniture is arranged, the timing and content of meals, the temperature of the bath water, prohibited items in residents' rooms (e.g., candles and alcoholic beverages). Interpretation of the regulation that no more than 14 hours shall elapse between the last substantial meal of the day and the first meal of the next day even dictates the time one gets up in the morning (Childress, 1990). Interpretation of what constitutes an adequate standard of supervision and protection leads, in some facilities, to constant surveillance. In many states, retention rules in board and care homes require that residents be discharged if they reach specified levels of disability (e.g., if they are bedfast for a certain number of days, become incontinent, or lose the ability to transfer).

A certain amount of interpretation is involved in applying long-term-care regulations. Most commentators have horror stories about judgments rendered in the regulatory process: for example, the facility that is cited for not having on file a recipe for buttered toast, or the facility that is cited for allowing a resident to use her own cherished but battered and unsightly chest of drawers (which had more than the requisite number of scratches and was thought to harbor germs). These kinds of easily parodied judgments result from inept applications of the rules.

Some regulations that affect the freedom of residents in minute ways are really designed to protect staff. For example, the regulations of the federal Occupational Safety and Health Administration require that the contents and instructions be provided for all items used in the workplace. It then becomes easier to mandate particular soaps and other toilet articles than to have staff use items that residents choose. Food and Drug Administration regulations can also affect residents' ability to choose, either because of their wording or the way they are interpreted.

Regulations tend to be pitched to the lowest common denominator of long-term-care clients, particularly if the regulations refer to group settings. For example, if some residents are incapable of handling over-the-counter medications or poisonous toiletries, the rule will be that no residents may have such items.

The force of regulations goes beyond the written word. The justification for many of the protective routines and requirements present in nursing homes cannot be found in regulations. As far as I can determine, no regulation ever required that residents be physically restrained, although, when the 1987 reforms put limitations on the use of restraints, many practitioners believed that their customary use had been a response to regulatory requirements in the first place.

A combination of forces make regulations potentially destructive of personal autonomy. The general risk aversion of health care providers means that they will act so as to minimize the likelihood that regulations will claim their care is substandard. If reimbursements are low or perceived to be inadequate, facilities may also claim that the regulatory requirements minimize the amount of individualized planning that is possible. If it is taken as a given that most residents should not go outside unaccompanied, be in a bathtub in privacy, have a glass of wine without a doctor's prescription, or stay awake in a chair watching a late movie, it is not because specific regulations prohibit these events. Rather, it is because providers fear that untoward consequences will be judged as neglectful or substandard care. They may also believe that only an unaffordable level of staff supervision and attention would make individualization of schedules possible on a widespread basis and that residents should not be left alone on any account.

Regulations Can Foster Autonomy

Despite the preceding comments, regulations can also be and have historically been used to enhance autonomy. Therefore, regulation cannot be categorically indicated. Though part of the problem, regulation can be made part of the solution. Several categories of autonomy-enhancing regulations can be identified.

Regulations Requiring Information and Disclosure

Information is a precondition of autonomy. Any regulations that require that residents or potential residents be informed about their choices, their care options, and the financial arrangements that undergird their care have potential to enhance autonomy. Similarly, requirements that residents' rights be explained in clear language is autonomy enhancing. To take an example, the work of Ambrogi and Leonard (1988) on contracts used in nursing home admissions led to regulatory and statutory reform in California governing the way contracts were written and explained.

Regulations Requiring Resident Participation in Care and Governance

Expectations embodied in regulations that require residents or their agents to have the opportunity to participate in their care plans have the potential to enhance autonomy. Such provisions offer residents a chance to provide input into and question the care plan. On a systemic level, regulations requiring resident councils, requiring mechanisms for appeal of care decisions, requiring that residents be consulted on room or roommate changes all have the potential effect of increasing residents' voices and power within the facility. It would be naive to think that requirements such as these are a panacea; the way they are publicized, encouraged, and administered will make the difference. But they do provide a start, a foundation on which residents so inclined can attempt to exercise autonomy.

Regulations to Reverse Autonomy-Eroding Practices

It is usually easier to observe practices that abridge autonomy than to predict that they will have that effect. Therefore, regulations can be used to prohibit such practices. For example, Oregon's adult foster home rules eventually were modified to include the provisions that the sitting room used by residents must not also be used as sleeping space for a household member. Until this problem occurred in practice, the need for the regulation did not occur in officials' minds.

The most vivid example of a regulatory strategy to correct a problem that interfered with autonomy concerns physical restraints. No practice on the face of it restricts autonomy more than literally tying residents up or confining them to chairs that prevent their rising. This problem was tackled head on as part of the 1987 regulatory reform; henceforth, the use of physical restraints is not to be the norm. Justification for restraints was required, and reasons related to staff convenience or punishment were not allowed. Moreover, the rules associated with restraint use (loosening, ambulation) were sufficiently arduous that physical restraints could no longer be considered as cost saving because of reduction of personnel costs. Thus, a regulatory strategy—coupled with education and outside advocacy—was called into play to redress a grave affront to autonomy that had become almost standard practice. Although not eliminated, restraint use has fallen off in the last 5 years.

One could imagine other specific regulations to counteract observable autonomy incursions. They might concern medical matters or everyday life matters—for example, residents must be permitted to initiate telephone calls to primary care physicians and specialists; residents must be able to speak to their doctors alone; residents must be permitted to wear their own clothing, which must be laundered according to their instructions; residents must be offered choices of food; residents must be allowed access to telephone to make personal calls in private; and residents must be able to choose bedtimes and rising times and be offered a snack on rising. These and myriad other similar rules could be established. Some would be objected to on the grounds of safety and some (e.g., the laundry provision and the individualized care routines) on cost grounds. Many would be objected to because of the claim that persons with dementia cannot exercise judgment about, say, whom to telephone and when, what clothing to wear, or how to interpret a physician's remarks. One can argue, however, that provisions first should be developed for cognitively intact residents, to be followed by articulation of exceptions.

To some extent, the current regulatory standard on residents' rights fits this category. In recent decades, evidence mounted on observable violations of residents' civil rights on matters such as freedom of association, freedom to receive and send mail, the right to privacy of possessions (not expressed as freedom from search and seizure, but perhaps simply that), the right to vote, and the right to nondiscriminatory treatment. "Residents' rights" was, therefore, elevated to a separate standard to which nursing homes must conform as part of the 1987 OBRA reforms.

Environmental Regulations Enhancing Autonomy

Perhaps the most controversial way that regulation can enhance autonomy is by mandating minimal requirements for privacy and dignity of the environment. Arguably, such standards are needed for anyone to exercise autonomy when unrelated adults live together in a group situation. In my view, the minimum requirements in the U.S. cultural context includes a singly occupied room with a self-contained bath. Facilities are not prohibited from structuring themselves with single rooms entirely but are unlikely to do so under current market conditions. All facilities would first need to be required to provide that minimum standard. Yet single rooms and minimal amenities in terms of living space, storage space, and possessions may be requisites for autonomy, both in the sense of self-direction and in Agich's sense of continuity.

The assisted living rules in Oregon are instructive in this regard. When Oregon decided to reimburse assisting living care under its Medicaid waiver, the rules established that each unit be singly occupied unless by choice of the tenant; that refrigerators and cooking facilities, full baths with showers, and individual temperature controls be provided; that each resident be able to lock the door from the inside and from the outside with a key; and that residents be able to furnish the units themselves, using nonhospital beds and their own things. Although extremely disabled people are served, these provisions form the basis for an environment in which it is possible for a resident to fashion an independent, individualized, and normal lifestyle to the extent that her own conditions permits. In contrast, other states determined that such standards were unrealistic because of presumed costs and because of safety precautions. In Florida, for example, there was opposition to mandating such provisions as a door that locks from the inside in bathrooms located on a corridor and shared by many residents (Kane & Wilson, 1993). In Oregon, however, the environmental standards set for assisted living settings are not considered luxurious frills or dangerous departures from safety, but rather autonomy-enhancing minimal requirements.

Some of the environmental standards mandated in public buildings by the Americans with Disabilities Act also promote autonomy by making free movement physically possible.

Autonomy-Fostering Regulations Are Hard to Develop and Enforce

I have argued that regulations can both impede and enhance autonomy. Realistically, however, it is much easier and more likely that regulations will have a net negative effect on autonomy rather than a positive one. First, the general risk aversion of long-term-care providers and public officials who pay for long-term care means that the urge to protect will be strong. Second, regulation is a frequent response to catastrophe; any well-publicized adverse event is likely to engender protective regulations that require more supervision and surveillance, and more prohibitions. Third, almost all autonomy-enhancing regulations have escape hatches including the resident quality of life standard now in place in nursing homes since the 1987 reforms. Although rhetoric emphasizes residents' rights of choice of treatments, of food, of lifestyle, the caveat always defers to medical judgment. This leaves the way open to conservative interpretation of the rules. Fourth, within the welter of sometimes conflicting regulations, providers discern which are taken most seriously. They will probably be prudent to judge that they are better off, when in doubt, to risk violating the residents' rights or quality of life, than to be accused of violating quality of care (perhaps in the wake of a death or serious accident). Fifth, negative outcomes are much easier to notice and count than positive ones; bedsores, decubiti, and depression are charted; poor hygiene and bad odors can be observed readily; happiness, social involvement, zest for living, and sense of identity and worth are difficult to notice except in their absence.

Moreover, as far as direct regulations about autonomy go, one cannot enforce autonomy by fiat. An ethicist Nancy Dubler frequently remarks, "you cannot drag a person kicking and screaming into autonomy." Those who have attempted to regulate toward autonomy in health matters in general (e.g., a Massachusetts law that states that women with breast cancer must be offered choices of treatment) have found that many people prefer to leave such choices to professionals or family members. Elaborate regulatory mechanisms could be developed presumably to force choice and, in their application, end up being an empty shell. The Hospital Patient Self-Determination Act, though perhaps a useful start, illustrates how an enormous regulatory effort has so far accomplished something rather perfunctory that does not really increase the sum total of personal autonomy for hospital patients.

Similarly, although Minnesota law requires that all nursing home residents make a choice on do-not-resuscitate status, the enormous effort needed to ensure that each choice is informed has been lacking. To comply with the letter of such a law, one more box must be checked on the resident's chart. To comply with the spirit of such a regulation, however, it would be necessary to develop a technology for soliciting the preference and a way to establish that the resident had made a choice. There would also need to be a provision for those residents who, for whatever reason, declined to make the choice and deferred to a professional or an agent. Such regulation and its enforcement are difficult and unfamiliar work.

Regulations Can Be Used as Scapegoats

A final proposition is that regulations are often blamed unfairly for autonomy incursions that are not regulatorily mandated. For example, hospitals often lead their Medicare patients to believe that the diagnostic-related group regulations mandate a discharge after a specific length of time, when, in fact, regulations only set the lump-sum payment for the residents' stay based on the average length of stay for residents with that condition. Similarly, in nursing homes regulations are blamed for routines, for facility-developed house rules, and for cost-saving measures. Regulations may require that residents' hygiene be maintained, but no regulation mandates the time of the bath. No regulation requires that residents be deprived of the power of their checkbooks when they enter a facility, though providers and family alike may find a representative payer convenient. It is important to render unto regulations what can be accurately ascribed to them. Facilities do have the right to establish conventions based on presumed commonalities of interest (e.g., some facilities expect temperance, some expect that residents observe religious dietary laws), but these must surely be clearly announced so that an autonomous resident (or her agent) can choose another facility if the practices are not compatible with her own. Arguably, too, even religious institutions that accept public funds must provide some recourse for residents of different religions. It is improper to mandate that residents attend chapel. It may also be improper to require that a resident in a kosher facility be deprived of nonkosher products in his or her own room.

Possible Solutions

Only a fanatic would wish to abandon all regulation in long-term care. As has been pointed out, some regulation directly enhance autonomy. Moreover, some regulation that provides for minimal standards of safety (e.g., proper precautions against infectious disease, prudent provisions to prevent or minimize the effect of fire, provisions for adequate refrigeration of food) would have few detractors. We expect such safeguards to govern hotels and restaurants that we, as members of the public, use, and we should also expect them in nursing homes.

So, To use regulations in the service of autonomy what steps might be helpful? The following might be considered:

- Make distinctions between regulations that require behavior change in the resident and those that do not. The former would include a regulation that a diabetic resident must not eat chocolate, whereas the latter would include a regulation that all food meet standards of need for a regulation that requires behavior change (e.g., in personal habits or routines). To take another example, a regulation that requires bath water to be tepid deals with behavior and demands that all residents conform to that standard regardless of preference; thus, a compelling justification is needed. Conversely, fire doors are innocuous protectors, unless they are designed so they control resident's comings and goings.
- Develop ways to appeal for exceptions to regulations on the grounds that they infringe on a particular resident's autonomy rights. Such mechanisms should be designed to minimize the hassle experienced by facilities, which probably means that the issues should be decided *before* a citation is issued.
- Avoid lowest-common-denominator regulations. Some regulations should pertain only to persons who are substantially cognitively impaired and should not be imposed on all residents (e.g., blanket prohibitions against shoe polish, shampoo, and aspirins).
- Immediately examine the environmental prerequisites for personal autonomy with a view toward mandating them in new construction or substantial renovation.
- Develop public dialogue in states and communities about the judgments that will be made about negative events. Falls are less likely if residents are immobilized or confined to wheelchairs, but a certain number of falls occur in the community. Under what circumstances will facilities be held harmless, therefore, if a fall occurs?

- Explore the legal ramifications of waivers of liability. Although one cannot waive one's right to quality care, in a nursing home, care should probably not be extended to include every facet of the resident's life. If warned about the risks of various decisions, cannot residents make a decision to take their chances?
- Examine the extent to which professional practice acts and orthodoxies are forcing a style of home care that can never be cost effective compared with nursing home care. Explore, too, the extent to which such rules inappropriately limit long-term-care clients' ability to purchase the help they want and need at the price they can afford. If systemic problems exist, consider how they can be solved while still providing some threshold of protection.
- Develop demonstrations with waivers of regulations to test autonomy-enhancing changes in practices.
- Keep an open mind about regulation in other sectors of long-term care. Nursing home regulations provide a cautionary tale of what can go wrong.

References

Agich, G. (1993). *Autonomy and long-term care.* New York: Oxford University Press.

Ambrogi, D. M., & Leonard, F. (1988). The impact of nursing home admission agreements on resident autonomy. *The Gerontologist 28,* 82–89.

Childress, J. (1990). If you let them, they would stay in bed all morning: The tyranny of regulation in nursing home life. In R. A. Kane & A. L. Caplan (Eds.), *Everyday ethics: Resolving dilemmas in nursing home life* (pp. 79–88). New York: Springer.

Collopy, B., Boyle, P., & Jennings, B. (1991). New directions in nursing home ethics. *The Hastings Center Report, 21*(Suppl.), 1–16.

Kane, R. A. (1990). Venerable and perhaps vulnerable: The nature and extent of vulnerability among the aged. In Z. Harel, P. Ehrlich, & R. Hubbard (Eds.), *The vulnerable aged* (pp. 4–17). New York: Springer.

Kane, R. A., Illston, L. H., Eustis, N. N., & Kane, R. L. (1991). *Quality of home care: Concept and measurement.* Minneapolis: University of Minnesota School of Public Health, Division of Health Services Research and Policy.

Kane, R. A., & Wilson, K. B. (1993). *Assisted living in the United States: A paradigm for residential care for frail older persons.* Washington, DC: American Association of Retired Persons, Public Policy Institute.

Harrington, C., & Grant, L. A. (1990). The delivery, regulation, and politics of home care: A California case study. *The Gerontologist, 30,* 451–461.

Hawes, C., Wildfire, J. B., & Lux, J. L. (1993). *Regulation of board-and-care homes: Results of a 58-state study.* Washington, DC: American Association of Retired Persons.

Institute of Medicine. (1986). *Improving the quality of care in nursing homes.* Washington, DC: National Academy Press.

Lidz, C. (1992). *The erosion of autonomy in long-term care.* New York: Oxford University Press.

Tobin, S. S. (1991). *Personhood in advanced old age.* New York: Springer.

Chapter Seven

The Medical Model and Its Effect on Autonomy: A Comparison of Two Long-Term Care Settings

Charles W. Lidz and Robert P. Arnold

A t the present moment, hundreds of thousands of Americans are spending their last years in nursing homes across the country. In a nation that values its individualistic traditions as much as we claim to, it would seem that we would put special emphasis on supporting the autonomy of those individuals (Agich 1993; Collopy 1988; Hofland 1988). Unfortunately, as has been documented elsewhere, that is not the case (Diamond, 1986; Fontana, 1977; Gubrium, 1975; Kane et al., 1990; Lidz, Fisher, & Arnold, 1992; Moody, 1988). This chapter examines what inhibits, rather than promotes, autonomy.

The concept of autonomy is a tricky one (Dworkin, 1989). Its proper application to long-term care has been reviewed elsewhere (Collopy, 1988; Agich, 1993). Our own formulation of the problem has been laid out in our book (Lidz, Fisher, & Arnold, 1992) and extensively revised and elaborated in a recent paper (Lidz & Arnold, 1993). For our purposes, being autonomous involves the ability to direct one's own life, values, commitments, and goals. The word "autonomy" is derived from the Greek *autos* (self) and *nomos* (rule or governance or law), and was first used to refer to self-rule in Greek city-states. In this context, it refers to ruling or governing one's own life. The President's Commission on Bioethics defined autonomy or self-determination as "an individual's exercise of the capacity to form, revise and pursue personal plans for life" (President's Commission, 1982, p. 30). Without belaboring the point, such a concept of autonomy potentially involves much more than simply the presentation of information about decisions that some have sought to adapt to the nursing home setting from the ethical model of informed consent (Lidz & Arnold, 1993).

The study reported here examined the differences between two long-term-care settings, a nursing home, and a residential care facility. Autonomy in the nursing home was limited. The general picture is clear from a description provided by one of the patients, Ms. K. She has just mentioned that staff members are disrespectful to patients.

Observer: How are they disrespectful?

Ms. K: Well, they don't respect people as. . . . They dehumanize people. "This one, this one, this one . . . go to bed." They don't ask if you want to go to bed, or if you'd like to stay up a little longer. . . . A lot of these people . . . they [staff] just manipulate them. I hate to see people manipulated. You know . . . to the chair . . . to the bed . . . then back to the chair. And that's all their lives consist of. And they [staff members] decide where you're going to be at a certain time. I don't like that. They're still human beings. I think they should be asked if they want to do it. I feel that if I get like that, and I pray to the good Lord that I won't, that he'll take me. Because it's just like an assembly line at night. This one goes to bed and that one goes right down the line.

Observer: So it feels like an assembly line?

Ms. K: I'm not on an assembly line. Don't treat me like that! I'm a person.

Observer: Do you tell them that?

Ms. K: I told them that. I said, "Don't treat me like I'm on an assembly line because I'm not." That's why they don't like me. . . .

As we see later, this picture contrasts sharply with what we saw in the residential care setting. Our problem is to understand why. In this chapter we suggest that the medicalization of nursing homes constitutes an essential difference between the two settings, and it substantially affects the nature of role relationships in nursing homes and how these relationships limit residents' autonomy.

Methods

The data on which this description is based comes from a 6-month-long ethnographic study of two nursing home units and a personal care facility, all run by the same nonprofit hospital group. We selected the setting because the facility had a reputation as an excellent, but not innovative, nursing facility. Our theoretical interests in the relationship between the nature of care and patient/resident autonomy required an intensive study of the relationships between patients/residents, their families, and the staff in skilled, intermediate, and residential care.

Our data collection technique, a type of augmented ethnography, lent itself well to these goals. It has been described in detail elsewhere, but we can summarize it here briefly. Two researchers spent approximately 300 hours observing both settings during both days and nights, and on weekdays and weekends. Most of this time was spent sitting on the units and informally watching and talking with staff, residents, and family. Rather than relying on observers' ability to remember key aspects of observed interactions, the observers recorded conversations using a form of speed writing, which has been shown in previous studies to result in near-verbatim transcription and have a high degree of interobserver reliability (Lidz et al., 1984). The observers also attended regularly scheduled conferences and meetings that dealt with patients'/residents' care and disposition. Overall, we observed 60 nursing home patients and 30 residents.

Our use of participant observation techniques was more successful in the nursing home than in the residential area. There was almost nothing to observe unobtrusively in the residential communal areas because of the physical structure of the setting, which had little communal space, and the considerable amount of time that residents spent in their rooms and outside the facility. We, therefore, supplemented our approximately 50 hours of observation with resident and staff interviews. Overall, we interviewed 9 upper staff (administrative and nondirect care professionals), 12 line staff, and 6 residents.

In addition to observations and interviews, we collected two other types of data: assessment rating scales and medical/demographic information. To gather systematic evidence of the staff's views of patients'/residents' capabilities, we asked staff to provide us with ratings of each patient/resident on six dimensions of their capacity to function independently (e.g., ability to make rational decisions). We also coded a variety of medical and demographic variables including diagnosis, medications, ADL evaluations, and sociodemographic data from the patient/resident records.

We began our analysis with a sequential reading of all participant observation and interview notes, roughly 1600 pages of text, as well as the more structured data. Based on this review, we developed a set of 62 content codes. Then, using the Unix Text Analyst, a computer program developed for the review of such coded textual data, we prepared a summary of the findings for each content code, using excerpts from the text as examples. These reviews were read and discussed among the research group, and modifications of the analysis were made. When completed, the reviews were combined into memos, which were critiqued and rewritten by each author. This chapter focuses on our findings concerning role relationships in the nursing home and the residential area.

Setting and Population

The research was done at a relatively large geriatric facility owned by a nonprofit health system. We studied two patient units (one intermediate and one skilled/intermediate), each housing about 30 patients at any one time. For our purposes here we do not distinguish between these two units and refer to them both as the nursing home. We also observed all residents in the residential area. During the study period 30 residents lived on two different floors.

The patients and residents were similar in age, race, sex, marital status, and the number of diagnoses on their charts. However, intermediate care patients had more chronic stable conditions, such as dementia, Parkinson's disease, hypertension, arthritis, and cardiovascular disease, than skilled care patients. Although residents also had chronic medical conditions, they were less likely to have dementing illnesses.

There were also differences in the staff's assessments of patients' and residents' capacities. In general, residents' capacities were rated higher than patients' capacities (see Table 7.1).

TABLE 7.1 Impairment of Patients' and Residents' Ability to Perform Certain Tasks

Item	Patients impaired (%)	Residents impaired (%)
Rational decision making	82	33
Mobility	51	20
Assertiveness	65	35
Activities of daily living	37	20
Independent living	89	83

Clearly, however, there was a significant degree of overlap between patients and residents on each dimension, and many residents had significant cognitive and physical impairments. This is particularly important because we contend that the differences in autonomy in the two settings were not exclusively due to the greater impairment of the nursing home patients. The social construction of one setting as a medical facility and the other as a place to live played a major role in the differences in autonomy in the two settings.

Role Relationships of Patient and Physician

Although physicians play a relatively minor role in the care and management of patients in a nursing facility, the social expectations guiding the physician-patient relationship are central to our understanding the role expectations governing the behavior of the elderly in nursing homes. A dominant feature of the culturally defined patient role is the need for help (Parsons, 1951). Patients are seen as representing deviance from the culturally defined ideal of physical well-being. Although the patient is not responsible for being ill, she is responsible for seeking help. The sick role assumes that the necessary help cannot be provided by the patient or other laypersons, but must be obtained from designated health care professionals. The inability of the patient either to determine the nature of the problem or to choose the scientifically best treatment is seen as justifying the sick person's dependence on the health professional's judgment. Patients must cede to health care professionals' authority for what is normatively defined as out of their control. If they fail to do so, it is appropriate (even expected) for family, friends, and health care professionals to use sanctions to change their behavior.

This conceptualization of the patient's role and its ethical import has been the subject of intense discussion within medical ethics over the last two decades (Appelbaum, Lidz, & Meisel, 1987; Faden & Beauchamps, 1986; Katz, 1984). This description of the patient's role most accurately portrays the situation of acutely ill patients. When the patient is suffering acutely or is in need of emergency help, the physician must act with little input from the patient. Unfortunately for nursing home patients, this model has potentially greater adverse consequence for them than it does for acute care patients. When a person needs care for the indefinite future and care is defined as encompassing almost all aspects of her life, then this abdication of responsibility signifies not just a loss of autonomy over a specific event but a loss of control over a significant component of life.

Nursing Home and Medical Model

Nursing homes, including the one that we studied, are clearly intended to be health care facilities (Diamond, 1986). The physical layout was reminiscent of a hospital—long corridors with flanking rooms and a centrally located nursing station. Patient rooms looked like hospital rooms. Rather than allowing patients to bring their furniture to the nursing home, each room was furnished identically with hospital stock furniture. The beds had side-bars, a call button, and mechanical controls like those in hospitals.

In addition, the nursing units were reminiscent of hospital wards. Most of the staff wore the white uniforms characteristic of nurses and hospital aides. As in hospitals, the direct care staff on patient units were registered nurses, practical nurses, and personal care aides. For each shift, one nurse, usually the one with the most formal training, was designated as the "charge" nurse and was responsible for supervising the other nurses and aides. Moreover, the nurses had the same training as nurses who work in hospitals.

Though this training included some discussion of the routine aspects of care and long-term care, the emphasis was on the management and treatment of clinical conditions.

Many of the routines in the nursing home were borrowed from the medical setting. This emphasis on "medical care" was made clear through a variety of subtle and not so subtle institutional rituals. Individuals who lived in this setting were referred to by staff as "patients" or by their medical condition rather than by their name. Individuals' identities as "patients" dominated almost everything that was done to and for them. For example, when they were admitted to the nursing home, they underwent a standard "history and physical examination" that was "charted" in a format clearly borrowed from hospital record keeping. At the discharge and planning meetings (at which most of the substantial decisions about patient care were made), an upper staff member would routinely present the case for consideration by the other staff members. A typical example follows:

Upper Staff 1: OK, this is W. B. She is 54, and this is her second admission here. She was home just one day, fell, and fractured her hip. She also has multiple other problems including a skin disease, congestive heart failure, COPD (chronic obstructive pulmonary disease), a deep venous thrombosis (clot in leg). . . .

Most instructions for their care were charted as "orders" and, formally, had to be given by doctors. Moreover, as in a hospital, patients were not allowed to take their own medications. Instead, medications were passed out by nurses in the same manner found in a hospital. These features of the setting conveyed to all concerned that this was a medical facility. Patients were often no more differentiating about staff than staff were about patients. Patients primarily saw the facility as a medical institution; many referred to all of the staff as "nurse," irrespective of their training. For example, despite considerable efforts at explanation, our female observer was sometimes called "nurse" even though she wore street clothes and provided no nursing care.

We have emphasized these obvious facts about the medicalization of the nursing home because we believe that they are key to understanding the nature of the relationships in the nursing home.

Closer examination clarifies how the medical model affected individuals' expectations about who was to do what and how this, in turn, affected the elderly's autonomy. We then contrast this with how the elderly were cared for in the residential area, a nonmedicalized setting, and consider how the different situational definitions and role expectations influenced individuals' autonomy.

Role Relationships in The Nursing Home

The role relationships between patients and professional caregivers within the nursing home drew heavily from the normative structure imbedded in the medical model. Like other health care professionals, nursing home staff conceptualized their primary obligation as maximizing patients' health, particularly their physical well-being. For example, in response to a global question about possible caregiving improvements within the institution, an upper staff member volunteered suggestions solely related to physical well-being.

Upper Staff 3: ... things like mouth care. I'm not saying that it's not done. I'm saying that it is not done as frequently as it should. Cleaning your teeth, cleaning your gums, rinsing your mouth out. ... Feet care. These are two of the things that are left for last. ... [Institution staff members are] really quite good about major components of care. ...

This medicalization of the patient's identity did not appear to be specific to upper staff but, rather, crossed staff lines. Among line staff (i.e., registered and practical nurses, and aides), the medicalization of tasks was reflected in their preference for acute treatment of remediable, biomedical diseases rather than custodial care of chronic conditions (i.e., basic support for activities of daily living) or talking with patients.

Observer: Is it better here than at other places where you've worked?
Nurse: Uh-huh. Absolutely ... it's the way this center is set up. ... Some parts of it are still really acute care oriented, and that's the really good part about this place. ...

This preference also was observed in staff/patient interactions. Staff responded positively to situations concerning medically reversible problems.

Because cure of the body was often not possible, staff focused on preserving the body's more basic functions, and most of the staff's time was spent on the mundane custodial tasks related to helping patients get out of bed, go to the bathroom, eat their meals, and so forth. In response to the perceived need to maintain patients' physical integrity, staff restricted patients' autonomy. These restrictions included physical restraints as well as institutional rules regarding patient-patient interaction, patient mobility within the nursing home, and a variety of restrictions on patient disposition.

However, just because staff members spent most of their time preserving physical health does not mean that they enjoyed these tasks. In the following example, an intermediate care charge nurse expresses her feelings about having to help prepare a patient for bed.

Observer: (An unidentified aide rolls the new patient [Mr. B] down the hallway. The nurse gets up from her chair in the staff room and follows. They roll the patient to his room.)

Nurse: And we've got to put this monster [Mr. B] to bed? . . . Look at him! He's disgusting!

Observer: (. . . the patient in question is an elderly white man. He appears to be in his late 70s or early 80s. He is lying on a gurney, dressed only in a hospital gown. He appears to be completely "vegged out.")

Another indication of the staff members' negative feelings about chronic care or improving patients' ability to act autonomously was their lack of interest in the rehabilitative work necessary for the recovery of lost skills or the development of new skills. Although medical techniques designed to prolong life were commonly and enthusiastically used, techniques focused on helping patients recover lost skills or develop new ones (e.g., walking patients on the unit or encouraging patients to do as much for themselves as they could) were not. As is typical in hospitals, rehabilitation was seen as the responsibility of the Physical Therapy Department and not part of the unit care tasks. For example, to help her husband

improve his functional status as much as possible after a hip fracture and subsequent illness, one patient's wife was forced into a
running battle with the staff.

Observer: So he came back home from the hospital?
Mrs. A (patient's wife):   Well, no. [He was at a] nursing home at
   first for 3 or 4 weeks.
Observer: And stayed there and then came back here and that's
   when he started walking?
Mrs. A: Yes. . . . They [staff members] were very antagonistic to
   me when we went into [the institution]. . . . I wanted to get him
   walking. I wanted him to have therapy. They said that he
   couldn't possibly handle their therapy program. He wasn't in
   good enough shape. I said, "Couldn't he walk?" And they said,
   "That would take three people. We don't have that much staff.
   We can't afford to spend three people walking him up and down
   the hall." First I said I could do it. They said, "You couldn't
   possibly do it." I said, "I've done it before. I brought him back. I
   can do it." So I went in and got him out of the chair. Nobody
   helped me. They didn't help me get him out of the geri-chair,
   which is a big heavy thing. I could hardly handle [him]; they just
   watched me. Antagonistic was the word. I don't know. . . . Finally
   they decided that the therapist would walk with him three times
   a week. That was wonderful. I had thought of it everyday. Always wanting more. I [asked,] "Don't they ever walk any of these
   people?" I was talking to the social service worker and the nurse.
   I said, "This isn't just your problem and my problem. This is the
   problem of the whole elder society who are in nursing homes.
   They're turning into vegetables. And I think something should
   be done about it. And I began to get a little action. Once in a
   while they'd walk with him. Now they're walking him twice a
   day. . . .

There are other comments in the data that indicate that staff
found their cognitively impaired charges to be less than ideal human beings. In the following example the nurse is partly joking and
her concern is not without some medical warrant, but the metaphor
of contamination is very strong:

Observer: (The aide goes back down the hall. I tell the nurse that I'll be passing out cookies during the afternoon.)

Nurse: How are you going to do it?

Observer: I thought I would just leave trays of them in the TV lounge for those who can help themselves, and then go room to room for the others.

Nurse: Oh, I don't think you should do that. You don't know where their [patients'] hands have been. (pause) Unless I can have mine first. Then I don't care. (laughing)

Staff's acceptance of the medical model thus resulted in health care providers' belief that "good care" consisted primarily of providing acute, medical therapies. Custodial tasks (e.g., feeding, toileting, and bathing) and individual attempts to help patients accomplish their goals were responded to, at best, without enthusiasm and, at worst, with anger and resentment. Psychosocial assistance of any sort, including promoting autonomous activity, was simply not part of the task as the line staff understood it.

The staff members' acceptance of the medical model can also be documented by analyzing their statements about patients' behavior. Although upper staff were often supportive of patient autonomy, there was not a single comment from line staff (aides, licensed practical nurses [LPNs], and registered nurses [RNs] who provided direct care) that reflected support for patient autonomy. Instead, line staff spoke approvingly of patients only when they complied with staff recommendations. Patients were referred to approvingly as "taking all his meds," "a real gentleman," "never complains," "behaving better," and so forth. In fact, all but one of the line staff's positive comments reflected approval of patients' compliance.

Moreover, two thirds of the negative staff comments about patients dealt with patients who interrupted the routine with what the staff thought were unreasonable requests that interfered with proper patient care. For example, patients often kept food and other trinkets in their rooms. The staff, who were more concerned with pest control than patient individuality, would go into their rooms and throw these objects out when the patient was not there. One would not think of doing such a thing to one's friends or neighbors; however, in the context of the institutional requirements for order and sanitation, this behavior seemed to the participants to be not only acceptable but laudatory. Being independent or wanting things your own way typically earned line staff's condemnation:

Observer: I saw Mrs. C roll herself down the hallway. That's the first time I've seen her do that.
Aide: Fortunately, she's usually in a geri-chair. She's a feisty one. As sure as you tell her you don't want her to do something, that's exactly what she does. We have some real feisty ones down there.

The other major implication of staff's acceptance of the medical model was their expectation that patients would defer to them regarding medical decisions. Elderly individuals living in nursing homes were seen as "sick patients." Staff members were, on the basis of their medical expertise, seen as the decision makers for almost all aspects of patients' lives. Patients were expected to cooperate with all recommendations in an attempt to "get better."

Most patients accepted the parameters of these role relationships. In general, patients exemplified the traditional patient role—they passively accepted health care professionals' assessments and followed their "orders." Thus, patient initiated interaction with staff consisted almost exclusively of patients asking staff permission for something. Moreover, when there was disagreement between patients and the staff about what should be done, both sides usually recognized that staff had the final authority to make decisions (cf. Diamond, 1986).

Patients were also encouraged by family members to cooperate with staff recommendations.

Mrs. A: (reconstructing conversation with her husband) "You ought to cooperate with them. You don't want to be difficult to get along with. You'll get better care if you cooperate. . . ."

Not all patients accepted these expectations, and some systematically failed to cooperate. The following example concerns a patient's response to being force-fed a medication by a nurse. On this unit medication was sometimes administered by crushing it into ice cream.

Observer: (Nurse brings a container of ice cream to Mrs. W, who is sitting in front of the television. The ice cream contains crushed medication. The nurse takes a spoonful of the ice cream and tries to put it in Mrs. W's mouth. The patient appears to refuse to open her mouth. The nurse then drops the spoon back into the ice cream.)

Nurse: Then you eat it. . . . (angrily)

Observer: The nurse leaves the ice cream on the table and leaves the television lounge. She walks back down the hallway. Mrs. W watches her leave . . . [and] picks up the spoon and begins to eat the ice cream. . . .

"Noncompliance" or violating the medical norm that patients should cooperate with treatment was disvalued by staff. The following took place at a weekly discharge/planning meeting:

Physical therapist: I'm not sure, I'm not seeing much progress, I'm trying to. . . .

Occupational therapist: Good luck! She does what she chooses. She won't even dress herself. She has her private duty nurse do it. That's why she is paying her.

Physical therapist: That's right, she doesn't cooperate in physical therapy either.

"Feisty" patients whose demands interfered with, or even were irrelevant to, the provision of "medical care" were viewed negatively by the staff. Here is one nurse's response to patient demands:

Observer: (Aides and a nurse are in the staff lounge. The nurse is writing in a chart. I go in and sit down. From the lounge, we can hear Mrs. Z yelling).

Mrs. Z: Nurse! Nurse!

Nurse: (mimicking) Nurse! Nurse!

Observer: The nurse then makes an obscene gesture. Everyone laughs.

In summary, we found that staff, and most patients, recognized a defined role for patients, characterized by compliance and cooperation rather than autonomous self-direction. Although not all patients accepted this role, in practice it dominated staff-patient interaction. There was some discomfort with these role relations on both sides, but there was little or no effective challenge to the traditional health care provider-patient relationship.

Role Relationships in the Residence

In contrast to the nursing home, the personal care section of the institution, called "The Residence," did not resemble a hospital. Although each of the three floors consisted of a hallway with small rooms set on both sides, the hallways were carpeted and decorated with pictures. There were no formal staff stations but rather one small office on each floor where staff met at staff changes. All the rooms were designed for single occupancy, more like a hotel than a hospital. Although the rooms were approximately the same size as those on the patient units, residents were encouraged to bring in their own furniture rather than decorating rooms with hospital-issue furniture.

Most caregiving was done by aide-level staff called "monitors" with supervision by two LPNs. Although some monitors had experience in health care services (e.g., as a home companion or an assistant to the mentally handicapped in group homes), most were housewives looking for additional income. Rather than requiring formal training in the clinical sciences, they learned the needed skills on the job by spending shifts with their supervisors or other monitors. Although the monitors occasionally assisted residents in various activities of daily living, most of their time was spent accompanying residents to the dining hall and other facility activities, making medical appointments, and arranging transportation for outside activities.

The atmosphere on these units was closer to an apartment complex than a hospital. The individuals living there were called residents rather than patients. There was little evidence of the medical routines so commonly seen on the nursing home side (e.g., the ritual of passing of medications to patients from a cart wheeled down the hall to each room in turn or the routine taking of vital signs).

This difference in atmosphere had important implications for the monitor-resident role relationship. Residential monitors valued independence and self-determination among the residents, and did their best to facilitate and encourage these behaviors.

Resident Monitor: I'm here to help them retain what little independence they still have. That's the only way I can describe it. If they need me to help them do something, I do it. But not take it away from them. If they're still able to move those extremities. . . . Even if it is messed up, but they're trying, they still feel that they did it themselves. You don't want to take that away from them. That's what I feel I'm here for—to help them retain what little bit they still have. . . .

This basic philosophy extended to monitors' evaluation of residents' behavior. In the following example, a monitor expresses approval of the behavior of one of the more independent residents.

Resident Monitor: . . . then we have Mrs. T. She's 96. An Italian lady. Now there's a self-sufficient one. Oh, my. You get her towels ready and she gets in that tub and bathes herself. . . . If I would put an apron on her, she would run the vacuum and dust the furniture. She's a typical mother. We do very little for Sophia. And then she'll start yelling at these people. "All you do is sit. Exercise! Exercise! Walk! Walk!"

Staff routinely encouraged residents who at least made attempts at self-sufficiency. The resident monitor gave this description of a resident who alternated between cooperation and noncooperation relative to self-care.

Resident monitor: . . . his memory. Long-term is good, but his short-term. . . . No. And it depends upon how he feels about things that day. Sometimes he has an attitude where, "I don't care." And other times he makes an effort. He'll get up and say, "Good morning," and "I made my bed." "You made your bed!" (says monitor). "I'm shaving" (resident). "You're shaving!" (says monitor). . . .

Supervisors in the residence shared the monitors' sentiments; self-sufficiency and independent decision making were valued and, thus, routinely encouraged.

Observer: (Mrs. S. heads toward the elevator.)

Resident nurse: (to observer) She's a real resident. She came in here herself. She wasn't sick. She takes her own meds. She's really on the go. . . . We encourage decision making over here. "What do you want? What do you want to wear. . . . to do?" They don't do that over there [intermediate care unit]. . . .

In the context of our concerns about role relationships, the phrase "she is a real resident" is particularly interesting. The resident nurse was defining the features of the normative role, by example, and the emphasis was on autonomy and activity.

Staff's complaints about resident behavior also reflected their assumption that residents should be more rather than less autonomous. Consider the following comment by a residential nurse concerning a resident who she did not think belonged there:

Nurse: She was a very dependent person before she came in here. Very dependent (with emphasis). She won't do anything for herself. . . . This is not the place for her.

Observer: What would be an appropriate place for her?

Nurse: I don't know. (pause) I guess intermediate care would be more right in a sense. She constantly walks and needs a place for that. She's not incontinent and she feeds herself. . . . (pause) It's her restlessness and her desire to be dependent on someone else. . . . They [intermediate care] can provide for that over there.

Although the nurse notes that the resident meets two of the formal qualifications for living on the residential side (qualifications that some other residents she values do not meet), the reasons she gives for her assertion that the resident does not belong emphasize the importance she places on autonomy.

The limits of the monitors' sense of entitlement to direct the residents' lives is clearest in those cases in which they disapprove of specific behaviors. The monitors often express ambivalence about behavior that, although autonomous, seems misguided.

Resident monitor: Yeah. You know . . . they are all adults and they are all responsible for their own thing. We're just here to monitor. It may upset us a lot to see how they're throwing their time away. We have activities that we encourage them to go to. I can name some that will not go even if you stand on your head. They choose to stay in their little rooms.

As we have noted, despite physical and cognitive screening and a mobility criterion, quite a few residents exhibited both physical and mental deterioration. Although residents were supposed to be continent, mobile, and cognitively able to manage their own affairs, because of the recent expansion of the independent living area and the need to fill beds, the only criterion firmly enforced was physical mobility.

This did not go unrecognized by the monitors.

Resident monitor: . . . technically they are supposed to be self-sufficient. They are free to come and go, to make their own doctor appointments. But not too many of them can. If they get a doctor's office [that is playing a] recording, they're [residents] saying, "I don't understand." And then we intercede for them. . . . So they're not as independent or self-sufficient as we'd like them to be.

In some cases, the impairments created only minimal extra work for residential staff and, in these cases, an approach that maximized residents' autonomy and protected their self-esteem without sacrificing physical well-being was generally adopted.

Resident monitor: . . . Mrs. M. goes and falls asleep, and wakes up and thinks it's breakfast time when it might be supper time or lunch, you know? My philosophy is that they aren't patients. They are free to come and go, as long they are not hurting themselves, or endangering themselves, or disturbing their fellow residents or hurting them. I kinda let them go. If I know they are off the unit I kinda spot-check them. I'll keep an eye on them. But I don't try to confine them because I feel that only frustrates them more. So I give them some freedom as long as they're not in pain and hurting themselves, or causing pain or harm to anybody else. So, if a nurse calls and says, "Hey, I saw [a resident] down in the lobby," I say, "Thanks, I'll go down and get her. . . ."

However, other residents' impairments required a considerable amount of extra work by the monitors.

Resident monitor: Mary has become incontinent about urine. She wears Depends. She is so confused that she does not know how to put the Depends on, and she's been in them for months and months and months. . . . I have gone in I can't tell you how many times to find the Depend fastened around the small of her back. . . . Now the dirty band is on her back, and she thinks she's ready to start the day. . . . She sleeps in the nude with newspapers. . . . wrapped up in different dresses and housecoats. . . .

Considering the much lower levels of staffing in the residential areas (one resident monitor per 15 residents), common sense suggests that encouraging residents to be independent and self-sufficient would help the units to run smoothly. Perhaps this has something to do with it, but the logical extension of that approach would dictate the removal of residents no longer able to function on their own. However, we found that resident monitors frequently compensated for failing physical and cognitive functioning of residents so that they could remain on the residential units. The willingness of staff to pick up the slack for failing residents appeared to be a function both of the unit's basic philosophy and the close relationships that developed between many residential staff and residents.

Observer: It sounds like you know these people pretty well.
Resident monitor B: Yea, I love them. I really do. . . . I just see them as human beings. . . .
Resident monitor J: . . . we're . . . supposed to be able to maintain a relationship between the family and them [residents]. We're supposed to keep in contact with the family, the members of the family, the friends, you know. We are their family. We take them in and we surround them. Do you understand what I'm saying?
Observer: Yes.
Resident monitor O: That's our job. . . .

Staff-resident relationships built on the conceptualization of residents as unique individuals help seemed to buffer the impact of physical and cognitive deterioration. We saw many examples in which monitors inconvenienced themselves to help such residents continue to live semi-independently.

Applying the Lessons of the Residential Area to the Nursing Home

The effect of nursing homes on elderly persons' ability to structure their lives has been amply documented in the last 10 years. Our results are consistent with a number of other ethnographies of American nursing homes. As Shields observed:

> Though residents may want most of all to talk with the nursing assistant for companionship and alleviation of loneliness, the nursing assistant's perception of her job is to make sure her resident is bathed, toileted, and fed on time so that she will be able to perform similar duties on her other residents. Some nurses expressed to me their preference for residents for whom they could perform real nursing. They liked the skilled-nursing floors better than the intermediate care floors because there were more procedures to perform. When specific nursing tasks are not called for, many nurses say their skills are not being utilized, and they are bored. Chart work and staffing take priority over talking to residents when specific nursing tasks are not pressing. (Shields, 1988, pp. 100–101)

What we found interesting, however, was how differently elderly individuals were cared for in the residential care setting and the nursing home. The different conception of staff and resident roles seems to explain many of the differences we observed. In the residential care setting, sustaining independent functioning, not health care, seemed the dominant value among line staff. Monitors were not trained as and did not perceive themselves as medical personnel. Instead, they saw their role as helping residents live their lives (as the residents defined them). Although some of the difference may be attributable to the differences in individuals' average mobility and cognitive capacity, it does not explain monitors' behavior toward the more severely impaired residents nor does it explain their willingness to allow residents to make decisions detrimental to their health.

Our descriptions of nursing and residential care facilities are not broadly different from what is reported elsewhere in the literature.

Some details differ; however, Morgan (1982) in his study of semi-independent apartment and nursing units also reported large differences in individuals' experiences in the two settings. However, he described a staff that had a more medicalized view of the situation and, therefore, there was ongoing conflict between residents and the staff over when the resident should be transferred to the nursing home: "The debate was a continuing source of frustration to the medical staff. They thought only a simple medical determination should be necessary" (Morgan, 1982, p. 42). The conflict led to an ongoing process of negotiation in which the residents attempted to disguise their disabilities to maximize their independence and staff attempted to monitor residents' disabilities to maximize their physical well-being. When physical well-being conflicted with resident independence, the staff, like the medical staff in the nursing home setting, opted for the medical model.

Summary

We have discussed some reasons for believing that the medical model of relationships between staff and elderly residents of nursing facilities undermines the latter's autonomy. However, eliminating the medical model will not, by itself, produce ideal nursing homes. Other commentaries have correctly pointed out that nursing homes are beset by numerous problems, ranging from commodification and devaluing of caring work (Diamond, 1976) to the social isolation of nursing homes in the community. Improving nursing homes will require major changes in the way we conceptualize and structure the care of the elderly in American society. Still, we suspect that separating the medical care function from the residential function of nursing homes would increase elderly individuals' autonomy, particularly among the less cognitively impaired inhabitants (Kane & Kane, 1991). Those staff whose job it is to facilitate residents' day-to-day living do not need nursing training. Those staff whose job it is to provide nursing care do not need to have daily responsibility for most residents beyond implementing treatment. Nursing care, like medical care and social services, can be a specialized, as-needed function. We need to abolish the idea that elderly people who are in some way disabled are full-time patients and should follow caregivers' orders full-time. Current efforts to conceptualize long-term care as a branch of the hospitality industry rather than as medical care seems like a good start in this direction. (For example, see the recent article in D. B. Wolfe's, *Maturity Market Perspectives: Hospitality, Health Care Hybrid Shows Marketing Promise*, which discusses several such recent attempts.)

In short, promoting the autonomy of the elderly in nursing facilities requires that we severely restrict the authority of the medical model to provide direction over residents' day-to-day lives. We need to rethink the model that we use in organizing routine care for the disabled elderly in institutions. This will not be easy, and it will require us to compromise frequently between the often competing principles of physical well-being and human freedom. However, if we seriously believe that those individuals who must live in nursing homes are human beings like the rest of us and that their experience of life is precious, then we must attempt such a change.

Acknowledgment

The research on which this chapter is based was supported, in part, by a grant from the Retirement Research Foundation. We would like to thank Lynn Fisher, MA, and Steven Jarvis, MD, who did the field observation, and George Agich, Jason Baim, Louis Burgio, Jay Gubrium, Brian Hofland, and Rosalie Kane for their comments on earlier drafts

References

Agich, G. J. (1990). Reassessing autonomy in long term care. *The Hastings Center Report, 20,* 12–17.

Agich, G. J. (1993). *Autonomy and long-term care.* New York: Oxford University Press.

Appelbaum, P. S., Lidz, C. W., & Meisel, A. (1987). *Informed consent: legal theory and clinical practice.* New York: Oxford.

Collopy, B. J. (1988). Autonomy in long term care: Some crucial distinctions. *The Gerontologist, 28* (Suppl), 10–17.

Diamond, T. (1986). Social policy and everyday life in nursing homes: A critical ethnography. *Social Science and Medicine, 23,* 1287–1295.

Faden, R. R., & Beauchamps, T. L. (1986). *A history and theory of informed consent.* New York: Guilford.

Fontana, A. (1977). *The last frontier: The social meaning of growing old.* Beverly Hills: Sage.

Gubrium, J. F. (1975). *Living and dying at Murray Manor.* New York: St. Martin's.

Hofland, B. F. (1988). Autonomy in long term care: Background issues and a programmatic response. *The Gerontologist, 28* (Suppl), 3–9.

Kane R. A., Freeman I. C., Caplan, A. L., Aroskar M. A., & Urv-Wong, R. K. (1990). Everyday autonomy in nursing homes. *Generations, 14* (Suppl), 69–72.

Kane R. L., & Kane, R. A. (1991). A nursing home in your future? *The New England Journal of Medicine, 324,* 627–629.

Katz, J. (1984). *The silent world of doctor and patient.* New York: Free Press.

Lidz, C. W., Fischer, L., & Arnold, R. (1992). *Erosion of autonomy in long term care.* Oxford University Press, New York.

Lidz, C. W., Meisel, A., & Munetz, M. (1985). Chronic disease and patient participation. *Culture, medicine and psychiatry, 9,* 1–17.

Lidz, C. W., Meisel, A., Zerubavel, E., Carter, M., Sestak, R., & Roth, L. (1984). *Informed consent: A study of decision-making in psychiatry.* New York: Guilford.

Moody, H. R. (1988). From informed consent to negotiated consent. *The Gerontologist, 28* (Suppl), 64–70.

Morgan, D. L. (1982). Failing health and the desire for independence: Two conflicting aspects of health care in old age. *Social Problems, 30,* 40–50.

Parsons, T. (1951). *The social system.* Glencoe, IL: Free Press.

President's Commission for the Study of Ethical Issues in Medicine and Biomedical and Behavioral Research. (1982). *Making health care decisions.* Washington, DC: U.S. Government Printing Office.

Shield, R. R. (1988). *Uneasy endings: Daily life in an American nursing home.* Ithaca NY: Cornell University Press.

Wolfe, D. B. (1989.) Hospitality, health care hybrid shows marketing promise. *Maturity Market Perspectives,* (Nov./Dec.).

Chapter Eight

A Resident's View of Autonomy

G. Janet Tulloch

"**C**an you spend an hour or so sitting with me to explain things? I feel so confused," sobbed Mrs. A., who had moved into the nursing home that morning. She had been agitated and crying since her daughter had departed after lunch. "Goodness, no!" said the overworked LPN, " I have medicine to give to 24 residents. Nurses never have time to play games."

When a new resident enters a nursing facility, she enters two places. A domicile—a home, a place in which to belong, to be accepted for herself with the baggage she has brought. It is also a place where she expects health care—good doctors and, especially, good nurses who will cater to her every command at the first touch of the call bell, which has been conveniently placed within easy reach.

We are all guilty of perpetuating this myth. Stories, articles, and television programs depict either the very worst conditions of nursing homes or this dream-like environment of utter perfection. The new resident has had the ideal chosen and described to her. Advocates as well as caregivers perpetuate these myths, aided by state and federal regulations.

In our efforts of almost 5 years to "make OBRA work" we also have fooled ourselves. Perhaps it is time we determine why some things have gone wrong and celebrate our victories.

I entered the Washington Home in 1965 at age 42 after the death of my mother. Because it was my own decision, I continued to exercise the independence that had been ingrained in me by my parents and teachers. For a time, however, this was a liability instead of an asset. Now I see this conflict and pain as having been necessary to continue my life with the philosophy and activities that had always been "normal" for me. I have managed to achieve a divergent, and sometimes contentious, degree of autonomy.

One of the possible reasons for my continuing sense of independence is that I did not have to deal with the physical and psychological devastation of a severe stoke or the debilitating diseases of multiple sclerosis or Parkinson's disease. Because many nursing home residents with these diseases previously lived normal lives integrated into society, with careers, marriage, and children, they have fewer coping mechanisms to deal with new, awesome physical disabilities. Added to this is the patronizing environment, which is overwhelming in itself. Their autonomy is within new frames of reference. A major decision once may have been whether to drive the car or to take the subway to work, whereas their new role is either to learn to propel a wheelchair or decide which staff member is likely to respond positively when asked to push the wheelchair into the recreation room so that they can play bingo.

This may be why residents of today, once known for gray-flannel suits and their sense of correctness, experience a series of psychological traumas. All the changes in their lives—physical, psychological, and social—when experienced together produce what is misinterpreted by caregivers as a "behavior problem." Could it be that these so-called problems are a cluster of wounds caused by environmental stress?

Social workers and psychiatric consultants who consider residents' behavior seldom consider the root causes. They use the word "behavior" when they really mean "misbehavior." Many residents are falsely typecast into negative roles, which they assume almost as an obligation to retain their compatibility with those on whom they are totally dependent.

Perhaps another word, "home," also has been overemphasized and misused. None of us would have chosen a group of sick and elderly people with whom to live at any other time in our lives. For the man in the gray flannel suit, changes in lifestyle were experienced as rises on the ladder of success.

One important aspect of long-term care today is the lack of rigid enforcement of residents' rights. This goes hand in hand with the impatience and resentment that caregivers feel for the Long-Term-Care Ombudsman Program. Although both the rights and ombudsmen were federal law long before the passage of OBRA in 1987, providers have not fully accepted them for their importance in ensuring a peaceful environment, contented staff, and residents who are able to realize their personal autonomy.

If residents' rights were fully enforced, the environment would be very different. One of the more ready excuses for not emphasizing rights is that "everybody has rights"; the implication is, "why should those of one group be more important than those of another?"

The answer to this question begs for much indulgence and patience. For many of our caregivers, "rights" is a loaded word heard in the context of injustice and cruelties dating back for two centuries. Perhaps we need another word, yet on searching we discover there is no other word that does not carry connotations of the ongoing struggle for justice.

Does this tell us that residents' rights are the same kind of crusade? It does. For the autonomy implicit in residents' rights means to surrender for caregivers who are fervent in their sense of responsibility. Good caregivers can become overly concerned for their residents. And it is often good caregivers who are most responsible for the loss of autonomy. Like overprotective parents, they use their power to prevent residents from becoming independent. Seldom is this a conscious action, yet seldom is a conscious action taken to foster autonomy. How often do we hear a certified nursing assistant say, "Do you want to be bathed and dressed now or shall I let you sleep for another hour or so?"

Professionals in long-term care have their own lists of stressful situations, and their own ideas of how they might contribute to "bad behavior." What is most important is that we understand that residents do undergo stress and learn to lower the pressure.

We realize that the gray-flannel era cannot be reproduced in current facilities administered by a generation of baby boomers. However, the consciousness of that period can be honored in many small ways. For instance, caregivers often make physical independence a primary goal for the resident. "You know how to brush your teeth." Within the dimensions of struggling with a new handicap and with the loss of environmental control, the individual is caught in an awesome dichotomy that makes complete surrender very tempting. Physical independence comes naturally when autonomy restores a sense of control over every facet of life. The people who managed the affairs of the post–World War II world were perfectionists. Families did not have to question their values.

Added to this is the humiliation stemming from the unconscious embarrassment felt when the physical self does not perform in the conventional manner. Not being able to execute simple procedures, such as tying shoes, buttoning a shirt, cutting food, or propelling a wheelchair, and especially being bathed and diapered—the largest trauma and the one that is never discussed openly—all bring subtle feelings of shame and inadequacy. The whole area of elimination becomes a guilty embarrassment, especially to the perfectionist in the gray-flannel suit.

Possibly because of this background of perfectionism, depression is often the first indication that a nursing home resident is experiencing severe trauma and a total loss of autonomy. Added to a sense of helplessness and hopelessness is the sight of other residents in various states of fragility. This evokes anger, the reverse side of depression, because the resident immediately knows, "that is my future." This manifests itself in the withdrawal from relationships with other residents.

Although many residents are inclined to band in groups—mostly for negative discussions of staff—others avoid intimacy. This is because they cannot tolerate what other residents may be experiencing in physical or mental deterioration. Indeed, this withdrawal is often accompanied by a covert byplay of "My condition is worse than yours." "You can at least read. I am legally blind." These remarks are more loaded with self-recrimination than with challenge to the resident to whom they are directed. Such residents are experiencing an identity crisis.

Individualization should begin at admission so that personal needs are met in a timely fashion through staff use of the minimum data set (MDS) and resident assessment instrument. The new resident is oblivious to the evolution of a care plan. Gray-flannel people, once very adept at making their own decisions, are seldom aware of the process or ready to participate actively on a decision making level. This increases their sense of helplessness, because they do not understand the impact it will have on life in the facility.

Because *giving* control also carries the sense that control can also be withheld, the environment must offer every opportunity for the resident to *take* control (Pringle, 1987). Autonomy, like control, is never an allowed thing; it is a surrender from one person to another.

Caregivers must be highly skilled and feel very secure within themselves to accept residents' refusal of care gracefully. Can the staff always honor the resident's expression of personal choice, which may sound too demanding or nonsensical for the reality of the facility? Although institutional living requires some rigid schedules for meals, nursing, and activities, they can be made flexible on many personal levels. Requiring residents to leave telephone numbers when signing out is an example of overprotectiveness infringing on autonomy. Signing out to leave the facility ("on pass") for a social engagement can be replaced by having the resident assume responsibility for canceling meals and making prior arrangements with staff for any help needed to be ready for the occasion. Having the resident assume responsibility is enforcing autonomy.

One of the most important steps toward autonomy is resident input and involvement with the care plan. All residents should participate in the conception, augmentations, and periodical changes in their care plans. These legal documents not only provide information and instruction to all levels of staff; they are the assurance that appropriate care will be given every day—no matter who is on duty.

Sometimes care plans appear to the resident as a "tool of terror" with the result that the MDS is used as labels for a resident's "misbehavior." This may be because staff fail to look for root causes when the resident is reacting normally to a situation. Negative language such as "screams," "abusing other residents," and "complaints about staff" are not understood within a valid frame of reference. Misbehavior is automatically exacerbated because the resident is enmeshed in feelings of shame, guilt, and embarrassment. These feelings are understood by Clarissa Pinkola Estes (1992, p. 176) for men as well as women:

> The most destructive cultural conditions for a woman to be born into and to live under are those that insist on obedience without consultation with one's soul, those with no loving forgiveness for rituals, those that force a woman to choose between soul and society, those where compassion for others is walled off by economic tiers or caste systems, where the body is

seen as something to be "cleaned" or as a shrine to be regulated by fiat, where the new, the unusual, or the different engenders no delight, and where curiosity is punished and denigrated instead of rewarded only if one is not a woman, where painful acts are perpetuated on the body and called holy, or whenever a woman is punished unjustly, as Alice Miller puts it succinctly "for her own good," where the soul is recognized as being in its own right.

A more positive approach is to involve residents in "environmental autonomy," that is, readiness to involve themselves not only with daily activities and personal care, but with caring for and ensuring that their surroundings are appropriate. Caring for plants and birds, or saying yea or nay to such seasonal decorations as valentine hearts being pasted on windows fosters a concern for the community. Residents who have been offered access to the *Physician's Desk Reference* can learn to identify side effects of their medications and offer suggestions for alternative dosages. Remaining in bed for a day is a method of controlling routine activity and interpersonal involvement within the community by "time off" (Tulloch, 1990).

This "time off" is not a seclusion as implied in, "Yes, I understand she's in pain and feels neglected, but she shouldn't take it out on the rest of us. Why doesn't she go in her room, close the door, and stay there until she feels better?"

Often we hear such remarks from frustrated staff. I say "frustrated staff" because many times they do wish they could help a resident in misery but cannot because they are overly tired and frustrated themselves. More often, they lack the skills to express the sensitivity such a situation requires, or they lack appropriate compassion because compassion has become an overused and seemingly negative term.

Some of you may remember the encounter groups of the 1970s when being "touchy-feely" was all the rage. People revealed past and present pain with no compunction. The revelations were met by others in the group with warm hugs, and tears were shed by all. Accusations of self-indulgence, and being too maudlin and overly sentimental soon put an end to these bathos groups.

Although such things, especially when they deal with feelings, do have a tendency to get out of hand, we should not have tossed out the need with the bathos. We now disallow the autonomy of open expression of feelings, even from residents who know they have reached their terminal stage. This has happened because staff-resident interaction is seen as a dangerous no-no.

Such forms of autonomy are best achieved and nourished within a supportive community of both residents and staff. Henri J. M. Nouwen (1989, pp. 43–44), the French *abbé* who joined Toronto's L'Arche for mentally disabled adults, has pinpointed an important element of long term care:

> Medicine, psychiatry and social work all offer us models in which 'service' takes place in a one-way direction. Someone is served. Someone else is being served, and be sure not to get the roles mixed up! But can anyone [help] those for whom he is not allowed to enter into a deep relationship? [Help] means making your own faith and doubt, hope and despair, courage and fear available to others as a way of getting in touch with [life] . . . yet the so-called 'helping professions' have been so thoroughly secularized that mutuality can only be seen as a weakness and a dangerous form of role confusion.

As Nouwen points out, we have become a culture that over-analyzes and overscrutinizes every friendship with suspicion instead of celebration. Although intimacy in the workplace has traditionally been considered a taboo, residents have an instinctive tendency to seek staff as surrogate family, an extension of a previous autonomous lifestyle. This should be seen for what it is rather than as grasping attempts to curry special favor to assure adequate care or special attention. On another level, residents who can be responsive to staff with a cheery "good morning" or a sincere "thank you for the great shower" set a stage for staff attitudes that carries over to residents who are less able to be positively responsive. Physical care is not complete when given in a sterile, impersonal environment without a recognition of individuality and without a tenderness that promotes a true quality of care and a viable equality of life. The need for displays of affection becomes a chief deprivation. Nobody ever kisses a resident good night. Yet these feelings go unobserved and unrequited. Echoes of loneliness can be heard in the sounds of "My husband always pecked me on the cheek before he got the morning paper."

Because we cannot endow autonomy, we must find other ways of stimulating residents with the desire to exercise their independence and rights. This means cultivating and conserving the environment in which we encourage and nurture the resident "to maintain his highest level of psychosocial well-being."

This catch-all phrase of OBRA sounds great on paper or when mouthed as a goal for group or individual residents. However, I very much fear that very few caregivers know what "highest level of psychosocial well being" means. Very few citizens ever achieve it. Does Hilary Rodham Clinton have it? What has it cost her, and is it a worthwhile toll on her psyche? Is it worth the cost for any of us, especially the frail elderly?

Today, my own highest level of psychosocial functioning is possibly the few minutes it will take to have this chapter read for me at a conference. As I sit writing it with the wintry January sun at my window, I am enjoying the anticipation. The adage about "getting there is half the fun" will be working for me for many months. I have a goal. Somebody wants something only I can offer. However, my life is not about writing a speech and traveling to Oregon. It is about what I write today to make a trip worth the effort of others as well as myself.

As with my usual writing, I set small goals for myself as I eat breakfast—try this on institutional coffee! Today I plan to write two pages on anticipation, do my laundry, read for fun (*Women Who Run With the Wolves* [Estes, 1992]), do some board reading for a National Citizen's Coalition for Nursing Home Reform article, or write the short piece for St. Alban's Church. This is somewhat the manner in which most people function barring all the variables of unforeseen circumstances.

Among the variables that permanently inhibit this control (which is another word for autonomy) is the onset of age or a serious illness that brings the need for long-term care. Somehow the nature of these new circumstances seem to terminate all desire to anticipate life in the manner we did unconsciously before entering a nursing home.

What helps you regain your incentives? Money? Achievement? Recognition? Self-satisfaction that fosters a healthy degree of self-worth? All these rewards stem from anticipation, which involves optimism, confidence, and hope. These breed faith and confidence. These are the words we rarely hear spoken of residents. Are they ever used on care plans? Perhaps these words do mean "highest level of well-being."

Federal regulations do not mention autonomy either. However, when we peer at them with attuned sensitivity, we discover many little roads that guide us to our own ingenuity. The seemingly benign Carter Williams forged one of the paths with her insistence that OBRA use the word "individuality" when speaking of resident care.

We may yet see the day when autonomy means a wider area of choices extending not only to certified nursing assistants, but to social workers and physicians as well. Facilities affiliated with hospitals usually provide two or three physicians designated for specific units. Residents who find they have poor communication with their assigned physician should be given other options. Social work, being a personal service, should also provide the same area of choice without judgmental comments such as, "She wants you, thank goodness; she is *so* difficult."

OBRA tells us that every resident's room must have a highly visible clock and calendar. Families usually provide clocks—either a digital one with large numerals or a bedside clock radio. The large numerals are important should the resident be prone to diminishing vision, but the clock radio is a boon for sleeplessness.

Engagement calendars are seldom thought of as necessities for nursing home residents. Their use can restore a sense of self-esteem and individuality, and promote a sense of autonomy. One innovation on this could be space for individual resident activities—when a specific volunteer is to come; going out to the eye doctor; when to expect a flu shot; physical therapy appointments; what day and time a niece usually telephones; a grandchild's birthday, when an antibiotic was begun and when it will terminate; shopping list for the sundry cart, such as kleenex or tooth paste; and when to go to the cashier before the weekend.

A ready response to this suggestion is going to be, "Who is going to write these things in a resident's engagement calendar? Staff already has too much paper work."

A volunteer may enjoy negotiating the next visit with the resident and marking the date. Medical reminders will protect staff from continuous questions, and the notations can also be used as reminders to themselves, "That's right, you have physical therapy today." Nurses will also know when to put the telephone near the resident and may remind a resident that she is nearly out of kleenex.

You may have noticed that things listed as personal items are all things one can consider negotiable. The volunteer should ask if the visit will be convenient next Tuesday; the trip to the eye doctor and the flu shot can be refused; physical therapy should be scheduled for the time of day when the resident finds treatment most beneficial; relatives negotiate a time and day when a telephone conversation is mutually agreeable; and a child's birthday can be recognized through a gift, a card, or a telephone call. The resident can determine for herself without asking when a temporary medication will be withdrawn, and we all make shopping lists and prepare to pay for our purchases.

Most important is that the calendar can be a tool for autonomy. The person, whether staff, family, friend, or outside professional, must negotiate by having a discussion before writing an engagement. The resident becomes truly engaged in her engagements. Daily living has returned as a decision-making process.

Finally, because engagement calendars are meant to reflect our future and the different roles we have to play day by day, year by year, the calendar may note on what day a special friend died or the day we remember losing family members. Although this could seem macabre, comfort is found as residents approaching death are reminded of life's measurements and are gently ushered into their own future.

References

Estes, C. P. (1992). *Women who run with the wolves.* New York: Ballatine Books.

Nouwen, H. J. M. (1989). *In the name of Jesus.* New York: Crossroads.

Pringle, D. (1987). *Control and care of older people.* Unpublished manuscript, University of Toronto.

Tulloch, J. (1990). Autonomy and long term care: From inside a nursing home, a resident writes about autonomy, *Generations,* (Suppl. XIV) 83–85.

Part II

Strategies for Enhancing Autonomy

Chapter Nine

The Gråberget Model of Care

Ulla Turremark

S weden, like most of the industrialized countries, has more elderly persons than ever before, and the proportion of elderly in the population continues to grow.

Gothenburg, with 450,000 inhabitants, is the country's second largest city. The growth of heavy industry and technology has changed Gothenburg from a shipyard town to a factory town. The major employers include Volvo (vehicles, food, and pharmaceutical products), SKF (ball bearings), Hasselblad (cameras), transport companies, and a large service sector.

People living in Gothenburg visit physicians more often and are off work sick more days per year than the average Swede; consequently Gothenburg invests more resources in health care, per capita, than other health authorities. We also have more beds in our hospitals than the average.

Gothenburg also has more old people than the national average. The basic philosophy of care for the elderly in Gothenburg is that they should be helped to live at home in their own environment for as long as they wish. For those who cannot manage at home, we have nursing homes.

The Gothenburg health care system is divided into five districts, and there are several nursing homes in every district. The idea is that those who need long- or short-term nursing home care should be able to get the care in the neighborhood where they live. In Gothenburg we have 16 nursing homes with 2,700 beds. Many of those older than age 85 live in the center of the city, where the Gråberget nursing home is located.

121

In Gothenburg there are two geriatric hospitals. Gråberget nursing home belongs to one of them, the Vasa hospital. The research on health problems of the elderly done at this hospital is well known.

The Gråberget Nursing Home

The Gråberget nursing home was built in 1978. With 210 beds and 204 full-time employees, it is one of the largest in Gothenburg. The nursing home has seven wards for long-term care and one for day care. Physiotherapy, occupational therapy, a central kitchen, a cleaning department, and administration are essential features of the nursing home. The nursing home is associated with the Institute for Long-Term Medicine and Geriatrics at Gothenburg University. A good deal of research and teaching are carried out at the clinic and at the nursing home. The patients, therefore, have contact with students in different areas of health care, who conduct the practical part of their studies at the nursing home.

In 1978, it was incredibly difficult to find people who would like to work in a nursing home. We had to start up Gråberget with only 2% of the nurses' aides having previous experience in nursing homes. Many of them were not at all interested in elderly people, but they were interested in getting a job; we hired them and gave them education for 2 weeks.

The care was given by a staff that strictly followed routines according to the schedules outlined; this meant, among other things, that all residents were awakened and had to go to bed at the same time every day. The schedules divided the day into the same routines for all residents. The staff had to work efficiently according to these schedules, which caused a lot of problems. For example, most of the staff took their meals and breaks at the same time.

Residents with a tendency to wander got into other residents' rooms and rummaged among their things. This happened all the time. Sometimes it was very noisy in the wards. Many anxious residents walked around the hallways, and others sat in their wheelchairs, knocking on the tables.

The environment was very different from what we have today. The rooms were standardized with hospital furniture, well functioning but covered with dull plastic material and mass-produced artwork on the walls. There were no carpets on the floor, and the curtains were exactly the same in every room.

Relatives and friends were not permitted to visit the residents more than a few hours a day, and the nurses did not cooperate much with them.

In short, the nursing home was like an acute care hospital in organization and environment, and it gave absolutely the best care we could provide for elderly sick people at that time.

Ten years ago we realized that the residents would grow older and older, and eventually would need maximum help. As a matter of fact, the average age of the residents at Gråberget has increased during the last 10 years from 75 to 87 years; 75% are females. More than 70% of the patients have two or more disorders and are not able to walk by themselves. The most common diagnoses are stroke, heart failure, cancer, and dementia. The average period of care (i.e., the period from the day on which a resident is admitted until he or she leaves the nursing home) has shortened from 4 years in 1985 to 11 months in 1992. Today almost all of the residents die in the nursing home.

Also, in the early 1980s, a new law strengthened the resident's position. The new law stipulates that residents must have influence over their own situation and that care must be individualized. The law also stipulates that the care must be of good quality, give the resident a feeling of security, respect the resident's rights of self-determination, provide continuity in the relationship between resident and staff, provide all the information the resident needs and understands, and be easily accessible.

So, we decided in the early 1980s—pushed by new health laws and the changes we saw in the residents—to introduce a new philosophy of care. We also decided that the organization and staff schedules had to be changed.

The Nursing Home Today

The Environment

Gråberget's rooms look like rooms in a home, with furniture and artwork from an era that feels right for the resident. Decoration of rooms is based on the resident's desires and taste; no two rooms are alike.

All rooms have connections for telephones so that residents may bring their home telephones. There are also two public telephones on each ward, one stationary and one movable.

We have abolished visiting hours, so that family members may come at almost any time and as long as the resident likes. The "Birthday Room" is a pleasant meeting room on the entrance level where residents and family members can get together for celebrations.

At mealtime, residents help themselves to food and beverages, if they are able. If a resident wants some special food, he may order a "wish dish." Those who enjoy a glass of wine with their meal or liqueur with coffee arrange and pay for these extras themselves.

Management and Organization

The director of the nursing home today has total responsibility for the budget, the staff, all activities for patients, and the building.

The nursing home employs more than 250 people, many of them part-time. In each ward there are 35 residents. A head nurse has the responsibility for a ward including the nursing staff—3 RNs and 20 practical nurses—and the ward budget. The budget for a ward is today almost $1 million (U.S.) and for the nursing home it is around $10 million.

Nursing care is now organized according to the principle of team nursing, with three teams in each ward. An RN is the team leader; she has responsibility for care planning and the education of her team. The ward staff works individually and that means that every staff member's shift is related to the residents' needs and demands. Therefore, the residents may choose when they wish to get up in the morning, have breakfast, and so on.

Rehabilitation plays an important role in our care. In addition to the staff, we have physiotherapists and occupational therapists working on rehabilitation. They all work closely with the ward staff, and residents have opportunities to improve their flexibility, strength, balance, and general condition, sometimes individually and at other times in groups, depending on the residents' needs and desire for help. Each resident also receives assistance in training to do things that are difficult for him or her. This might be dressing oneself, managing normal hygienic routines, moving about, or participating in leisure time activities. Occupational therapy address-es these needs. Occupational therapists also work with residents to find the most comfortable chair for each chair-bound person. A variety of chairs and arrangements of pillows and footstools are used, and seating is highly individualized.

Physicians at the geriatric clinic are responsible for medical care at the nursing home. A physician visits the nursing home every weekday, and we also have contact with the on-duty physician at the geriatric hospital during evening hours and on weekends.

Alternatives to Full-Time Institutional Care

Given the increasing number of elderly, it is important to develop alternative types of care and to facilitate normal independent liv-ing. Elderly people need more care than others; because we are not building any more nursing homes in Gothenburg at the moment, we have to use all the existing beds very effectively. Intermittent care is a form of alternative care for elderly people who despite diseases and handicaps still want to live at home. What this means is that the resident lives at the nursing home for 2 weeks and then lives in his or her own home for 2, 4, or 6 weeks according to a preplanned schedule.

Intermittent care was started in 1983 by Harriet Berthold, RN, MD; nowadays intermittent care is an accepted form of care at Gråberget nursing home. Intermittent care must provide good nursing care, qualified medical treatment, and rehabilitation to ensure a satisfying life for the elderly and their relatives. The criteria for intermittent care residents are the following:

1. Fairly stable medical condition
2. Absence of anxiety, memory disturbance, or confusion
3. Ability to stay at home at least 4 weeks in a row

We have 12 beds for intermittent care and 60 residents in the system. With flexibility, cooperation, knowledge, and planning in-termittent care is a good alternative to permanent nursing home care.

In addition, elderly living at home attend daytime care for the support necessary to be able to continue living in their own home.

One ward is devoted entirely to daytime care. Here, the elderly have access to nursing home personnel, physicians, physical therapy, occupational therapy, entertainment, and the company of other elderly.

The Gråberget Approach to Care

Our new philosophy of care is based on four cornerstones: knowledge, respect, individual care, and the environment.

Knowledge

To provide this kind of care prescribed in the 1980 health laws, staff must understand that these elderly sick people are really no different in their thinking and feelings from any of us. Therefore, for many years we have invested a lot of money in educating and training staff to change the attitudes toward the elderly and increase their factual information on aging. All staff, from cooks to nurses, are included in these educational efforts. Emotional support is given to the staff in regular sessions during which they can unwind and share the burdens they are feeling. Support is also given in the form of lectures and discussions on the wards. It is important to have these discussions every day.

Everybody working in the nursing home must have a comprehensive view of the residents' care and be aware that not only is medical treatment important, but also the psychological, social, and cultural aspects of care are vital. Many of the RNs alternate between work and periods of study at the nursing school and the university. We who work at Gråberget have made an agreement that we are all working toward the same good and based on this, a knowledge inventory is carried out so that we know what education is required for the staff.

Respect

All residents are individuals with their own special needs and desires. We have to listen to them to understand them and see problems from their viewpoint. This is the basis on which our work is founded. Respect will also help us with the main questions involved in daily living, particularly regarding the relationship between resident and staff. Many times, especially in the care of dying residents, we have a dilemma when the resident's wishes conflict with medical regulations.

The staff also must respect all professions involved in care and cooperate well with all of them.

Individual Care

In response to increasing demands from The National Board of Health and Welfare for full documentation by nurses of treatment and nursing care, we developed a Swedish model of nursing diagnosis, based on work by Doris Carnevali of Seattle. According to this model, every person is unique, and we have to care for each resident in the way that suits him or her best. The model requires nurses to integrate data on an individual's or family's functional capacities and external resources with data on the individual's current and future daily living requirements. These capacities and resources must be sufficient to meet the individual's needs. Daily living can be divided in four subcategories: activities of daily living, demands of daily living, the environment for daily living, and values and beliefs affecting daily living. A care plan is drawn up for each resident, together with the resident and, in some cases, family members.

During the first week after admission to the nursing home, a resident is assigned an RN who will be responsible for the resident's nursing care and a special contact who is more involved in the resident's activities and daily living than other team members. A concentrated effort is made to know the resident's customary daily living and to understand preferences and incorporate these in the nursing care plan. To reach a high level of nursing, good contact with the resident's relatives is essential. If a resident suffers from dementia, it is even more important to have contact with the family because this is the only way to get the basic knowledge vital for treatment. We cooperate with relatives individually, in groups, and together with the residents.

Nutrition for the resident is a major focus of care. No other part of the care is so interwoven with all aspects of daily living, and especially self-determination. Creating a domestic environment around meals and setting tables beautifully mean that residents eat better. The staff joins the residents at meals to assist them and create a good social environment.

In Sweden we have a law stating that only physicians can prescribe retraints for a patient, and restraints are seldom used in long-term care. Today at Gråberget we have no residents in restraints, though some of them use a tray or table in front of their wheelchairs. The chairs are designed to be comfortable, and with attention to individual needs. Occasionally residents fall and get fractures; however, we must accept this risk, or otherwise quite a few residents would be in restraints. We are all exposed to risks every day. Conversely, we have to try to prevent accidents and injuries, and, therefore, we identify and carefully supervise the high-risk residents. Through individual nursing care planning, risk factors are specified. For example, the clothing and shoes of a patient must be inspected and, if necessary, corrected, just as technical equipment is inspected.

Most of the residents die in the nursing home, and terminal care is of great importance to us. Terminal care involves a complete change of priorities for nurses. Their aim is not any longer to cure the resident. Instead, they work to keep him or her comfortable. Both the medical and emotional needs of the resident have to be met effectively. If we can, we involve the family to help the nurse with feeding, turning, and washing. With good terminal care, a resident can die without distress. After the death we are very careful with the body and handle it with respect, almost as if it were still alive. By inviting relatives to come back to give voluntary help, the ward staff are able to help some bereaved relatives. Often they have visited the nursing home over a considerable time, and they know the ward routines and many of the other residents.

Environment

Improvements cannot be achieved without sufficient funding. The nursing home must be viewed as a whole, where the atmosphere of the premises influences the behavior and well-being of the residents as well as the staff and visitors.

For any improvements actually to benefit the residents, the staff must help and instruct them. This requires time and knowledge on the part of the staff, and thus changes in the physical environment provide excellent opportunities for further education of the staff.

It is important for our philosophy of care that residents participate in the design of their environment. This is the reason why the decoration of rooms is centered around the patients' desires and tastes. We encourage residents to bring their own furniture, paintings, and other personal items from their homes to their rooms at the nursing home to give them a home-like atmosphere.

The Change Process

All changes take time—often much more time than one expects. The whole staff must go through all the steps of change and must understand and accept the new system. We developed a seven-step process to help staff change. The first step involves learning about the new system. The second and third steps require staff to understand and then to accept the new system. Step four involves consequences of change, and in step five staff members realize the new part they will pay. Step six involves recognizing one's own need for development, and, finally, step seven is working with the new system.

To carry out all the changes, leadership is of vital importance. The main point is to understand that the best resource is professional staff members, who have a strong feeling of responsibility for the patients and are interested in the work.

Summary

Like many other countries, Sweden now is experiencing economic stagnation, resulting in reduction of funding to the public sector. The consequences for health care and nursing homes are that we all have to save money. In this situation priorities must be set. Despite the shortage of funds, the elderly sick people in the nursing homes must have a feeling of security and self-determination, and must be treated politely and always individually. All people working in a nursing home must be flexible and aware of the needs of the residents.

Progress in the care of elderly people must continue; therefore, we must continually work on improvements. A flexible staff who can accept these changes is a necessity to provide our elderly people with the good care they need.

Chapter Ten

The Skaevinge Project: A Model for Future Primary Health Care—The English Summary

Lis Wagner

Primary Health Care in Denmark

Denmark is a relatively small country with a mere 5 million inhabitants and a long tradition of public responsibility in health care and health services. The Danes are well educated and traditionally have favored public health research activities. Medical research is thus well developed, and data on health-related problems have been collected by public and private agencies for a long time.

Since Denmark signed the Strategy of "Health for All" developed by the World Health Organization in 1984, the importance of primary health care (PHC) has been emphasized throughout the country. And with the rising cost of health care, PHC is considered even more important because it is able to offer quality care at lower costs.

The Danish Ministry of Health is responsible for health services administration at the national level and is assisted by permanent committees serving in an advisory capacity. Administratively, the country is divided into 16 counties and 275 communities, almost half of which have fewer than 10,000 inhabitants. Most health services are free to the individual; they are paid for through taxes, which are between 48% to 67% depending on income. In addition, there is a 25% Danish sales tax on virtually all purchases. Consumers pay part of the costs of dental care, prescribed drugs, and physiotherapy. General practitioners are reimbursed by the National Health Insurance Scheme in part according to the number of patients on their list and in part on a fee-for-service basis.

County authorities are responsible for hospitals, but care for the elderly is handled by communities. The hospital sector takes care of medical treatment; however, when the patient no longer requires this, social welfare agencies take over and ensure that treatment and care are provided. This means that, in Denmark, there are no hospital wards for the long-term ill, or for frail or disabled elderly persons. The needs of these people are taken care of by local authorities through preventive health services, home nursing, nursing homes, home help services, aids/appliances, meals on wheels, and so forth. An important feature of Danish legislation on social welfare is that it merely sets up the framework for care; concrete social measures are drawn up by local authorities. This means that the organization of care for the elderly may differ from one local authority to the next.

Model of Care in Denmark

All the elderly in Denmark receive an old-age pension sufficiently large to enable them to live solely on their pensions. To cover their stay in nursing homes, the elderly must pay all of their pension plus 60% of other social income; in return, everything is free of charge, and each resident receives a sum of "pocket money." In recent years this system has been debated at great length in Denmark, because there are indications that it leads to an inactive life devoid of responsibility, which was not the intention of the system when it was created.

As a result, during the last 10 to 15 years, there have been significant changes in care for the elderly; since the 1980s, there has been a tendency to move away from institutional care toward home services: We are done with the "institutional syndrome."

Indeed, in the last few years the trend has been toward staying at home as long as possible. Also, efforts have been to strengthen the influence of the elderly on their own life by ensuring continuity and the greatest possible measure of self-determination.

The main consequences of the gradual aging of the Danish population are changes in the relations between the economically active and the nonactive, and a movement away from child care toward care of the elderly. There is also an increasing number of older frail people; this increase will have a powerful impact, both socially and economically, on society as a whole.

However, it is easier to accept this change because older people today are not like those of previous generations: Most of the "new elderly" are better educated, healthier, and less dependent on public and private assistance, and, therefore, far more active than their parents or grandparents. They cannot be considered a specific and separate class; it is both in their interests and in the interests of society as a whole that they remain fully and completely integrated into the community.

Such an integration has been attempted in a small Danish municipality, Skaevinge, and here I describe how this has taken place. Using Skaevinge as a model, I concentrate on how a given structure within PHC may be changed.

Skaevinge is a rural municipality with a population of 5,000, of whom 10% are old-age pensioners. The purposes of developing an experimental program of housing and care for the elderly were to (a) offer health benefits to all community members, regardless of where they lived; and (b) give priority to preventive action, to support the individual's potential for preserving and strengthening health and quality of life. The result has been a new structure in which the nursing home has been turned into a 24-hour community health care center, open to all citizens. Within the community health care center, the elderly residents have private apartments.

Planning Phase

First of all, a project team was formed, made up of one member from each of the following fields: home help, home nursing, public health nursing, and all nursing home staffs, plus representatives elected for and by the elderly. I was the project leader from 1984 to 1988. The project team's tasks were (a) to strengthen the professional/technical bases for the project; (b) to ensure that coherent health benefits were offered to the people in the municipality, and resources were optimally used; (c) to participate in planning of training/seminars/meetings parallel to the development of the project;

(d) to contribute ideas, criticism, and creative thinking in the adjustment process; and (e) to ensure the exchange of information and dialogue with individual professional/technical groups through their representatives.

During the planning phase, all the professional/technical groups were involved: home help, public health nursing, home nursing, nursing home staffs, and the representatives of the elderly. These meetings showed that coordination and cooperation among staff from different fields were deficient, and no common objective existed in the care of the elderly population. Closer collaboration and better knowledge of the other groups' areas of work were needed. Time was an important issue, and self-criticism and a sense of humor were important components.

At first, the team found it difficult, in fact, almost unthinkable, to move away from the existing structure of care. The team discussed ideas and suggestions that could form the basis for change; in this we were guided by three key concepts: a philosophical view of humans, a framework for organization, and the need for 24-hour service. The team soon discovered that it was difficult to handle the concepts of organization and 24-hour service in a creative manner. Their conclusion was that we needed a common view of the individual as a basis for planning and preparation. The view of human beings who served as our common ground for ideas and creative thinking was based on the Orem's concept of self-care (1980) and on the World Health Organization's health-for-all strategy.

Orem sees human beings as rational, problem-solving, and need-satisfying individuals. Self-care is based on the idea that a human being is a free, independently thinking and acting individual—a responsible person capable of making decisions concerning his or her own life. In this view, the role of health care staff is consultative. They are responsible for passing their technical information on to individuals so that they may acquire the knowledge and skills needed to continue being responsible for their own life.

Many discussions preceded the decision to implement the self-care concept. A few of the questions raised were: What do we—the health care staff—do wrong in an institution? Why is the nursing home an outmoded institution? One of our answers was that health care staff suffer from the "maid-servant syndrome." They have acquired deep-seated habits of "helping" and "taking care of" instead of encouraging nursing home residents to do as much as possible for themselves. Further, nursing home residents expect these services because health care staff is paid to perform them.

Our conclusion was that the structure of the nursing home was a "service package solution" and, therefore, not consistent with the project team's view of the individual. Regardless of residents' needs, medicine was administered three times daily, meals were served at fixed hours, and residents were no longer in control of anything.

It took 1.5 years of education and dialogue to reach an agreement on this new theoretical basis for PHC, in which all barriers to autonomous development in the care of the elderly were dismantled. Implementation of the Skaevinge project called for considerable adjustments on the part of health care personnel, including continuing education, because they also wanted autonomy and self-determination in planning and carrying out their work. A total of 120 interdisciplinary staff members went through 80 hours of training before intervention in practice took place in 1986, 1.5 years after the project started (Wagner, 1988).

Implementation Process

The concept of a nursing home was dismissed. The nursing home was turned into private two-room apartments, each with a bath and toilet and cooking facilities. In addition, there are two guest apartments and one day/night room for persons requiring temporary care—for example, an elderly person with flu and high fever who does not require hospitalization but cannot be left ill and alone at home. All residents now receive their pensions directly and are expected to pay for food, hair dressing, personal purchases, medicine, newspapers, and so on. A health care center was set up, with home nursing, public health nursing, and a day care center under the same roof, serving everyone in the municipality from 0 to 100 years of age. That is, the center serves not only the inhabitants of the 63 private flats but also other citizens. For example, prenatal care and well child care are both emphasized in the health center. On weekdays, a nurse is available at a call station in the health center from 8:00 a.m. to 4:00 p.m. to coordinate work in the municipality. This responsibility is rotated among the home nurses. Everyone in the municipality, not only the elderly, can call and get advice. The nurse at the call station coordinates duty hours and ensures that information is passed on to all sectors of the health care center. Three district groups of nurses, auxiliaries, and home helpers have responsibility for one third of the citizens including those in the apartments in the former nursing home. During the evening and night shifts and on holidays and weekends, the municipality is considered one large district.

Some apartment residents require 24-hour service: not only the senile or demented, but also those who cannot go to the toilet or take a bath alone. These same people may, however, be capable of looking after their finances, preparing breakfast, and calling the doctor.

The health care staff and the resident decide together the health care needs in each individual case, following an overall assessment. The principle is that everyone can get exactly the help they need. Nobody is automatically channeled into a network of support measures, which may deprive them of control over their own lives.

No two residents in a nursing home are alike, and the social behavior of the residents has changed considerably since the nursing home was turned into apartments. They can now choose to participate in group activities and parties, and can even do special favors for friends, like baking a birthday cake. Most residents now have more money and can make their own financial arrangements. Many residents prepare their own breakfast. An increasing number make their own sandwiches for the evening meal, asking the home helper to do the purchases or go shopping with them. Most of the residents now have more money, and some have been able to buy a television and other necessities, and even have a telephone. In short, as a result of the changes, each individual resident stands out in a unique way.

The project team has been surprised by the level of acceptance of the changes in organizational structure, and how smoothly these have worked. All nursing posts at the nursing home were transferred to the 24-hour home nursing service. The two ward sisters and the nurse in charge of home nursing are now district nurses. Health visitors work as consultants to the whole population. A nurse with advanced education was appointed to coordinate the entire health division.

As a result, there is now one coordinator for all speciality areas, with closer cooperation and better use of the technical and professional groups. There are also possibilities of greater flexibility to meet needs for assistance at any given time.

Experience Gained from Skaevinge

The Skaevinge project created a new interdisciplinary structure that turned a nursing home into private apartments and introduced 24-hour health services for the entire community. There is continued communication between staff and the population, which means that the project receives input from both staff and citizens.

An evaluation has been carried out based on information on costs; and a questionnaire has been given to citizens older than 67 years on their satisfaction with the new system, number of hospitalizations, use of health insurance, and status reports. As a result of the 24-hour service throughout the municipality and more information on help in their homes, many elderly have chosen to remain at home.

It is important to emphasize that the objective of the Skaevinge project has not been to save money for the municipality, but to allocate resources, both human and economic, so that more people may benefit.

Denmark no longer builds nursing homes. Forty percent of those older than 65 years who live in private homes live with a spouse, but more than 50% live alone. The bulk of practical assistance and care for the elderly living in private homes is provided by the spouse, if there is one, or by home help and the district nurse service, which, in an increasing number of communities, is on a 24-hour basis. This is a flexible system and can be adjusted to meet the changing needs of clients. Institutional services, such as nursing homes and sheltered housing, are being replaced by private apartments, specially designed for disabled persons and linked to flexible home care services.

The nursing homes of the past were, so to speak, a "package" of services. In the new system, housing and care have become separate functions. Housing is now upgraded from one room and a bathroom in a nursing home to a specially designed two-room apartment with modern conveniences in a health care center. Care services in these private apartments are adjusted over time to meet the needs of the elderly person in question, and include a system for sharing decision making and responsibilities.

If the Skaevinge project is used as a model for larger municipalities or other countries, it might be advisable to subdivide areas into districts the size of Skaevinge. However, it should be noted that the success of a project of this type depends on geographical, cultural, and political and economic conditions.

To make these changes, it is crucial to separate care and housing, and eliminate institutional solutions for the elderly, such as nursing homes. Private homes need to have easy access to services from the primary health care sector, regardless of housing conditions. This is more satisfactory both for the elderly and for staff.

References

Orem, D. E. (1980). *Concepts of nursing practice.* New York: McGraw-Hill.

Wagner, L. (1988). *Skaevinge-projektet—en ny model i primaere sundhedstjeneste.* Copenhagen: *Kommunetryk.*

Chapter Eleven

Assisted Living as a Model of Care Delivery

Keren Brown Wilson

One of the fastest-growing options in long-term care today in the United States is assisted living. An assisted living facility is an apartment where residents are provided nonmedical services and support, often in increments as their conditions warrant (Kane, Illston, & Kane, 1990). The popularity of assisted living is growing even though it is not well defined, its regulatory future is unknown, and financing for such shelter and services are difficult (Kane & Wilson, 1993). The growth is a response to three dominant concerns in long-term care that are the focus of enormous attention in political, academic and practice settings today.

The first of these concerns is the burgeoning cost of Medicaid, which is predicted to increase 120% between 1990 and 1996. The aged, who make up only 5% of Medicaid recipients, consume nearly one fourth of all Medicaid expenditures. Moreover, the $17.7 billion expended on institutional long-term care in 1990 represents less than half of the money spent to cover chronic care costs for that year. Although the elderly pay privately for more than half of their long-term-care costs, picking up the tab for the rest has state governments on the verge of panic (Ladd et al., 1992). This panic increases when increases in future costs are calculated based on projected demographic changes.

A second concern related to long-term-care services is consumers' growing expectation that a variety of alternative care models will be available. In the United States a generation of advocacy, coupled with increasing personal wealth among a segment of the young old, has fueled the aggressive growth of service options for middle-class older adults trying to avoid nursing home placement. Coupled with state policy designed to control the growth of nursing home beds, this consumer expectation has generated multiple models of in-home care and supportive housing.

A third concern is the growing recognition that the paradigm of a "continuum of care" is inappropriate for long-term-care services (Wilson, 1993). This paradigm has three major conceptual flaws.

1. It assumes a linear progression of disability/disease.
2. It separates services from housing.
3. It engenders misuse of the therapeutic milieu.

One result of this approach has been the development of a dichotomous service delivery system that medicalizes, institutionalizes, and professionalizes long-term care in ways never originally envisioned. Thus, a costly, unappealing system has become an entrenched way of providing long-term-care services.

Assisted living is, in essence, a response to these concerns. In its broadest definition, assisted living is a reconceptualization of long-term-care services for special-needs populations including the frail elderly, physically disabled, developmentally challenged, and emotionally impaired. This reconceptualization underlies a redefinition of the role of the environment, the enhancement of care service capacity, and, perhaps most important, a shift in values about how care is provided. Taken together, these alternations with the approach to care illustrate the unique characteristics of assisted living.

Normalization of the Environment

Clearly, one of the strongest values in North American culture is that of home. Although we normally think of home as a "house," it is defined uniquely for individuals by numerous characteristics. There are, however, common themes for individuals regardless of their age, ethnicity, race, or gender. These themes define the elements of an environment that make it feel more "home-like" for individuals.

The first of these themes is the appearance of the setting. Appearance gives rise to the concept of a "tenantial" feeling—as opposed to a commercial or institutional setting. A tenantial model of assisted living requires the following:

1. An architectural style that is commonly associated with places where people have lived and that they recognize thematically as being tenantial
2. Community common space with recognized public functions
3. Accommodation of cultural preferences for privacy and control of personal space
4. Amenities in public and personal space in keeping with lifelong experiences
5. A scale appropriate to support tenantial feeling
6. Features to enhance the ability of the individual to age in place

In most care settings—apart from individual homes—most of these elements are violated to some degree. Indeed, it is the violation of many of these elements that leads, in part, to the classification of space as institutional or commercial (Regnier, et al., 1991). New housing and facilities built for the aged, in particular, have violated most of these elements. Often these settings are large; devoid of personalization; and inappropriate in scale, design, and functionality. The effort that has been made to create a tenantial ambiance has focused largely on the outside of the building in the common spaces within the building. Private space has often been a shared room without control over access, temperature, or even how the space is furnished. Assisted living, at its best, supports the normalization of the environment, as defined in the six preceding points.

Perhaps the most central of these points is control of personal space. This typically means single-occupancy units, shared only by personal choice. Ideally, this private space has defined areas for sleeping, living, and preparing food, as well as a private bath. It has a locking door and individual temperature controls, and is furnished completely with personal belongings. These features are necessary amenities in the life experience of most older adults. The tenant maintains a large degree of control over lifestyle and social structure. Access to and use of personal space are determined primarily by the tenant.

Additionally, assisted living residences should represent the predominant character of a community. Just as the facade should not be that of a flat roofed box or upscale hotel, the architectural mode should respect regional and age-sensitive thematic influences. For example, porches and victorian design may fit some regions, whereas patios and mission style architecture fit others. Even in this context, it is important to understand that older persons are not living in the past, even if they enjoy remembering it.

Appropriately designed assisted living offers individuals the choice to use their unit as a base for the conduct of their daily lives or to take advantage of interior community space. Done well, assisted living balances personal and community space demands and use. Moreover, community space is developed to recreate those public spaces most likely to be patronized by persons residing in the community.

Finally, elements of universal and adaptable design are used in unobtrusive ways to support individual functioning. Some features need not be unique—lever door hardware, door width, window height, and so on. Others may be special—specialized storage for medical supplies or incontinent laundry. Appropriately incorporated into the function and design of the setting, these elements do not stand out as special.

Although the need for these elements may seem fairly self-evident, they are *not* standard features of current design and organizational practices in supportive housing and care arrangements in North America. In most long-term-care settings, for example, it is typical for individuals to have roommates assigned, share bathrooms, sleep in hospital beds, or be forbidden to store food in their space. In many supportive housing arrangements, it is uncommon for individuals to have kitchens, baths, or locking doors. Pets, overnight guests, alcohol, and cigarette use typically are prohibited or restricted.

Little thought has been given by policy makers, architects, and providers to the adverse impact of imposing such non-normative elements on special-needs populations. To illustrate, many problems, such as incontinence and aggression, can be managed better with private living space and bathrooms (Wilson, Ladd, & Saslow, 1988). Further, kitchenettes or kitchen galleys encourage use of lifestyle skills and facilitate continued social patterns of interacting. In essence, individuals may feel a revitalized territorial stake in their surroundings.

Enhanced Service Capacity to Foster Well-Being

The separation of housing from services is tightly bound to the assumption that medical services are the primary focus of long-term care. This assumption is reinforced by reimbursement mechanisms that define health in terms of treatment for illness or disability.

Assisted living focuses more broadly on the following:

1. Competence as measured by the ability to perform instrumental activities of daily living (IADLs) and activities of daily living (ADLs)
2. Appropriate interventions to manage the effects of chronic disease or disability
3. Aggressive medical treatment for episodes of acute illness
4. Overarching concern with all aspects of well-being
5. Responsibility for the management of care across all domains

Traditional long-term-care settings differ notably from assisted living in all these areas. These differences are, in large part, due to the dominance of a medical model. Consider, for example, the type of tools used to assess needs in traditional care settings. They are all disability or problem based. Eligibility for services and, more important, reimbursement are both based on level of impairment. Although it is important to know what is needed, this approach often has two adverse effects on the individual. First, disability in one domain (e.g., mobility) is often assumed to create incompetence in another (e.g., cooking). Second, by focusing on what individuals cannot do for themselves as opposed to what they can do, the image conveyed is often negative, fostering perceptions of incompetence and engendering learned helplessness.

Moreover, most assessments and interventions are weighted in terms of physical functioning. Although clearly the ability to perform critical ADLs, such as transferring, toileting, and eating is vital for survival, seldom is adequate attention paid to the other domains, and even less attention is paid to their interaction with physical functioning. This interaction is illustrated nicely by the example of the incontinent, arthritic, insulin-dependent diabetic who cannot get out of bed because she has no motivation to do so. Her depression significantly increases her need for physical care.

Interventions, especially for the very old, tend to be reactive and attempt to reduce the impact of illness. Assisted living suggests that integration of a broad array of services ranging from individual socialization to regular nursing care is more appropriate. At a minimum, assisted living must be able to meet a wide array of needs 24 hours a day. The services to meet these needs fall into four categories: hotel, personal care, nursing, and care management.

The first, and least intensive group of services, are hotel-type services, such as meals, housekeeping, laundry, social events, and transportation. These services typically can be scheduled and provided in a group; they do not necessarily require special knowledge of disease or disability. Although these services are very helpful, unless the individual needs protective oversight as a result of cognitive or emotional disorders, the survival of the individual is not necessarily threatened if the services are not there.

Personal care, the second category of assisted living services, are those ADL tasks needed to get basic needs met one or more times daily. Many are enduring needs, and they cannot easily be scheduled. Most require some special training; few can be provided to more than one person at a time. Along with medication management, these services—help with toileting, mobility, eating, grooming, personal hygiene, and dressing—make up the bulk of long-term-care services. Many persons with these needs end up in traditional long-term-care settings, because without such services, their level of risk is higher.

The third category of assisted living services is nursing care. Many care needs are unpredictable and must be performed with a fair degree of specialized skill. The greatest ongoing need is for readily available observation and assessment to ensure appropriate management of chronic disease or intervention for acute illness. Some diseases or illnesses may result in conditions requiring skilled treatments, such as catheter or ostomy care. These care needs are perceived to be most efficiently met in nursing-type facilities. However, with proper training and supervision of non-licensed staff, these needs can also be appropriately met in a tenantial setting. Assisted living can meet most of the nursing needs if permitted to do so by licensure criteria.

The fourth type of services in assisted living include individualized assessment, planning, and implementation of programs to manage the problems associated with functional or organic psychopathology and case management of ancillary health care needs. Ability to perform these services adequately sets assisted living apart from most tenantial programs, just as the environment sets it apart both from most tenantial programs, and from most nursing or medical facilities. When all four categories of needs are addressed in a tenantial group setting, a merger of housing and services is achieved.

Shift in Values Orientation to Preserve Self-Worth

In long-term care, it is easy to be overwhelmed by meeting physical needs, and to overlook emotional, social, intellectual, or spiritual needs. Perhaps the most radical aspect of assisted living is a shift in values orientation, which results in redefinitions of consumer empowerment, best practice concepts, and quality. This shift in thinking supports human principles, such as dignity, choice, and privacy, that are easily violated when individuals are dependent on others for care.

Part of the reason it is easy to violate these principles is that the concepts of autonomy, reciprocity, and empowerment are confused and misused. Objectively defined, autonomy is the ability, willingness, and opportunity to make and act on decisions. Reciprocity implies a balance of giving and taking in relationships. Reciprocity demands that the individual's needs and preferences be balanced against the needs and preferences of others including the caregiver. Empowerment is the redistribution or restoration of opportunities to promote reciprocity and autonomy for those in society labeled as disabled, disenfranchised, or dependent. Assisted living is uniquely positioned to support fundamental change to achieve empowerment of frail, often significantly impaired adults.

This empowerment is achieved by embracing the concepts of shared responsibility, bounded choice, and managed risk. Without these grounding precepts, empowerment cannot be achieved. They enhance the potential for reciprocal actions and reduce objections to autonomy for individuals whose ability to act independently is compromised. Shared responsibility assumes that rights and responsibilities are balanced. The degree of autonomy exercised in the decision-making process is weighed against the degree of responsibility accepted for the outcome of the decision. Bounded choice reflects the recognition that personal capacity, societal limits, organizational capacity, and situational circumstances set the parameters of autonomy for all individuals. Managed risk is a process that defines the responsibilities and choices associated with empowerment.

The vehicle for achieving this model of empowerment is the service planning process. In assisted living, service planning and delivery of care are based on shared responsibility, bounded choice, and managed risk. The individual actively participates, to the extent possible, in setting priorities, proposing strategies to meet his or her needs, and agreeing to service parameters as a part of the plan. The plan is negotiated by the individual, the provider of service, and advocates (if necessary) who reach consensus. Central to this process is thoughtful, thorough analysis of the "need" or "problem" from several viewpoints—those of the provider, the individual, and the society, as well as others who are directly affected.

Such a process encourages integration, competency-based task assignment, service incrementalism, and familial involvement. Assisted living thus provides new opportunities to embrace approaches in congregate or group living that have always been used in home care situations. This redefinition is important because not only does it enhance the independence of individuals, but it also leads to better use of limited resources.

For example, in assisted living, the adjustment of services to accommodate individual needs and preferences precisely often actually results in less service. This happens because many services are given based on professional assessment of need that does not sufficiently consider individual differences. These assessments often reflect cultural or professional bias toward an acceptable care standard rather than actual need or even preference of an individual. A more incremental approach to services also makes it easier to identify and support the continued involvement of families or significant others in the provision of care. Unable to take full responsibility for a given set of needs, dependent individuals and their families often want to stay involved in a meaningful way. Traditional care settings have often served to discourage that involvement.

In assisted living, best practice is not defined by staffing ratios or types of licensed professionals on staff. Rather, assisted living fosters the use of specially trained staff to assess and identify potential strategies for intervening with identified needs, and teach other staff who have day-to-day responsibility for helping individuals manage clinically unique needs. This approach helps to ensure consistency of intervention across need areas and produces more integrated care responses.

This redefinition of best practice and the focus on consumer empowerment lead to new ways of thinking about what constitutes quality services or care. Although not yet well developed, the criteria focus on adherence to a normalized setting, client-based service delivery techniques, enhanced program capacity, consumer satisfaction, and appropriate use of ancillary health services.

Model in Practice: The Oregon Experience

Assisted living, as described earlier, is policy in the state of Oregon, which is recognized in the United States as having one of the most innovative service systems for older and physically disabled adults (Kane & Wilson, 1993).

In 1984 Oregon's Senior and Disabled Services Division (SDSD) granted a program waiver to an assisted living program, addressing both environmental and program capacity standards.

This first assisted living program, 112 units with all private pay clients, was so successful that a second facility was opened in 1986 with 127 units. This program had 20 units set aside for Medicaid clients as part of a demonstration project. The state selected 20 clients eligible for nursing home placement to participate in the program; they had a variety of diagnoses including cognitive, functional, and health-related problems.

After 1 year, a study was conducted to examine the outcomes of placement in the assisted living program. The state looked at client status, discharge experience, and cost. Based on data that pointed to improved functioning, lower turnover, and decreased costs for services, the state determined to make assisted living available to Medicaid clients on a statewide basis. However, the state decided to first put special rules for assisted living in place. The rule-making process took approximately 1 year. Providers, consumers, advocates, and other regulatory entities (e.g., the fire marshall, building codes, and the health department) joined SDSD in a series of task force meetings to develop the assisted living rules. The process resulted in an unusual degree of interagency consensus on what standards were needed and how duplication of agency responsibility could be reduced. The rules established environmental and service standards, and legitimized the shift in values orientation to emphasize consumer autonomy.

Since 1989, more than 1,400 units of assisted living have been licensed in 25 buildings throughout the state. Of these, 6 are retrofitted congregate or nursing facilities (400 units) and 19 are new construction (1,000 units). An additional 1,000 or so units are in various phases of development. Licensed capacity ranges from 15 to 105 units, with typical projects ranging from 25 to 50 units. Interestingly, most development has been in the more rural parts of the state, outside the Portland Standard Metropolitan Statistical Area (SMSA).

Tenant Profiles

On average, tenants of Oregon's assisted living programs have significant impairment. Medicaid clients must be eligible for nursing home placement to receive authorization for service. This generally means being dependent in two or more activities of daily living. Thirty-four percent of the tenants are older than age 85, and the average age in most projects in the high 80s. Assessed needs include need for bathing assistance (89%), mobility impairment (84%), behavioral/cognition problems (59%), toileting needs (52%), and medication management (80%). Tenants average 3.4 dependencies in ADL functioning; most are virtually dependent in all IADL related activities. The following are a series of typical tenant profiles:

- Mrs. X, a widowed female, age 85, relocated from her own apartment. She often feels misunderstood, has disturbed sleep, and is occasionally physically and verbally abusive. She is typically unable to get along with others. Mrs. X is totally dependent on staff to orient her to time, person, and place. She has very poor short-term memory and poor long-term memory, and she requires frequent reminding and constant oversight because of judgment. She is hearing impaired and severely visually impaired, and she needs assistance with eating. Mrs. X is dependent in all IADLs and two ADLs.

- Mrs. Y, a widowed female, age 84, relocated from a nursing home. She has disturbed sleep, suffers from fatigue, finds life uninteresting, is unhappy, and feels plotted against to a significant degree. Mrs. Y is controlling and manipulative, exhibits dependent behavior, and is often depressed, anxious, irritable and pessimistic. She is resistive to care and does not adapt well. She requires frequent reminding and exhibits poor judgment. Mrs. Y is visually impaired, and uses a walker and wheelchair. She requires total assistance with two ADLs and all IADLs, and is oxygen dependent. Her health problems include arthritis, hypertension, heart disease, COPD, diabetes, and a history of falls. She has frequent episodes of hospitalization and takes 11 drugs at least daily.
- Mr. A, a divorced male, age 86, relocated from a nursing home. He has occasional functional disorders secondary to a mild alcohol-related dementia. Mr. A is frequently irritable, and he occasionally experiences uncontrolled frustration and is verbally abusive. He has a limited social support system and is withdrawn. He is generally alert despite some alcohol-related dementia. He is severely visually impaired and uses a walker and wheelchair. Mr. A requires preventive skin care and has a history of falls, fractures and heart disease. His health history includes paralysis from a cardiovascular accident (CVA) and arthritis. Mr. A requires assistance with all IADLs.
- Miss B, a single female, age 78, relocated from the geropsychiatric unit. She has functional disorders secondary to mild neurological impairment. She suffers from some depression and anxiety, is frustrated and generally easily agitated, and is occasionally resistive to care and verbally abusive. She requires minimal behavioral intervention and has a limited social support system. Miss B is generally alert but has inappropriate speech patterns. She is visually impaired, and uses a walker and wheelchair. Her health history includes seizures, CVA, gout, arthritis, heart disease, and cancer. She requires assistance with IADLs and is totally dependent on staff for four ADLs. She requires a special diet but is noncompliant.
- Mrs. Z, a widowed female, age 90, relocated from a foster home. She has functional disorders secondary to severe dementia. She is frequently resistive to care, irritable, un-

cooperative, anxious, and physically abusive; she abuses alcohol. Mrs. Z requires supervision to promote stability. She is totally dependent on staff to provide social structure, and to orient her to person, place, and time. She has very poor short- and long-term memory, and a limited ability to communicate. She suffers from poor appetite and digestion, and has a problem with weight loss. Mrs. Z is totally dependent in all ADLs and all IADLs.

Generally, the state has targeted persons such as these, at a midlevel of impairment, for placement. Placement priorities are as follows:

1. Private-pay spend-down (to Medicaid), already living in assisted living
2. Hospitalized status but awaiting nursing facility placement
3. Eviction from other setting based on care needs
4. Nursing facility placement seeking relocation
5. Own home

Approximately one third (32%) of all current assisted living tenants are Medicaid clients. The average public pay rate is $1,390 per month. Of this, the average state contribution is $900, with the balance paid by the tenant from personal funds.

Turnover averages from 20 to 30% annually. Move-out experience for mature projects (1 year after full occupancy has been achieved) indicates that half the tenants are dying in the project or after a brief hospitalization, 10% go to skilled care, 30% return to more independent living (typically surviving spouses), and 10% move to similar levels of care, such as another assisted living or foster home. Nursing facility placement typically is the result of need for intravenous therapy, a catastrophic health event that leaves the person bedridden and unable to communicate, uncontrolled acute psychosis, or an unstable medical condition (Oregon Assisted Living Facilities Association, 1992).

Service Needs/Preferences

Although generally there is no such thing as a typical package of services, they often parallel those required for license (see Table

TABLE 11.1 Oregon's Assisted Living Service Provision Rules

Oregon's rules require the following:

1. Capability of assessing, planning, implementing, recording, and evaluating for necessary support services of the tenant's choice and independence
2. Capability of providing or coordinating three meals daily, 7 days a week, including diets and evening snacks appropriate to the tenant's needs and choices
3. Capability of providing or coordinating personal and linen laundry (including incontinent laundry)
4. Capability of providing or coordinating opportunities for individual and group socialization and use of community resources to normalize the environment for community interaction
5. Capability of providing or coordinating medical and social transportation
6. Capability of providing or coordinating personal care to assist the tenant in performing all activities of daily living including bathing, eating, dressing, personal hygiene, grooming, toileting, and ambulation
7. Capability of providing or coordinating routine nursing care, such as medication management, injections, nail and skin care, dressing changes, health monitoring, nonskilled catheter care, and other nursing tasks as might be delegated under the (Oregon) Nursing Delegation Act
8. Capability of providing or coordinating services for tenants who have behavior problems requiring ongoing staff support, intervention, and supervision
9. Capability of providing or coordinating the ancillary services of medically related care (e.g., physician, pharmacist, therapy, and podiatry), banking, barber/beauty, social/recreational opportunities, hospice, and other services necessary to support the tenant
10. Capability of providing or coordinating the household services essential for the health and comfort of tenants (e.g., floor cleaning, dusting, bed making, etc.)

11.1). Although the state has five service levels, as represented by a tiered payment system, most private pay providers offer two or three service packages.

The basic services available would typically include all hotel type services (e.g., meals, laundry, housekeeping, etc.) plus scheduled personal care, such as bathing or medication assistance. Many tenants using this level of service are either physically impaired or mildly confused.

Midlevel services typically include hotel services and regular unscheduled personal care, such as toileting, protective oversight, or ambulation assistance. It is not unusual for tenants at this level of service to have significant confusion or to need transfer assistance. Thus, these tenants often also need special programmatic interventions.

Higher levels of service generally include all hotel and personal care as well as regular nursing interventions or significant special services. Tenants at this level might need blood sugar checks, skin care, and ostomy or catheter care. Often they are both physically and cognitively impaired.

Because service plans must be individualized, generally services are not offered as packages at a fixed price. Two common methods of organizing services are the "a la carte" and the "buffet." In the "a la carte" system, tenants pay a base price, with add-ons based on the service used or for increments of time. The "buffet" provides a range of services, and the tenant picks any combination of the services that falls within the pricing ceiling allowed. Tenants may refuse services, do things for themselves, or have family members provide care. All of these factors are considered when the service plan is developed.

Enhancement of Autonomy

The shift in values orientation acts to enhance the autonomy of frail older adults. The rules in Oregon (and other states) now actually legitimize the role of values in supporting a higher quality of life. The values typically associated with assisted living are both implicitly and explicitly aspects associated with autonomy.

1. *Individuality* involves recognizing variability in human need and having the flexibility to organize services in response. Individuality is supported in the physical environment by providing unfurnished private units. It is supported programmatically by providing a range of services to meet differing needs.

2. *Independence* involves supporting tenant capabilities and facilitating use of those abilities to the broadest extent possible. Independence is supported in the physical environment by barrier-free structures and careful design of assistive

devices. It is supported programmatically by systematically determining areas of competence for which the individual can retain responsibility and providing support to enhance areas of functional disability.

3. *Dignity* involves providing support in such a way as to validate the self-worth of the individual. Dignity is supported in the physical environment by a structure that allows support to be provided in the tenant's living unit or a private area designated for the purpose. It is supported programmatically by providing special training for staff and services that reflect tenant preferences.

4. *Choice* involves creating viable options for tenants to enable them to exercise greater control over their lives. Choice is supported in the physical environment by providing sufficient private and common space to allow options in selecting where and how to spend time. It is supported programmatically by policies and procedures that encourage tenant selection of services and scheduling of services in response to client preferences.

5. *Privacy* is defined as designated areas and times that are not shared and over which the tenant maintains a large degree of control. Privacy is supported in the physical environment by living space that is not shared with others, except by personal choice. It is supported programmatically by program policies and procedures that address the tenant's civil rights.

6. *Home* is defined as a living environment that creates, to the extent possible, an atmosphere that closely resembles the personal definition of a socially and spatially cohesive unit. Home is supported in the physical environment by the use of tenantial building codes, materials, and furnishings wherever possible to replace commercial or institutional ones. It is supported programmatically by policies and procedures that reflect the tenant's status as a tenant, not an inmate or patient.

In summary, assisted living recognizes the importance of engendering as many aspects of autonomy as possible in the day-to-day lives of individuals dependent on others to help them meet their needs in long-term-care settings.

References

Kane, R. A., Illston, L., Kane, R. L., & Nyman, J. (1990). *Meshing services with housing: Lessons from adult foster care and assisted living in Orgeon.* Minneapolis: University of Minnesota Long-Term Care Decisions Resource Center.

Kane, R., & Wilson, K. (1993). *Assisted living in the United States: A new paradigm for tenantial care for frail older persons.* American Association for Retired Persons Public Policy Institute.

Ladd, R., Mollica, R., Dietsche, S., Wilson, K. B., & Ryther, B. (1992). *Building assisted living into public long term care policy: A guide for states.* Portland, ME: National Academy for State Health Policy.

Oregon Assisted Living Facilities Association (1992). Discharge Summary. Unpublished document.

Regnier V., Hamilton, J., & Yatabe, S. (1991). *Best practices in assisted living.* Los Angeles: Long Term Care National Resource Center at UCLA/USC.

Wilson, K. B. (1993). Assisted living: A model of supportive housing. In P. R. Katz, R. L. Kane, & M. D. Mezey (Eds.), *Advances in long-term care:* Vol. 2. New York: Springer Publishing Co.

Wilson, K., Ladd, R., & Saslow, M. (1988). Paper presented at the 41st Annual Scientific Meeting of the Gerontological Society of America, San Francisco, California.

Chapter Twelve

The Politics of Autonomy: Lessons from the Lazarus Project

Nancy Kari, Pam Hayle, and Peg Michels

Autonomy in long-term-care settings is commonly understood as the resident's ability to make personal decisions or, at the very least, to have choices about personal care in the routine of day to day life. This is an elemental but also restrictive view of its meaning. To expand our definition of autonomy in nursing home settings to include participation in self-governance is to acknowledge that the meanings of autonomy go well beyond the ability to decide individually what activities to participate in or when and where to eat meals. Defined as participation in governance, autonomy for residents and staff includes building relationships based on interests, assuming problem-solving roles, and making contributions. It means creating and participating in the traditions and rituals that name what is important in life both individually and collectively. And if one chooses, autonomy also includes the opportunity to engage actively in the human struggles and drama inherent in the aging process. Ultimately this leads one to come to terms with death. These important developmental life tasks of old age, when resolved positively, can bring a sense of integrity and meaning to life (Erickson, Erickson & Kivnick, 1986). Accountability for actions is central to self-governance in this sense.

Institutions have public roles to play in providing spaces and opportunities for people to learn and practice the arts of governance. When institutions create positive environments for this kind of serious problem solving, the institutions themselves become more effective and more responsive to the needs of the larger public world. In this chapter we argue that the service and medical models that typically govern nursing homes now cannot create the kinds of environments that promote autonomy in its fullest and richest sense. The Lazarus Project developed in the Augustana Home of Minneapolis has a vision and conceptual framework for addressing issues of autonomy both individually and institutionally. We present this as an alternative nursing home model, called the public community model.

One reason autonomy has become an issue in nursing homes is that it mirrors the dilemmas of self-governance in society. To understand the premises of the Lazarus Project, the broader social context needs examination. America today is dominated by a "clientized" culture. Clients, who are consumers, customers, patients, and receivers of services, stand outside the decision-making process. In these roles people are primarily passive, buying goods, receiving services, or engaging in "therapeutic" relationships of one-way remedial intervention. As a result, identities are narrowly defined in individualist terms. On the other side of the equation are roles as professionals—the expert, consultant, physician, or nurse. In an effort to solve problems, disciplinary experts "package" information into programs or services. In these roles people do not normally see themselves as a part of or within the problem to be solved, so the interests and skills of collaborative, reciprocal interaction are likewise narrowed. What is lacking in a clientized society is the notion of a civic identity and empowered citizenship. Fortunately, the United States has a rich heritage of citizen involvement in public life through institutions, and we can draw on this heritage as we struggle to redefine citizenship in a health care environment.

America has had in the past many examples of public-spirited organizations whose civic quality today has largely eroded. Despite their frequent limitations of parochialism and exclusiveness, institutions like colleges, settlement houses, voluntary associations, and neighborhood schools once were more explicitly *civic* in their mission and practice, teaching skills of public interaction and leadership. The story of medicine in America, as Paul Starr (1982) has described it, forms a dramatic case in point. In the 19th-century, American medical and health practices included many contending and diverse approaches, from home medical traditions and popular healing practices (including many descended from native american experiences) to more formal and "scientifically" credentialed medicine. The result was an environment in which physicians and other health professionals functioned in far more interactive, reciprocal, and public ways than came to be the case in the 20th century. Health professionals commonly worked *with* people rather than simply providing services *for* them.

In his book, *Commonwealth: A Return to Citizen Politics* (1989), Boyte argues that our current lack of civic identity and skills to participate effectively in public problem solving is due, in part, to the loss of public spaces and the general erosion of public life, both of which are essential for the development of skills for citizenship and governance. This societal shift has occurred over time, and is both complicated and multifaceted. Major factors influencing the change have included the exponential growth of specialized, fragmented knowledge detached from civic identity and context, advances in scientific technology, the development of professional expertise, and changing patterns of education. Contemporary institutional environments, including nursing homes, have both influenced and been influenced by this set of circumstances. Today health service settings focus primarily on providing programs and therapeutic services. We need to reclaim health settings as places where the community is involved in lively debate about the causes and solutions to problems affecting them. This will require expanding roles to include problem solving, contribution, and public debate—the very heart of what it means to embrace the ideal of autonomy and self-governance.

Traditional Models of Governance in Nursing Homes

Models of governance are important in shaping the mission, decision-making structures, and power relationships within an organization. The model of governance is embedded within an institution's philosophy and procedures. Associated with it is a powerful language that is used to frame problems, define solutions, and provide parameters for possibilities. Health care organizations, including long-term-care facilities, are typically governed by the medical model or its derivative, the therapeutic/service model (Kari & Michels, 1991) (see Figure 12.1).

The therapeutic/service model is frequently used in rehabilitation and other therapeutic settings to identify the psychosocial and physical needs of the client and determine appropriate services. It is appealing to many care providers because it engages the client in making some choices and generally approaches helping from a holistic perspective, considering the physical, emotional, and spiritual dimensions of the client. The Lazarus Project acknowledges the importance of appropriate therapeutic programs and medical services for residents in nursing homes. However, it challenges the idea that the whole of residential life can be effectively organized by either of these models and still create an environment that practices the ideals associated with autonomy. Both models are hierarchical and dominated by professional expertise and service delivery. The primary roles are therefore limited to care provider and client. If the essence of autonomy is agency, then individuals and communities of people must reconceptualize and expand their roles beyond expert and client to citizen; that is, they must learn how to engage with diverse perspectives to name problems and contribute to the design of solutions in a fluid, reciprocal, interactive fashion. This requires developing the capacities of residents, staff, and others who have a stake in the work of the nursing home to establish a set of relationships, take actions, and participate in ongoing evaluation of the common work.

An educational approach cannot alone produce the changes in power relationships necessary to establish an empowering environment. However, the dynamics of organizing to change power relationships in health environments, where authority resides in knowledge that cannot simply be given away or transferred, are different from the dynamics in traditional community-organizing or advocacy politics. Confrontation and polarization rarely work well to bring about lasting or wide institutional democratic change. Strategies for democratization have to develop a sophisticated approach that brings together diverse groups whose many interests in making change differ. *Civic organizing* is an approach that has been used with some success in health care environments including a nursing home setting. Using civic concepts, this approach pays attention to the ways in which people reconceive their identities, roles, and patterns of interaction. The develop-

	Medical Model	Therapeutic/Service Model	Public Community Model
Focus	• "Acute" care, disease and disability, attention to physical needs	• Provision of a variety of services based upon clients' needs	• Capacities, leadership development and ability to contribute among staff, residents and family members
Roles and Accountability	• Facilitates dependency on staff; holds staff responsible • Organized hierarchically	• Facilitates dependency on staff; holds staff responsible • Organized hierarchically	• Encourages interdependency among all members; holds all accountable • Organized democratically
Information and Knowledge	• Seen as technical expertise	• Compartmentalized and perceived as serving the client	• Come from many sources including experience and technical expertise
Language	• Uses specialized language which creates dependency	• Uses therapeutic language which creates dependency	• Recognizes diverse languages; privileges none
Approach	• Reductionistic, scientific	• Programmatic; fragments spiritual, physical and social well-being; emphasizes residents' rights	• Wholistic; addresses physical, social and spiritual well-being
Activities	• Geared toward improved physical functioning • Staff intensive	• Geared toward personal development and contentment • Staff intensive	• Create spaces for practicing public judgment and doing public work • Includes all community members
Outcome	• Empowers staff	• Empowers staff	• Encourages relational empowerment

FIGURE 12.1   Models of organizational governance.

ment of public leadership is key. Public strategies that include a wide range of people in solving common problems is important as well. The Lazarus Project has demonstrated that nursing homes can be places in which residents and staff alike develop and use these civic skills.

Lazarus Project

The Lazarus Project, begun in 1989, has developed through collaboration of the residents and staff of the Augustana Home of Minneapolis and Project Public Life (PPL), which is housed at the Hubert Humphrey Institute of Public Affairs, University of Minnesota. PPL is a national theory-building and practical initiative to redefine and revitalize citizenship and civic education in a variety of arenas including health. Working collaboratively with policy makers, higher education, community organizations, and sites such as Augustana, PPL has provided a testing ground for civic concepts and civic organizing, demonstrating that ordinary people can take on serious roles in everyday environments.

The Augustana Home of Minneapolis is a large metropolitan skilled care nursing home in downtown Minneapolis that employs an administrator, 15 managers, and 500 staff members for its 370 residents. The facility is part of a larger campus that includes 400 apartments in four adjoining high-rise buildings. The apartments and nursing home share a variety of services, including a small grocery store, coffee shop, bank, and health clinic. Augustana is a nonprofit institution supported by 12 area Lutheran churches. Its history, values, and institutional mission reflect the strong influence of a Lutheran care and service tradition. To this point, the work of the Lazarus Project has focused almost entirely on the nursing home and has not included the people who live in the adjoining apartments.

The major purpose of the Lazarus Project is to help create a public vision and practice, linking citizenship with health care for elderly people, that can be embraced by long-term-care institutions. Its second purpose is to create a conceptual framework for an alternative model of organizational governance for nursing homes—the public-community model.

Lazarus Conceptual Framework

The first 1.5 years of the project was dedicated to developing an understanding of PPL concepts applied in a nursing home setting. Although the democratic values of the Lazarus framework are not incongruent with the values implicit in health care, their explicitly political and civic nature and associated practices often challenge the habits and practices of the nursing home culture. The three concepts that form the core of the public community model proposed by the Lazarus Project are *public, diverse interests,* and *power* (Michels, Kari, Hayle, & Mitchell, 1993). Each concept is associated with a set of practical skills termed public or citizenship skills. Creating and sustaining change depends on people learning both conceptual and public skills. Concept means literally to conceive, give birth. This definition connotes the creative powers inherent in the ability to understand and integrate conceptual knowledge. Conceptual understandings can be transformative because they teach people to "map" their environments and their own roles in more generalized, effective, and multidimensional ways. In the Lazarus Project, skills and tools are always taught in relation to the conceptual framework.

Public is an important concept because it both challenges and dramatically enhances work within health care environments, which otherwise have a privatized, intimate quality. The concept of public adds a different dimension to settings where the focus is almost entirely on individual interventions.

Public is key to the public community model. It refers both to public as agency (a group taking actions and producing change on common problems) and public as a kind of heterogeneous social environment or place in which diverse groups of people debate, render collective judgment, and organize to shape that environment. Public is distinct from but linked to private life. A primary strategy for implementing change is establishing public spaces where people can practice the skills of citizenship that lead to self-governance. Public is an important concept in reconceptualizing and expanding the roles of client and service provider, and in recontextualizing professional activity within a larger set of civic interactions.

The notion of *diverse interests* draws attention to the wide and particularized set of life experiences, traditions, knowledge, and values that bring people to public settings. A distinction is made between interests (sometimes called self-interests), selfishness, and selflessness. The word interest comes from *interesse,* which means between. Hence, self-interest means self among others and is a public concept. The concept of self-interest, while it draws attention to the idiosyncratic personal narratives and particular concerns which motivate individuals, thus also understands the individual as part of larger, diverse wholes. Interests as defined here are important because their recognition and enlargement create stakeholding and participation in public roles.

The concept of diverse interests is difficult to integrate into health care settings because it raises conflicts and breaks the norms in health cultures. But it is also a powerful concept that can help people redefine their work in much broader terms and more meaningful ways. Skills associated with the concept of diverse interests include learning to listen for the interests of others, negotiating differences to create an agreed-on public goal, and using conflict to solve problems.

Power is central to public leadership. Power comes from the word *poder,* which means, literally, to be able and denotes the capacity to act. It is a concept integrally linked to autonomy in that individuals who are autonomous act with effect and self-direction.

The language of power is unsettling in health cultures. Power relationships between professionals and patients are often masked and unnamed. Empowerment, conversely, is a buzzword in health cultures. The use of this term sometimes implies that it is an attribute one can give to another. Power, in contrast, is a dynamic capacity that one develops: It cannot be given; it must be actively acquired. Nursing home personnel can create empowering environments, but they cannot give power to residents who are passive. Patterns of power relationships within organizations reflect the predominant governing model.

In the Lazarus Project power is reconceptualized from its more traditional hierarchical definition of power through position, which is static and one directional (one person has it; others do not) to the understanding that power is both dynamic and relational. This concept helps problem solvers know that relationships are not simply built with individual allies but must be created with those who can influence the use of resources to solve problems. Power resources include knowledge, capital, and people. To learn to govern, people must have access to power. Moreover, being able to "map" the power relations in settings in dynamic relational terms highlights the fact that environments are in a constant process of change, in which anyone can intervene.

Public Community Model

The model created by the Lazarus concepts is called the public community model. It is based on the democratic ideal of shared governance. This requires that people have access to information, public spaces, and the skills to participate in give and take debate, deliberation, and action on the policies affecting them. It is a messy, gritty, organic process that engages diverse viewpoints in decisions that shape the nursing home community as well as the public work of the institution. Conflict, diversity, and power are accepted and recognized as necessary to healthy public life. The Lazarus Project believes it is in this kind of lively, diverse, public-spirited environment that people can see themselves as serious actors and begin to influence a larger world through their institutional relationships.

The public community model also has a strong communal dimension that overlaps with its public nature. Communities are important because they provide individuals with a base of support, nurturance, and a sense of belonging. They help shape and define individual identity, and are important in developing and sustaining autonomy. Membership in communities also assumes that all contribute to an agreed-on shared "good life." With community membership comes an implied obligation to care for and support others. Jameton (1988), who argues that responsibility and autonomy are linked, discusses the complexities of applying this in nursing homes, where many elderly people have lost some of their capacities and perhaps willingness to assume this kind of role. However, Jameton limits responsibility to the community; his tasks are personal and community tasks that lack a broader public connection.

In the alternative public community model, individual capacity is developed in relation to the community and the public. To accomplish this, nursing homes must create environments that offer opportunities for the development of both citizenship and communal capacities of residents and staff. In this way, institutions can become creative public institutions that contribute to society's understanding of large-scale issues rather than remain limited to individually oriented service institutions.

Lessons from the Lazarus Project

This description of the democratic values of the Lazarus Project must not mask the difficulties involved in making fundamental changes proposed in this chapter. The Augustana Home has not undergone institutional transformation. Its governing structure remains predominantly hierarchical. Staff members at all levels are skeptical about the potential for change. Administrative staff members express resistance and confusion about what a change in governance would mean to them. Residents also have mixed responses to the notion of assuming expanded roles.

What we have demonstrated, however, is that pockets of noteworthy change can occur within hierarchical structures. For example, changes that have occurred in the resident council suggest that a reconceptualization of governing roles can happen in nursing homes. The resident council is the formal governing body for nursing home residents. Typical problem-solving patterns often center around residents' critique (both critical and complimentary) of services provided by the staff and administration. When issues of common life are raised and named, the staff/administration is primarily responsible for "fixing" or at least responding to the problem identified by the council. In this scenario, the work of the council can be narrowly defined and perfunctory with little resident participation in creating new ways of doing things. At the Augustana Home we have taken a different approach. Resident council members discussed the public nature of the council's work, and acquired concepts and some of the skills for public action. For example, they learned how to set a collective agenda and how to lead effective public meetings. They practiced the rules of public debate and recognized the importance of diverse perspectives in understanding problems. Council members clarified and negotiated their roles in this process. Residents then chose the roles that suited them; they agreed to be accountable to each other.

In an early meeting, the issue of staff response to "call lights" came up—a perennial nursing home problem. (Call lights are used by the residents to summon help from the staff.) The residents' initial response was to recount a series of personal stories, commenting on the quality of the service (e.g., the amount of time before staff responded to the call) and identifying staff who were least responsive. But the chair recognized that a complaint session was not engaging resident participation in solving the problem. Thus she argued, "We are not going to present this discussion to the administration and just get a feedback of the regulation. We are going to really talk about this." As council members explored the issue, they realized that others were affected by the problem as well. Nurses and nursing assistants (who also were frustrated by the problem) were invited to join the public conversation. The diverse perspectives helped people see the issue of call lights in a fuller way. In fact, the "call light" was a symptom of a larger problem—what it is like to be dependent and what it is like to be depended on. The council decided to take a year to solve the problem through a series of actions—public discussions on individual units, one-on-one interviews with residents, and ongoing discussion at monthly council meetings to continue to evaluate the issue. They concluded that each floor, in its own context, should look at the issue and at possible solutions appropriate to their situation. The council will test and evaluate the solutions before making overall changes.

The important lesson in this example is that when people learn the basic concepts and skills of public life, they can also learn to practice self-governance and develop a deeper sense of their own efficacy and capacity. Such experiences of practical autonomy require public spaces and the engagement of diverse perspectives not only to solve problems, but also to define them. These dynamics increase stakeholding and establish the environment for rich discussion and debate. Without a public environment, the deeper discussion of dependence would not have happened in this council. Through their experience, a small group of residents and staff have come to understand the concept of autonomy in a fuller way. Council meetings have become more oriented to problem solving. Residents and staff are beginning to address the issues of their common environment through new roles and interdependent relationships that go beyond delivering and receiving services.

In another example, a resident current events group recently began discussing drug use among teenagers. As residents asked what they could do about this problem, they began to imagine they could practice citizenship in a world beyond the nursing home. Thus their imagined scope of agency, or autonomy, was stretched still further. Their discussion led them to think about other societal issues directly affecting elderly living in institutions. Plans are now underway to hold a series of public forums on topics, such as death and dying, restraint use, and responsible use of resources in long-term care. The nursing home residents, seeking to broaden their base, have decided to include elderly volunteers at the home, elders in corporate churches, and apartment residents in planning and participating in the forums. It may be possible to develop action strategies from these discussions and study groups.

As nursing home residents become engaged in meaningful work, staff members, who define their primary work roles as giving personal care, providing emotional support, and implementing therapeutic programs, also need to reexamine and redefine their own agency and effectiveness in the context of a wider repertoire of civic skills. The Therapeutic Programs Department at Augustana has developed processes that help staff structure this task. For example, each employee receives a periodic performance review. This feedback is typically a grading of the performance of employee duties as determined by the supervisor. Using the concepts of self-interest and relational power, the department supervisor has redesigned the review process to focus on an ongoing evaluation of the departmental work and the employees' contributions to it. Staff members are now asked to evaluate their work in relation to the public mission of the institution rather than just describing the services they provide to residents. They identify work-related problems and successes, and describe how their roles intersect with others in the department. This process helps clarify roles and increases stakeholding and accountability for goals set. The shared responsibility for problem solving helps staff create change rather than interpreting the need for change as inadequate performance.

Summary

A challenge we face as a society is to reclaim and create anew healthy, effective, and public-spirited institutions. Our institutional renewal must not only address contemporary societal problems, but as Robert Bellah and colleagues (1991, p. 6) say, "[also] become an indispensable source from which character is formed." Today the model of a health care system based on highly trained, specialized personnel and sophisticated technology is in crisis. In the case of long-term-care institutions, the challenge is to solve problems of increasing dependence, high staff turnover, spiraling costs, and public discontent.

At the same time, growing numbers of people are recognizing the need for a new approach to problem solving, an approach that broadens the base of those responsible for health care and prevention to include the people who actually use the system. This calls for a reinvigorated definition and practice of citizenship. If citizenship is to be a serious and effective basis for public contribution, then its arts need cultivation and practice in the places where we spend our time. Thus, citizenship in a complex, diverse world requires change in institutional settings. These "mediating institutions" hold potential for becoming the spaces where our values, interests, and capacities are linked to the larger world. The potential payoff will include an expanded, enriched capacity of citizens to become cocreators of our common environments, essential in health as elsewhere.

Long-term care, as it struggles with the notion of autonomy, can provide national leadership on issues of aging and make a significant contribution to a renewed understanding and practice of citizenship in the context of health care. To create this kind of change, residents, professionals and staff, families, educators, administrators, policy makers, and others associated with nursing homes need to reconceptualize and expand their roles as citizens, learn the skills of governance, and restructure relationships for more effective public problem solving (Boyte, Barber, Cotton, Morse, & Saunders, 1993).

References

Bellah, R., Madsen, R., Sullivan, W., Swindler, A., & Tipton, S. (1991). *The good society*. New York: Knopf.

Boyte, H. (1989). *Commonwealth: A return to citizen politics*. New York: The Free Press.

Boyte, H., Barber, B., Cotton, D., Morse, S., & Saunders, H. (1993). *The new citizenship: A partnership between citizens and government* (White Paper). Minneapolis: The Center for Citizenship and Democracy.

Erikson, E., Erikson, J., & Kivnick, H. (1986). *Vital involvement in old age.* New York: Norton.

Jameton, A. (1988). In the borderlands of autonomy: Responsibility in long term care facilities. *The Gerontologist, 28,* 18–23.

Kari, N., & Michels, P. (1991). The Lazarus Project: The politics of empowerment. *The American Journal of Occupational Therapy, 45,* 719–725.

Michels, P., Kari, N., Hayle, P., & Mitchell, M. (1993). Health and politics. Unpublished working paper.

Starr, P. (1982). *The social transformation of American medicine.* New York: Basic Books.

Chapter Thirteen

The Regenerative Community: The Live Oak Living Center and the Quest for Autonomy, Self-Esteem, and Connection in Elder Care

Barry Barkan

Autonomy, Self-Control, and Connection to Community: It's All About Change

If it comes to it, when I am old and feeble and perhaps disabled, I want to be in an elder care environment where people know who I am and where I have been. I would want the environment to be permeated by the belief that even if I am physically encapsulated by disease or crippled by cognitive disintegration, I still have at least a kernel of potential to make choices about my life, to grow, learn, develop and be in connection to others. If this wish is met, I trust my spirit will be preserved and my life will be as good as it can be.

This chapter is about transforming skilled nursing facilities and the combination of global vision, strategy, and process that is necessary so that elders within them can have the most meaningful life possible. For me this work is deeply personal. My earliest motivation was the haunting specter of my grandmother, Lottie Barkan, spending the end of her life in a cold, impersonal institution in Long Island, New York, in the late 1960s.

My focus is on the quality of life of the person living in the elder care environment and whether her or his spirit is nurtured and enabled to grow strong. The measure of quality of life is the extent to which a person has autonomy, self-esteem, and connection to a community that provides meaning and joy in life.

Autonomy, self-esteem, and connection to community are vitally interrelated aspects of a life affirming culture. In our experience you cannot promote one unless you are promoting all three.

Autonomy

Simply stated, autonomy is the experience of freedom in one's life. It is the solution to the problems of repression of will and institutionally cultivated dependence that make for our grimmest nightmares of life in elder care environments. In a dependent society, autonomy is undermined by consistent domination of the will of individual elders and their peer group by the expressed will of the institution, staff members and family members.

Choice is the bedrock of autonomy. It requires regular and consistent orientation at one's highest level of understanding to the place where one lives and is working, and one's rights and responsibilities within it. It requires access to information about how the system works, how it can be changed, and who is responsible for what goes on. To the greatest extent possible, given the factors that bring one to long-term care, elders need to be able to participate in the routine decisions that affect their everyday lives, and they need to have the ability to affect what goes on around them. This takes an understanding that every person, regardless of cognitive and physical impairment, is unique and special. It also requires the ability to suspend our own judgment about what a person is capable of doing or understanding. We need to remind ourselves constantly to act as if the individual is capable of making choices.

Another key aspect of autonomy is a healthy relationship to time in which residents live in the present, draw from the past, and prepare for the future. From our perspective, a life without stimulation, meaning, ritual, and an active relationship to shared reality relegates elder care residents to their reverie and their life in the past, a place where there is no freedom to make choices about contemporary life. When they have a framework for active participation in the present and are enabled to plan ahead, think about what they want to do in the coming weeks, and see their plans realized, the process of regenerating autonomy has begun.

Self-Esteem

Healthy self-esteem is one of life's most precious gifts. All human beings need to feel that we have intrinsic worth, that our thoughts, dreams, and actions are good and important. There is a direct correlation between our capacity to experience joy and peace of mind, and how we feel about ourselves. If throughout life, we have had both opportunity and learning that support our good feeling about ourselves, then we are more able to access the light in our dark places, and to survive loss and difficult transitions.

Even if we have been fortunate enough to have our sense of self-worth nourished from an early age, our sense of self, and, ultimately, self-worth may fall victim to the ravages of loss and disease that frequently accompany old age. Our lives are diminished by the loss of loved ones and the restriction of mobility and independence. It is difficult to feel good about yourself if you cannot dress yourself, or go to the bathroom on your own, or remember who you are or why you are here.

Institutionalization traditionally accelerates the deterioration of self-esteem. Institutions fetter the human spirit because they are driven by a functional rather than a cultural agenda. Particularly in nursing homes, everything needs to happen on time, and the needs of the human spirit often fall through the cracks as staff focuses on taking care of the larger agenda that is determined by regulation, financial constraints, and too few people to meet too many needs.

The regeneration of resident self-esteem needs to be part of the cultural agenda of the long-term-care environment. The ultimate message that needs to be conveyed by the culture of the facility is that you are somebody, your needs are important, you are lovable, you are loved, we are glad you are here—even though your body and mind are no longer your familiar lifelong friends.

Connection to Community

A culture that enables and supports participation in meaningful community is the antidote to the isolation and disconnection that accompany the trauma of loss, and are exacerbated by institutionalization. A community is a group of people nourished by their continued connection to one another. Regeneration is an ongoing process in which we experience learning, growth, and renewal at the highest level of what is possible for us at any given time. A regenerative community is a community assembled with the conscious purpose of helping its members to flourish. It provides its members with a cultural context within which they can bring past, present, and future into perspective. It connects them to meaning, themselves, and one another. It provides an opportunity for people to know one another, be known, and celebrate life together.

The culture that underlies the regenerative community is grounded in the belief that no matter how infirm and how physically or cognitively debilitated a person may be, a part of that person remains that is still healthy and capable of learning, growth, and renewal.

Open communications and the trust and fairness that enable an honest feedback loop provide the circulatory system through which flows the lifeblood of a healthy, minimally institutional, resident-centered environment.

In virtually every skilled nursing environment in America, the context in which resident quality of life is fostered or undermined is government established. OBRA (1987) mandated government to be the driving force for change in the way in which long-term-care is administered throughout the United States.

The goal of OBRA is to make each skilled nursing center an environment that is driven by the individual needs of each resident. In practice, however, it fosters a self-protective, paper-work–centered culture in facilities. So, unfortunately, while the intentions of OBRA and of much of the thinking that has gone into defining the elements of resident well-being and interdisciplinary care management are unquestionably excellent, the outcome has been that the regulatory process ultimately compels care centers to reinforce the worst aspects of institutions.

Institutions first and foremost protect their own status quo. Documented proof of performance takes precedence over care. Information is controlled rather than shared. The management framework is hierarchical and controlling rather than participatory. Institutions do not see a mistake as a learning opportunity; they seek to gloss it over and obscure it. Rather than liberate the creative energies of staff members, institutional culture causes the most committed and interested to burn out, lose their enthusiasm, and fight a daily uphill battle against demoralization.

We are long past the age when the good guys were the advocates and the bad guys were the venal nursing home operators with the regulators coming in to impose order on the corrupt nursing homes. Today, with the exception of the elders in our care, we are all part of the problem. This includes nursing home operators, lawmakers, high-level bureaucrats, inspectors, nursing home reform and advocacy groups, unions representing nursing home workers, individuals and funds investing in companies that operate nursing homes, and property owners and real estate investment trusts controlling nursing home properties. We all have had a part in creating a system plagued with problems. To avoid a return to the dark ages of nursing homes, we will all need to work collaboratively to create a solution.

Poetry of Everyday Life at the Live Oak Living Center at Greenridge Heights

The Live Oak Living Center at Greenridge Heights is an elder care facility that includes adjoining residential care and skilled nursing centers. It is located about 20 miles northeast of San Francisco at the top of a hill in El Sobrante, California. Behind the facility is undeveloped land abutting hundreds of miles of East Bay Regional Parks. On a clear day you can see the distant hills of Marin County across the San Francisco Bay.

At the Live Oak Living Center at Greenridge Heights, more than two thirds of our residents are affected by the cognitive disintegration that accompanies dementia. In varying degrees they struggle to remember who they are, where they are, why they are here, in what era they are living, and so forth. Their physical and mental condition mitigates against autonomy and self-esteem as they lose the capability to control their bowels and bladders, take nourishment and articulate their feelings about what is happening to their lives. Slowly and inexorably—and sometimes rapidly, they regress. The most articulate among those who suffer from these related diseases have moments of lucidity in which they can describe what is happening to them, and it is heartbreaking, terrifying, and bewildering to them and to those of us who are there to help them. In the midst of such tragedy people make a life, form relationships, and live out their days.

Those residents who are cognitively integrated bring their own baggage of struggle, loss, and grief. After all, to grow old is to survive those you have known and loved. Living in an elder care facility frequently involves loss of physical health and the opportunities, work, routines of a lifetime, and ability to remain independent. On the other side, those who survive loss and are able to come to terms with their life experience are often able to tap into a wellspring of strength and resiliency. It is a great life if you do not weaken.

Giving Voice to the Residents at the Live Oak Living Center

When the author assumed the management of the Live Oak Living Center at Greenridge Heights in the late winter of 1986, we needed to seed a regenerative culture within the facility on which we could develop the Live Oak program model. We needed to wake up the residents and to weave a community among them so that they could be reconnected to the contemporary world, their past, and their future.

The day we arrived, we called our first daily community meeting. Our purpose was to create a setting in which elders could gather daily to celebrate their lives and themselves, sing, exercise, build hope, do business, mourn their losses, get to know one another, and tune in to the current events of our own community and the larger world, and relate these to their own life experience. Our community meetings were always open to all. Participants included those who were well and those who were suffering from the ravages of broken bones that failed to heal, arthritis, Alzheimer's and other dementias, Parkinson's, advanced cancer, and other diseases.

We told the residents repeatedly that we saw (and we continue to see) ourselves as building a movement for change—right here in a nursing home at the bottom of society's pecking order. The underlying theme in our discussions was that no matter how disabled a person might be, there is still something healthy, alive, and vital within him or her that can grow and expand and promote healing in the self and in others. Our lifeline is in our connection to one another.

By design, we isolate the cognitively impaired from the cognitively integrated. They are all part of the same community. They participate in many of the same programs together. They are in relationship, and sometimes they build friendship. They know one another. Many in their own way develop caring and concern for one another. They mourn one another when death comes.

We never force people to participate, but we encourage them. People who are more well are told that in confronting those whose conditions they fear or find unappealing, they are provided with greater strength and resiliency should they suffer life's losses and find themselves in a situation in which they have fewer options for choice. For the most part, once people who are cognitively healthy begin participating in such a community, they expand their ability to grow, contribute, and participate with those who are stricken by loss of cognitive function.

Mostly we believe that if you create an environment in which people are accepted and treated kindly, they will grow beyond previous conditioning and learn to be their best selves with one another. A fundamental tenet of our corporate management culture is that you must show staff love and respect if you expect them to love and respect the residents.

Much conscious effort goes into building a culture that welcomes everyone and validates everyone's experience and origins. Our staff comes literally from the four corners of the world. At one time or another, everyone experiences feelings of victimization or prejudice or being less favored than the next one. It happens in families. It happens even more often in communities that are so markedly heterogeneous. We remain sensitive to such experiences and try to respond quickly to them.

We attempt to have an even hand, loving everyone. Yes, loving everyone. In the culture we are fostering, love is a primary function of management.

We need to model it, we need to live it, we need to express and show it. It is a proactive process. Everyone needs to be helped to feel that this is a place where they belong.

A few days after we initiated our daily community meeting at Live Oak, we began our first Live Oak Poets' Workshop. The purpose of the poets' workshop is to help people develop a powerful and eloquent collective voice. We chose poetry as the medium because it has the magical ability to give form to our dreams, memories, longings, and wisdom.

The poems are collectively written, and the beauty of the process is that one never knows where the next line will come from. On many occasions a person with Alzheimer's disease or encapsulated in isolation will amaze us by speaking just the thought we need at a crucial moment when the group is groping for a concept, word or line.

For the winter holiday season in 1990, the Live Oak Poets' Workshop published *In Our Own Voices: A Chronicle of Life Among the Elders*. The elders describe their lives at the Live Oak Living Center, sense of meaning, connection to the past and future, and relationship to the events of the world.

In the poem, "Memory," the elders express a sense of whimsy about loss of memory, a subject often relegated to clinical discussions in the long term care environment.

My memory?
Goodbye, I haven't got any . . .
. . . It's hard to accept
That it's so easy to forget . . .
. . . Where did it go?
I've forgotten . . .

The residents use poems to advocate for others around the world. In "Elders for a Wage That's True," the residents carried their concerns for justice for the people who serve them to their lawmakers and to the governor. They wrote:

We need them to watch over us,
    to make sure everything is right . . .
They make the beds, they do the laundry . . .
They scrub the floors, wiping sweat from their eyes,
    and they are expected to be in a good mood.

And yet these people who are so important to us
    bring home such a small wage.
Is that all they deserve for caring for seniors?
    Are we looked down upon because of our age?
It's crucial for us and for our future,
    that this important bill goes through.
As elders, we ask you urgently
    to vote for a wage that's true.

In our Live Oak culture, poetry is not only an art form, but it has emerged as an important tool for communicating important messages within the community. During a campaign to give residents an understanding of their rights, which are often very dense and difficult to absorb in the format mandated by the federal government, the residents decided to write a "Residents' Rights Song" to educate themselves and new community members.

The poetry of the Live Oak Living Center at Greenridge Heights, the daily community meetings, the memorial services, the participation of residents in welcoming new staff members, the caring community among staff members, our open door for family members and families' participation in the care of their family members, our family celebrations of the holidays, our values and our rituals all reflect a consciously developed culture that we call the regenerative community.

Developing the Regenerative Community Model

It is not difficult to develop a regenerative community in virtually any elder care or elder support setting. It takes common vision, commitment, consistency, persistence, and a willingness to learn as you go. Given these factors, the skill will come, and the community will flourish.

When we started out in our effort to develop a community among elders in a nursing home, it was with the faith that if you got enough people to come together at the same time every day, and talked to them about real things, sang with them, laughed with them, and reinforced their individual and collective self esteem, something good would happen. We believed, although there was little supportive evidence at the time, that people can learn, grow, change, become involved, and have new and meaningful experiences—no matter where they are in the continuum of mental, physical, and emotional regression.

Almost to our surprise we learned that the reality was potentially even more outrageous than our vision of what was possible.

To develop a regenerative community, we had to begin to alter the culture from an extended acute hospital governed by a medical model to a resident centered model. We have evolved a simple programmatic approach to resident community development that currently provides the operating program model for the Live Oak Living Center at Greenridge Heights. This programmatic approach involves three essential elements: (a) core values, (b) program development, and (c) committed change agents or community developers.

Core Values

Regenerative community development begins by carrying a vision and its message to the people we are working with. As we use it here, vision is the ability to look at what is and to see what is potential within it. Everyone has it. When we look at vegetables in a produce market and think of the salad they will make, this is an act of vision.

The Live Oak definition of an elder clearly articulates our message to our residents and the wider society about our potential in old age and the importance of the role of the elder: "An elder is a person who is still growing, still a learner, still with potential and whose life continues to have within it promise for, and connection to the future. An elder is still in pursuit of happiness, joy and pleasure, and her or his birthright to these remains intact. Moreover, an elder is a person who deserves respect and honor and whose work it is to synthesize wisdom from long life experience and formulate this into a legacy for future generations" (Live Oak Project, 1977).

There is yet another core value of regenerative community development. Regeneration is a lifelong process that can occur even when we are in physical, emotional, or mental decline. Implicit in this notion is the belief that though we may not be able to be who we used to be, every stage of life has its own potential for learning, growth, and development. Progress is a lifelong process even in the midst of such terrible maladies of old age as Alzheimer's disease. We always believed that this was true. Still, on some level, we are constantly surprised by the extent to which our belief system has been validated by experience.

Traditionally, the medical model has seen people in terms of what is wrong with them, and this defines the institutional vision of the people who are receiving care. Although it is important to anticipate and respond to problems, healing comes from the place where well-being exists. In a wound, the healing grows from the healthy tissue out rather than from the damaged tissue in. In wound care we protect the injured part of the flesh from infection and further degradation while strengthening the ability of healthy tissue to regenerate itself.

In the regenerative paradigm, we see change as growing from the part of the individual or group where well-being exists. If a person has Alzheimer's disease and a 98% disability, we focus on the 2% that is well. Often we see that despite the disease there is a potential for 10% wellness to emerge. If in our community meetings we can have only an attention span of 8 minutes, we try to make these 8 minutes as energetic and meaningful as possible. They then may expand to 10 minutes or 12 minutes, and ultimately to 1 hour or more.

Program Development Methods

The following programmatic activities provide the basic steps in the community development process:

- Begin each day with a community meeting in which all residents are invited to participate.
- Structure the meeting with predictable and ritualized routines, songs, and spirit-building activities. There needs to be spontaneity and you do not have to follow the routines each day, but have a predictable format. For example: (a) start with a song, (b) exercise, (c) sing again, (d) talk about the news of the home, (e) talk about the news of the world, (f) have a discussion or program of the day, and (g) end with a song.

- Ritualistically solicit participation from all members, regardless of their level of cognitive integration.
- Take each person's participation seriously, summarizing it to the rest of the group and building bridges. Help to fit what people are saying into the context of the group discussion.
- Welcome new residents, new staff members, and all guests to the community meeting with a song, an explanation of what goes on at the meeting, a response to questions, and a report to the community about who the newcomers are and where they have been. Establish a welcome song that becomes part of the ritual. Sing the "Residents' Rights Song" so that newcomers know they are not powerless. Read the "Definition of an Elder" or whatever other statement embodies the message of the group.
- Communally acknowledge and celebrate residents at every opportunity for their gains, progress, life passages, losses, illness and recovery from illness, return from absence, the way they look today, the role they take on in the community, birthdays, rites of passage within their family, just showing up, and so on.
- Talk regularly about what is current in the home. Talk about changes, challenges, and events, and involve residents whenever possible. Help the residents to make the changes they want in the environment.
- Talk regularly about the news of the wider community and the world, putting it into a historical context that residents can relate to, identifying news and issues that are particularly relevant to them.
- Have a discussion each day that involves and challenges members, builds bridges to contemporary society by helping them to understand modern social practices and morays and current events, and continually raises their consciousness about what is possible for them as elders, and their rights and responsibilities as residents and members of a community.
- Plan events and future activities in which residents are partners in development. Involve them in wider community issues and occurrences that affect them. Use the community meeting as a forum to help define the issues that are important for them to talk about in the residents' council. Involve them in planning activities, such as parties or outings.

- Have a memorial service for each person in the community who dies. These do not have to be elaborate or long winded. Ask the residents what they feel is appropriate for memorial services. The still all too prevalent practice of nursing homes in which people are silently removed when they die lest the presence of death upset the residents is an insult to the self-esteem and autonomy of residents. The message needs to be that the life of everyone who has dwelled among us is precious and worthy of remembrance.
- Once the community meeting is in place, develop small group activities to give residents a more personal sense of connection to one another, a voice, a sense of growth and development and, for those suffering from loss of cognitive capability, a communal opportunity for cognitive enhancement. Among these can be workshops for artists and poets, a happy hour, a friendship circle for cognitively impaired people, reading groups, singing groups, and welcome sessions for new members. Feedback from the small groups into the community meeting provides another opportunity to recognize and celebrate residents' lives.

Community Developer's Role

There is a crucial aspect of Live Oak Regenerative Community Development—the role of the change maker. About 10 years ago, when my wife and partner, Debora Cushman Barkan, and I sought to create a model for teaching others to develop regenerative communities, we defined the role of culture bearer or change maker as community developer. Anyone working in long-term care can assume this role—the activity director, director of nursing, the administrator, staff developer, restorative nursing assistant, nursing assistants, and so on. The role of community developer does not replace one's job description. It augments it and provides an expanded focus.

The Live Oak Community Developer has four major functions: teacher, leader, learner, and participant. Because we take responsibility to build community, we have to be teachers and leaders. Because community can only be developed from within, we have to see ourselves as participants. And because these are our elders that we are working with and the process is constantly evolving, we have to see ourselves not as experts but as learners, also constantly growing and evolving.

Perhaps the most important part of being a community developer is the commitment to being real and not separating oneself from the community one is serving by barriers of professionalism. The community developer is a new kind of professional, one who does not work to keep one's personal life separate from one's work, but, rather, shares who one is and one's beliefs and experiences as a platform for the practice of community building. Community development is a socially transformative experience in which the group is woven from the willingness of the community developer to encounter the group's members in an intimate, visionary, and consistent fashion.

Transforming The Culture of the Regulatory Environment: A Prescription for Change

The regulatory environment has a direct bearing on resident life in an eldercare environment and needs to be consistent with the common wisdom of society and the outcomes society desires. From my perspective as a community developer working in a small elder care facility, government and the regulatory process are currently among the biggest obstacles to creating environments that foster autonomy, self-esteem, and connection to community.

In California the defining factor in the implementation of OBRA has been conflict and distrust between the state and federal government, with facilities caught in the middle. As a whole new system of resident care and regulatory practice was being mandated, facilities were squeezed by a combination of overzealousness, chaos, and lack of clarity, at a time when the scope and complexity of the task required consistent guidance, common sense, and clear communication.

For us a telling example of the needless chaos created by the regulatory process was an experience we refer to a *leaky roofgate*. We call it that because it is one of those seemingly small, insignificant events that reflect something deeply inappropriate within our system of governance, something that goes against the grain of the fundamental values of our society.

Last year as a series of driving winter storms finally brought 7 years of drought in California to an end, we were constantly patching leaks with the expectation that when the rainy season ended, we would peel back the roof and make major repairs. Despite these efforts, a late-season 3-hour deluge opened up a few new leaks in the roof. The storm occurred late in the afternoon of June 4, a few days after new rules governing state and federal coordination went into effect.

The state surveyors came into the facility in the midst of the rain after a resident's family member called the ombudsman to express concern. When they came back a week later for an exit interview, we assumed that the surveyors would be satisfied that we had found and fixed the source of leaks within 16 hours and had documentation to show that we had worked on the problem all winter and that, indeed, we had already begun working with a contractor on major repairs. Instead, the surveyors gave us a $9,000 fine for putting at risk a resident who was nowhere near the leak and sent documentation to the federal government that our physical plant was out of compliance with federal standards.

The local office of the Health Care Finance Administration responded by putting us on a 23-day fast track for decertification from the Medi-Cal and Medicare programs even though the dry season had begun; according to the U.S. Weather Bureau, there was virtually no possibility of significant rainfall for at least 5 months.

The consequences of decertification would have been bankruptcy and the closing of the facility. This would have destroyed the habitat in which our residents live and thrive, and subjected them to life-threatening transfer trauma. As the clock ticked down on our decertification, we bounced back and forth between state and federal governments trying to get breathing room to do what we had intended to do anyway. The federal government told us the ball was in the state's court, and the state told us that it was the federal government that was holding things up.

Then, as we waited for building permits to be issued by yet another state bureaucracy, the Health Care Financing Administration (HCFA) lifted our ability to admit new MediCal Medicare residents and to readmit our old residents from the hospital. Fortunately, no one was refused readmission and subjected to transfer trauma, but the process took its toll on staff, family members, and residents who followed the drama in discussions at community meetings.

Live Oak is based on the assumption that we cannot significantly improve the quality of life within the long-term-care-environment unless we transform the culture of long-term care. The same truth applies to our regulatory system. The only way we will reform the system is by changing the culture of the regulatory environment— from a predominantly punitive system of policing people and organizations who are assumed have the worst possible motives to a regenerative regulatory model in which learning, growth, and socially responsible performance are facilitated and assisted by regulatory personnel. Otherwise, regulations and the pursuit of excellence will forever continue to be at cross purposes, and the American people will continue to be the losers.

We propose as a starting point for discussion the following *initiatives for change*. They have the potential to stimulate a creative process in which we rethink some core elements of our approach to government regulation. Although they are by no means definitive, the proposed initiatives for change go to the heart of the kind of cultural revolution that potentially could make governance compatible with resident autonomy, self-esteem, and connection to community.

Initiative for Change 1: Reaffirm Values of Participatory Democracy

We need to reaffirm democratic values and establish a standard for governmental regulation against which the performance of regulatory agencies and their employee performance can be measured.

There is no need to invent a new set of values on which to base regulatory reform. The values we need are deeply imbedded in our American tradition. For example:

- In our society there is an undercurrent of belief that all of us, including those in government, should treat others as we would care to be treated ourselves.
- We have long believed that public servants exist to serve the people and that their power derives from the consent of the governed.
- We have long believed that government must be accountable for what it does.

- We have long believed in due process and the presumption of innocence.
- We have long believed that people have property rights, and those who own enterprises have a right to make decisions about how their enterprises should be run.
- We have long believed that it is the legitimate function of government to protect consumers, our shared environment, and the weak and the powerless, and to advance the common good and common resources by establishing compliance standards for those enterprises that affect the common good.
- More and more as we stand on the brink of the 21-century, we are coming to believe that hierarchical, top-down decision making is inefficient and ineffective, and that a participatory, collaborative process involving all concerned yields the best results.

It is values such as these that need to be reaffirmed and translated into a standard of behavior on which performance is based. I can only imagine how different the process would have been for us if the regulatory performance during our recent inspections had been keyed to such a standard.

Initiative for Change 2: Shift From Regulation to Systems Management and Support Services

Historically, our operating paradigm has been a system of regulation in which change is achieved through a process that focuses only on what is wrong, and gives no consideration to what is healthy and progressive within a facility. We propose to shift the way we understand and define this task from *regulation* to *systems management and support services*.

The goal of regulation is control of negative outcomes and restriction of behaviors. The outcome of management is growth of the organization's capacity to achieve its mission. It involves the achievement of goals by encouraging certain activities and preventing others and the building of organizational structures to accomplish these goals.

The regulatory process is based on the use of power rather than empowerment of potential partners for shared objectives. It does not factor in the size of the wake created by the bureaucracy and the damage it can do to the small craft that cross its path. Good management needs to be aware of the impact of decision making and action, and help those it supports to own the process. Regulation functions through a narrow perspective; management must have both a narrow and broader perspective. Our nursing home reform efforts have moved from a broad catalog of thou-shalt-nots, which is the traditional format of regulation, to a whole series of positive commandments based on an enlightened view of who the elder in the nursing home is as a person and what she really needs. Unfortunately, the old paradigm of regulation through restriction and control is by definition incompatible with the new paradigm of supporting growth and development, and the system has thus come up against the inevitable necessity of its own evolution.

Initiative for Change 3: Shift From Hierarchy to Consensus and Diversity

A stultifying aspect of the hierarchical regulatory process is that basically it establishes a single way of accomplishing outcomes and then forces everyone into conformity. In America, our strength is our flexibility, pluralism, diversity, and ability to be creative. With opportunities for innovation that harmonize our differences in beliefs, styles, and practices into consensus around achievement of the common good, all our endeavors will continually evolve. This can not occur in a hierarchial model.

In a management model based on *consensus and diversity,* we envision personnel from the new *systems management and support services* helping people to organize themselves into *innovation zones* to develop successful elder care in which the intent and mandate of the legislation are actualized in the lives of nursing home residents. The process would involve forging a consensus about the bottom-line measurables of elder care and then helping local communities of operators, consumers, advocates for change, government personnel, practitioners, innovators, and perhaps an occasional philosopher, poet, or artist, to come up with models to apply social policy in this field—or in virtually any field of endeavor. These innovations can then be packaged as a menu that facilities can draw from, in a diverse system in which there are both common standards and genuine options for consumers.

Initiative for Change 4: Shift From Adversarial to Educational Regulation

Our regulatory culture presumes the worst from us. The adversarial nature of the system begins with the premise that facilities and their personnel do not intend to do the right thing. However, most of us in the proprietary and nonprofit sectors of the industry want to comply fully with the law—provided (a) it does not waste our energy and infantilize us; (b) we know what it entails; and (c) we have the resources to accomplish it. Most of us will strive to do the right thing, and only those who demonstrate a pattern of recalcitrance should be approached with an attitude reserved for those who have contempt for the law.

If we alter this fundamental assumption about the nature of the caregiving enterprise, the tone, style, and substance of government regulation will change. Imagine what would happen if the bulk of the huge sums of money spent regulating us had been used to provide us with education, training, and assistance to help us come into compliance with the intent and mandate of OBRA, teach us the process of inquiry that underlies the new federal assessment system, and come up with innovative and exciting ways of achieving the legislative outcomes.

With an educational approach we can be helped to identify our strengths, weaknesses, and goals for improvement, and then we can be provided with the guidance and technical support to implement policy, evaluate the outcomes, and improve ourselves during the next round. Ideally, our facility emphasis would shift from the ethos of CYA to a continuum of learning and organizational growth. Organizations that are busy growing in competence minimize the potential mistakes that threaten resident well being.

Even under the best of circumstances, society has yet to evolve to the point where everyone functions responsibly. With a predominantly educational approach to the implementation of socially mandated priorities, there will be those who avoid making the effort. They need a stick to drive them toward the carrot of freedom from the stick.

When it becomes apparent that a facility is not making sufficient effort to comply with regulations either because of incompetent management, corruption, or ill will, the policing function needs to be invoked. If a facility or company is poorly managed, misappropriates funds, or lacks the will or motivation to fulfill its mission, it will immediately show up in bottom-line measurables and in failure to participate earnestly in an educational process. This should trigger a negative review process reserved for those who require it. We need not even have a separate police force. Regulatory personnel working in an educational capacity with other facilities can put on a policing hat and provide that function when facilities require it.

Initiative for Change 5: Separate the Appeals Process from the Policing Process

Ours is a system based on due process. In the same way that the police department does not try suspected felons, the regulatory agency that issues citations for violation of regulations should not hear the appeal. Appeals should go to an impartial venue, outside the regulatory apparatus. The process of review should be independent, speedy, and inexpensive. A review should provide feedback to the highest levels of the bureaucracy about its shortcomings and be empowered not just to bring relief to the appellant but to bring remedy to breakdown in the governance process.

Initiative for Change 6: Study the Environmental Impact of Any Proposed Implementation

The process of developing changes in regulations should include a meaningful study of the impact of the proposed changes on the social environment in which care is provided. We would not think of building a cluster of houses on a hillside without an environmental impact report that looks at the nature of the environment as it is now, imagines the change that would be brought about by the new construction, and makes the best possible guesses about the impact on the environment. Based on this, a determination is made about whether the construction is worth the consequences of its impact.

Too frequently, the regulatory process produces an overall impact on the organizational environment and resident life that is the opposite of the intent of the legislation underlying the regulation. The art of regulation will not evolve until we begin to understand that the process of regulation is a key variable in the outcomes of resident care, and it needs to be studied and managed accordingly. Therefore, we propose that all changes in the way we manage the common good be subjected to a regularly updated environmental impact study that considers the impact of government regulation on the organizational environment.

Initiative for Change 7: Separate the Payment Function of Government from Its Regulatory Function

In a field like long-term care, where government is both the regulatory enforcer and the largest single payer, there is an inherent conflict of interest between the part of the government that pays for care and the part of the government that holds us to standards.

It should be the duty of the payment arm to pay the cost of care as mandated by law, and it should be among the duties of regulatory authority to assure that facilities are provided with the resources necessary to assure the common good as the law requires. As the system is now constructed, the payment and regulatory functions are combined both in HCFA and in the State Department of Health Services. Neither assumes the impact on compliance of failure to assess the cost of mandated services accurately. When payment and regulation are both in the same agency, there is no accountability: The payment arm fails to pay the cost of mandated care, and the regulatory arm holds us accountable without the will or ability to go to the source of the problem.

Initiative for Change 8: Pay the Full Cost of Legally Mandated Changes

Government has paid substantially less than the cost of implementation of the OBRA legislation. It is an abuse of power and a perversion of the democratic process for government to mandate standards of care, and then maneuver and manipulate itself free of the responsibility to pay the bill for those people for whom government is the largest single payer.

The whole question of how we determine the cost of care needs to be reassessed. In a consensus model, the entire community would have input into determination of the cost of care. If the resources are not available to manage in the way mandated, all concerned parties can reach a consensus on priorities.

Initiative for Change 9: Create a Field Response Force for Internal Review and Intervention Within the Regulatory Process

Regardless of the management approach used, regulatory authorities need internal review to assure that personnel are performing competently, and power is not being abused. Such internal reviews should go on both routinely and in response to complaints.

Throughout Leaky Roofgate we wished for a Field Response Force, a kind of systems-correcting SWAT team that could come on site and take the following steps: (a) suspend sanctions pending investigation; (b) evaluate the performance of government personnel; (c) remedy the situation if necessary, and (d) initiate steps within the bureaucracy to assure that should such practice prove to be inappropriate, it will not occur again.

Initiative for Change 10: In Internal Review, the Primary Approach Should Also Be Educational and Not Punitive

We would hope that the strategic shift from an adversarial model to an educational model would carry over to the performance of government bureaucracies. A model in which advancement is based on learning, growth, and professional development would enable the bureaucracy management to achieve its highest standards. Conversely, when members of the bureaucracy have performance problems, they should be enabled to respond to these by learning to meet appropriate job standards before they are subjected to sanctions. After all, we are all connected and any standard applied to one of us needs to be applied to all of us.

Initiative for Change 11: Cut All Paper Work by 50%

Systems management personnel need to get together with people in the field and specialists in computer technology, and establish zones of innovation to reduce the amount of time and energy devoted to paperwork. We need to ask the question: What of this do we really need to get the job done more effectively? Establishing a cap on how much paperwork government can require will bring a more effective learning curve for improving resident care, infection control, waste management, and outcomes in virtually any field of endeavor.

Extending the Regenerative Community; Its Much Bigger Than Nursing Homes

One does not have to be in an elder care environment to benefit from a regenerative community. Wherever we are in society we need healing, meaning, authentic roles, and connection to one another, to our traditions and to our future. Countless demographic, technological, and cultural changes have cut us adrift from the ways and traditions of the past, whereas a healthy, pluralistic 21st-century culture has yet to emerge.

Our Live Oak work is building culture. Our purpose is the development of models for the renewal of society's institutions. We truly believe that the restoration of the role of elders in our society will be the lynch pin of social transformation.

Our vision is to create an organizational vehicle called the Live Oak Elders' Guild to involve people, and help them grow and evolve. We envision hundreds of thousands, maybe more than a million, elders bringing a legacy of good to those who will follow behind. In virtually every environment in which we have worked, our experience has been that in the moments when residents are in the role of "elder," they are motivated by selflessness and good will, and are connected to a very deep wisdom. The poems of the Live Oak Poets' Workshop are drawn from a special garden of understanding that blooms when one is an elder.

We foresee the Live Oak Elders' Guild as a warm, friendly support community, a school of life, a self-help movement, a repository of lore and wisdom, a path to life mastery, and a vehicle for service and social change for people who take seriously the eldering path. We envision elders learning and teaching about how to create their legacy for future generations—investing their financial resources, wisdom, time, and love to leave a world behind for their children and their children's great-grandchildren that is an expression of the most meaningful truths distilled from long life experience.

With this vision before us, together with Rabbi Zalman Schrachter Shalomi of the Philadelphia based Spiritual Eldering Project, we have already begun to think about and test rites of initiation and passage for becoming an elder. At age 50, I have been initiated by my elders onto the path of eldering.

Imagine what a nursing home would be like if many of the people there have participated in such a conscious process of learning, growing, and serving many years before they enter the facility. The same Elders' Guild they belonged to in their home community would have a lodge in the elder care facility. The rituals and practices would be the same, providing constant reminders of one who has been and providing familiar landmarks for continued growth and becoming. Staff members or their parents, aunts, and uncles might be part of the Elders' Guild, and they would have learned the values of a culture in which elders are valued and empowered. The meeting place of the wider society and the elder care environment would be seamless.

Our greatest aspiration is to join with others to create the Live Oak Elders' Guild. We see this task as far greater than ourselves and something that can only be born of collaboration, consensus, and innovation.

We are standing on the foothills of the third millennium. It is an era that has yet to define its culture. Will it be a culture of peace or a culture of violence? Will it be a culture where every person has a human right to lifelong education and care when it is needed, or a culture defined by ignorance and strife? If we can be part of the creation of a powerful, wonderful cadre of elders, schooled in community development and committed to their grandchildren's grandchildren, the balance may very well tip in our favor.

Chapter Fourteen

Lessons from a Restraint Reduction Project

Joanne Rader, Joyce Semradek, Darlene McKenzie, and Mary Lavelle

The use of physical restraints on nursing home residents provides a graphic illustration of how individual autonomy can be limited in the name of good care—often without a sound scientific basis and without exploration of underlying problems or development of less restrictive alternatives. With funding from The Robert Wood Johnson Foundation, the Benedictine Institute for Long Term Care developed a comprehensive, collaborative 3-year program, (described in detail elsewhere [Rader, Semradek, McKenzie & McMahon, 1992]), to reduce the use of restraints in nursing homes in Oregon. The project was designed to

1. Develop criteria and guidelines for use of providers and regulators as they monitor progress toward physical and chemical restraint reduction
2. Provide training, protocols, and consultation for providers, regulators, and advocates to facilitate implementation of restraint reduction guidelines
3. Resolve problems that arise among consumers, providers, and regulators during implementation of the guidelines

Federal, state, and local rules regulating nursing home care, developed in response to past problems, are often viewed as barriers to change. However, the new federal nursing home regulations implemented in 1990 (OBRA 1987), encouraged dramatic changes in practice, focused on individualized care and outcomes, and provided an opportunity for us, through the restraint reduction project, to help transform nursing home care.

Despite the impetus provided by the regulations and the desire by nursing home staff to change, we discovered several obstacles to be overcome. These included conflicting regulations within and across governmental agencies, conflicting interpretations of regulations, uneven knowledge, and acceptance of new care standards among providers and regulators; lack of knowledge about alternative practices and no system of getting knowledge into practice or putting knowledge to use; a tradition of parental, "we know best" orientation among professional caregivers, families, and regulators; and organization of staff and work assignments according to a hospital model.

This chapter describes some situations that illustrate these obstacles and ways we found to overcome them. We believe the obstacles are not unique to Oregon, and hope the strategies we used will be useful to others who are confronting the challenges of changing practice to enhance the dignity and choices available to residents in nursing homes.

From its onset, the restraint reduction project was designed to foster collaboration. We structured educational opportunities and forums for sharing information among providers, regulators, advocates, and consumers so that all received new information at the same time. The main focus of the training and training materials was to encourage creative thinking about the provision of nursing home care. Those involved began to develop new working relationships as they discussed new standards of practice and identified barriers to change. In addition, we believed that information alone would not change practice and that those in positions of power must be involved in ongoing efforts to support change. Therefore, we established a project coordinating committee to serve as an avenue for collaboration and ongoing problem solving.

We also knew that nursing home staff would not or could not change unless they were assured that they had administrative and regulatory support for trying new approaches to care and for honoring the resident's right to choose to take risks. Collaboration has enabled providers and regulators to develop creative and sometimes "unconventional" approaches to individualizing and evaluating care. For example, placing mattresses on the floor to enhance mobility and prevent injury, and "allowing" residents to sleep through breakfast can now be done without fear of citation, and surveyors can spend more time interviewing residents and families, and encouraging creative solutions to challenging care problems. Comments from providers about changes in the way care is evaluated by state "survey" teams assures us that collaboration has resulted in changed attitudes among both providers and regulators.

Collaborative education and committee work have greatly improved provider access to those in charge of monitoring care and implementing regulations. Discussion and clarification of rules, and dissemination of this information through workshops and consultations have reduced misinterpretations of new guidelines. As an example, early on in the restraint reduction project we received several calls indicating that some surveyors and providers were viewing all residents who were in gerichairs as being restrained, for one draft of the federal OBRA regulations stated that *any* gerichair is a physical restraint. To involve key players in clarifying the definition and appropriate practice, project staff telephoned the head of the client care monitoring unit at the Oregon Senior and Disabled Services Division and asked her about it; her response was "Sometimes a chair is just a chair." In other words, if the resident had no ability or desire to get out of the geri-chair, it was simply a chair and not restrictive. This information was communicated to clinicians and surveyors through workshops and consultation so both groups knew that using a reclining gerichair for an immobile resident did not require a physician's order and was not a restraint. Something as simple as that kind of clarification saved an endless amount of time for both surveyors and providers. Everybody had a similar interpretation of the regulation and no time had to be spent debating it.

Collaboration has also helped when conflicting regulations functioned as barriers to change. Some facilities we work with have found that many of the things they want to do, in keeping with the OBRA emphasis on developing home-like environments, are impossible under current building and life safety codes. Specific problems are brought before the project coordinating committee and often are referred on to those who can offer solutions.

Conflicting interpretations of regulations can also cause difficulties. An example of this has been named the "chairs in the hall" saga. A local city fire marshall felt very strongly that facilities should not be allowed to place any chairs in the hallways even though the chairs were lightweight and easily removable, and there was a plan for removing the chairs from the hallways swiftly in case of fire. This local fire marshall interpreted the rules more conservatively than the state fire marshall or the HCFA Region X fire marshall. Several facilities had gotten approval for hallway chairs at the state level because many nursing home residents, especially those with dementia, liked to sit in the chairs. The chairs provided visual cues for residents who were pacing, a place to sit for residents who were restless and fatigued, and a place for residents to sit close by the nurses' station so they could see people and feel more secure and comfortable. But the fire marshall who took a strict interpretation was not in agreement with this decision. As a result, one facility was actually cited and fined for leaving chairs in the hallway.

The facility had been told to remove the chairs for a year or more, but had chosen to keep them in place while they requested a waiver. After the facility was cited and fined, they did remove the chairs. Up to this point there had been very few falls on the unit. When the chairs were removed, six falls occurred in one weekend. Also, several residents developed edema in their legs, and other became increasingly restless and agitated. The facility and representatives of the Senior Services Division continued discussions with the fire marshall, until a compromise was reached (comfortable, safe chairs with front wheels).

Our workshops emphasized the development of systems and practices that help staff learn about the individual resident, his or her past, likes, dislikes, and usual activities. We have found it useful to encourage what we call a "thoughtful process" of analyzing behaviors considered problematic and to discourage the use of terms such as "behavior modification," "behavior control" or "behavior programs," which imply a blaming, punitive and controlling approach. As Janet Tulloch says in Chapter 8, When people talk about "behavior" in nursing homes they are talking about misbehavior. We have conceptualized the process of analyzing behaviors and meeting needs as taking on a series of four roles—the magician, the detective, the carpenter, and the jester.

The first role is that of the magician. All of our manuals on restraint reduction come with magic wands becaue we feel that the magician's role is the most important staff role and the one that is most often missed. The magician's job is first to turn a resident's "problem behavior" into a symptom of an unmet need. As we have heard many times, all behavior has meaning; "problem" behaviors occur because the resident has some need that is not being met. When we can identify that need and find a new way to meet it, the chances are that the behavioral symptom will disappear. So the magician's first task is to change the behavior problem into a behavioral symptom of an unmet need. The second part of the magician's work is to "become the resident" and view the situation from the resident's perspective. For example, having a shower in a nursing home makes it clear why residents are aggressive during bathing, though taking the resident's perspective does not always require literally taking his place.

After staff members turn the behavior into a symptom of an unmet need and view the world from the resident's perspective, they are ready to become detectives. The detective's role is to look at what is going on inside the individual and what is going on in the external environment to see where that unmet need is coming from. The first question the detective asks is whether any physical problem or medication is causing the behavior. Then, the detective assesses the external environment. Generally in long-term care we do a good job at looking at what is going on inside the resident, but we have just begun to look at how external factors—the physical, organizational, and psychosocial environment—affect the behaviors of residents in nursing homes, particularly residents with dementia.

The third role that staff take on, after they look at what is going on inside the individual and what is going on in the external environment, is the role of the carpenter. In the past, staff wanted quick fixes: They wanted to fix things before they knew where they were broken. In this model, staff do not do the carpenter's work until they have done the magician's work and the detective's work. Then the carpenter decides what is the most appropriate intervention for the unmet need that is disguised as a behavior problem. For example, the carpenter has three categories of interventions to choose among for alternatives to restraints or psychoactive medications: changes in the organizational environment, the physical environment, or the psychosocial environment.

After the carpenter's work is done, the final role is that of the jester. If people do not go about this work with a sense of humor, they are not going to make it. It is important that the role of the jester imbues all the other roles, and that the magician and detective and carpenter know how to use humor with other staff and with residents.

As part of the thoughtful process, we have found it useful to help facilities identify ways in which their practice may be in conflict with their stated philosophy, the OBRA philosophy, or with the philosophy that they would like to put into practice. Their current practice was not achieving their intended goal of enhancing autonomy through restraint reduction, and their lack of awareness was an obstacle to change. For example, in one facility we worked with, there was a man who had had a stroke and who was aphasic. His preference was to take himself to the toilet. Even tough he knew he could ask for help, he did not want to ask for help; he wanted to do it himself. Sometimes when he was taking himself on and off the toilet—particularly off the toilet, he fell and bumped up against the wall and got some bumps and bruises. The day-shift staff members were comfortable with his level of autonomy, and they were working with him to remain restraint free. Unfortunately, the evening staff were not quite as comfortable with the inherent risks. One evening-shift nurse said, "My blood pressure can't take worrying about his falling on my shift." And what that nurse meant was that her emotional well-being and blood pressure were more important than the emotional well being of the resident. If we put it in that light for staff, they see the absurdity of the statement and their own attitudes, and this helps them examine the relationship between the new philosophy of care and their actual practice, to see where discrepancies might lie.

When that nurse said, "My blood pressure can't take it," she was also reflecting the traditional parentalistic, "we know best" orientation held by many professional caregivers, regulators, and families who feel that they are responsible for ensuring safety "at all costs" or fear blame for any negative event, such as a hip fracture. The nurses on the evening shift expressed concern about this man's risk of falling though they knew that he understood what was happening and was willing to take the risk. They knew because when he saw the evening shift coming on, he would hide on another unit to avoid being physically restrained.

Our parentalism tends to drive practice in a way that is in conflict with the philosophy of autonomy and restraint reduction. We believe we have to be completely, 100% responsible for everybody. Probably all of us working in long-term care have been told at some point, "You broke the resident's hip," as if we went up and pushed him when, in fact, it was simply that the resident was frail and at risk, and he fell. So there are real reasons why we felt that responsibility in the past. Not today. In "giving some autonomy back" to the resident we acknowledge that the resident might decide to make decisions that carry negative risks, such as falling. In exercising autonomy, the resident shares in the responsibility. The decision to be "totally responsible" is no longer ours to make.

It should be noted that there are several reasons why evening- and night-shift staff may be less comfortable with these changes than the day shift; one reason is that we still staff our nursing homes as if all residents were going to have surgery in the morning, with a high level of staffing on mornings and days, and fewer staff on evenings and nights. We do this even though we know that most residents have dementia, their behavior tends to become more difficult and complex in the evenings, and they do not sleep through the night.

Resistance to change is another obstacle we encountered. In the past, many individuals including physicians, nurses, regulators, and families refused to change their attitudes, beliefs, and practice, even in the face of overwhelming evidence that physical restraints were ineffective and even dangerous. We have found that making an analogy between the now-obsolete practice of using heat lamps to heal decubiti and using physical restraints often gets the point across. If a physician, nurse, surveyor, or family member insisted on using heat lamps as a treatment for decubiti, it would be challenged because it is recognized as an out-of-date, unsafe practice. Physical restraints will fall into the same category once those involved learn how to use alternatives.

The following example illustrates how staff in one facility challenged the unsafe practice of using rstraints and was able to come up with creative alternatives. In this facility a 99-year-old woman had two subdural hematomas as a result of falls that had occurred at home and in foster care. The doctor wrote in her chart "restrain at all times: the next fall *will* be fatal." At age 99 it is a sure bet that something is going to be fatal soon, and probably many of us think that if we had the freedom to walk and fall and hit our heads, that would be preferable to being tied up, and it might not be such a terrible way to go at age 99. This woman made it clear to her family and staff that she knew she was at risk for injury if she fell again, but she preferred to have her freedom—that was more important to her. During a staff inservice the woman was interviewed about the use of restraints, and again made her wishes clear. The staff decided to honor the woman's request not to be physically restrained. They talked with the physician, they talked with the family, and, most important, they talked with the resident before beginning a gradual process of restraint elimination. The woman expressed a willingness to wear a bicycle helmet, so the family purchased a helmet for her that she wore whenever she was up and about. She was restarted on a restorative program for walking. Staff also adapted her wheelchair so that it was more comfortable and provided a more solid seating surface, so that she was less likely to become restless and uncomfortable and fall forward in the wheelchair. She regained her ability to ambulate short distances independently and no longer needed or desired the helmet. This woman lived and died restraint free. She did not fall in the six restraint-free months before her death from stroke.

Under the old parentalistic philosophy, it would be difficult for a surveyor to argue with staff and physicians who justify the use of physical restraints for a woman such as this who has fallen numerous times and had subdural hematomas. But as long as care providers are willing to consider restraints appropriate, they may not think any further. The staff in this facility decided restraints were not an acceptable option, so they came up with creative, safe alternatives.

Ambiguity around who should pay for cost of change has also created an obstacle to change. There have been some unacknowledged costs of the move to restraint-free care, and as a consequence of this lack of acknowledgment there are no plans for distributing these costs. As the preceding story illustrates, we restrict and restrain people not only by tying them up with physical restraints but also by not providing appropriate seating and mobility equipment for them. Using the expertise of rehabilitation specialists and seating experts, it is sometimes possible to obtain needed equipment, or at least prescriptions for the equipment, but strategies to provide affordable, comfortable seating and mobility systems for residents are still in the planning stages.

One strategy for helping staff recognize when their practice is in conflict with the new philosophy of care is to encourage staff and others to identify residents' behaviors, such as hiding to avoid being restrained, that might indicate a violation of autonomy. Aggressive behavior associated with bathing, or pushing away food may also indicate loss of autonomy. Mary Lucero, a former nursing home administrator and current consultant in the care of persons with dementia, notes that we often treat residents with dementia as if they do not have the right to say no. Let us give you an example of how that was graphically brought home. The first author of this chapter was involved in a study on aggressive behavior during bathing, and because I believed in the importance of the magician's role, I decided that it was important to experience what it is like to have a shower in the nursing home. So I asked the nurse's aide to give me a shower. When I was thinking about getting this shower, I said to myself, "I'll do it with my bathing suit on, of course." Then I thought, "Do we go in and put bathing suits on our residents before we give them a shower? No, I don't think so." So I decided to do it the way the residents did it. I went into a room and took off my clothes and the nurse's aides came in and put me in the shower chair, which felt like a toilet seat. I had made sure to empty my bowels and bladder before sitting on that chair because I had seen a lot of incontinence with bathing. It was cold and although I was adequately covered when I was rolled down the hall sitting on that shower chair shaped like a toilet, there was a cool breeze blowing on my most private parts, and it felt as if I were not covered. Also, my feet, legs, and toes turned a purplish blue color, which makes you wonder about the design of the shower chair. We have seen that in people 80 or 90 years old, and here I was having the same experience.

When I later told people in workshops that I was showered in the nursing home, they said, "Oh, how brave you are, how brave you are to do that" and I thought, "Listen to that, do we say to our residents when they go in to take a shower or they've resisted or something, 'Oh how brave it is of you to go and take a shower'? No. If they show any kind of resistance at all we minimize that, saying, 'Oh what's the problem? It's no big deal, don't worry about it.' "

But we generally do not know what it is like to be cold, naked, and fearful. There is no other circumstance in which one human being can go into the room of another without his permission, go over to the bed, pull the covers back, drag the person out of the bed, take his clothes off, sit him in a chair, and drag him into another room despite his vebral and physical protests, with no one to help him even though he is protesting and screaming for help. In any other situation that would be termed assault. We are not sharing this story to make staff feel bad; we are saying that when looked at from the resident's perspective, being forced to take a shower feels like an assault. We need to look at the situation from the resident's perspective.

Viewing resistive behaviors of residents as an indication of the need to alter the way care is given encourages the use of alternative, nontraditional methods of providing care—such as towel bathing instead of tub and showers, and holding and rocking the person—which can make care activities more acceptable for persons with dementia. Here is a story presented in our workshops of a woman in a nursing home who was in a fairly advanced stage of dementia; she did a lot of crying, a plaintive sort of wailing, almost an animal cry. She had gone beyond the point where she could express her wishes verbally and was doing it through crying behaviors. The staff worked very hard at trying to figure out ways to make her more physically and emotionally comfortable. They tried several different activities—putting her bed out in the lounge area, music, things to hold, but nothing seemed to work.

It is difficult to listen to that for very long. You can feel the pain in the person's cry, and you feel helpless; after a while, you begin to feel irritated. I was working with the woman, and I was at the point of irritation when I decided to try something different. I went to the desk and told the staff, "Now look, don't call the protective services people, but I'm going to get into bed with this resident. I think she needs to be held. Let me just see if it works." The woman was lying in her bed on her side under the covers. I got on top of the covers with as much of my body in contact with hers as possible, put my arm around the woman's head and started stroking her brow. I told the woman what I was doing and asked if it was okay. Nothing in the woman's body language indicated that this was not all right with her, so I just lay there quietly talking to her saying, "You're okay, everything is okay now, there's nothing to be afraid of" and kept stroking her brow. After about 5 minutes, her crying stopped. There was a slight pause and she said, as clear as a bell, "How come you're so calm?" I was so startled, I let out a laugh and said, "I'm calm because there is nothing to be afraid of and you can feel this way too and I'm going to stay here until you do," and I stayed there with her and continued to stroke her and reassure her much as if she were a young child. In a few more minutes she fell asleep.

What that tells us is that there are ways to meet the needs of these residents, but they sometimes fall outside of what we have traditionally considered acceptable; we need to open our hearts and our minds and our care plans to commonsense, compassionate approaches, such as rocking and holding, and use those as caregiving routines for people who are distressed and restless and fearful. Interestingly, a Swedish study (Zingmark, Norberg, & Sandman, 1993) that looked at residents with dementia who felt homesick in nursing homes found that the residents liked very much to sit close to caregivers and in some cases even to sit on their laps. We know that residents will try to get in bed with other residents to get that same kind of comfort, but we have not established a way for staff or family or someone routinely to provide them with that kind of holding and rocking.

We also try to show staff the difference between guiding residents with dementia and trying to control them. People with dementia are usually very open to guidance, but they resist strongly being controlled—much like any other human beings. This makes it especially important to teach staff the intricate skills of communicating with people with dementia.

Let us conclude by sharing a story with you about a resident and a staff member who truly embraced the concept of individualized care, dignity, and autonomy. When Opal came into the nursing home, she was about 86 years old; she had dementia, but unlike most persons with dementia did not like being hugged or touched in any way, often pushing people away. The staff knew immediately that she was going to be a challenge. On her first evening in the facility, Opal refused her dinner and was asked if there was anything else she would like; she said she would like a little dry toast so staff went down to the kitchen and got her some toast, taking pains to get it back to her while it was still warm. She looked at the dry toast she had requested and said, "It doesn't have any butter on it." So the dry toast was taken back to the kitchen, and some new toast with butter on it was brought back to her. She looked the staff member in the eye and said, "I told you I wanted dry toast." Although Opal was demented and probably had some memory problems, there was more than that going on: Opal was testing the waters in her new environment.

Opal never believed she lived in a nursing home. She had been a business manager, and she thought she was running this particular unit; she would frequently bark out orders and tell people what to do. She was feisty, ornery, and sometimes downright mean. If she was sitting with something to drink in her hand, she had a habit of taking the glass of juice or water, milk, coffee, or whatever it was and throwing it on another resident or a staff person walking by. Sometimes she would wheel up behind other residents in her wheelchair and cuff them on the back of the head for no reason at all.

The staff always had to keep Opal within view so they could see what she was doing—not only because she might be imposing on another resident's well-being and space but also because she was at risk for falls. Opal was a member of the frequent faller club, but the staff knew that to restrain Opal would be to break her spirit and create aggression. The staff had embraced a restraint-free philosophy so fully that restraints became the "R" word and staff did not consider them acceptable, so they came up with a lot of alternatives. They placed Opal's bed very low to the floor and put a rug by the side of her bed; they made sure that when she was in a wheelchair her feet touched the floor so she could move herself. An alerting device was used so that when she would go from a sitting to a standing position, the staff would be alerted and could help her with whatever it was she was trying to do. The staff used that alerting device as a call light because Opal did not have the presence of mind to use the call light. Although she fell many times during a month, she was never seriously injured, but merely had bumps and bruises. She could not fall out of bed because her bed was so low she would just roll out of it. Sometimes she would roll out of bed, and then crawl over and get underneath her roommate's bed. She seemed to want to be in a small enclosed space.

As Opal got older and more frail, she was more at risk for falling and she would forget to set her wheelchair brakes, so staff put her behind the nurse's station so that when she stood up in her wheelchair she would have something solid to lean against. In addition, this position put other residents outside her reach and protected them from her unprovoked attacks. Also, while she was behind the desk Opal felt like she was in charge. She would naturally gravitate toward that area to be with the nursing staff anyway, because "she certainly wasn't a resident there, she was just part of the staff." Staff made that spot her space. There was a call system and a telephone there, and probably there were a few doctor's orders that Opal took that no one ever knew about. Opal would pull on the cords and the maintenance staff said she could not be left there, she needed to be moved before she destroyed the system. But the staff stood firm in the belief that the environment was there first for Opal and then for staff's convenience. They moved the telephone and call system wires over the side of the desk so that they were out of sight and out of reach of Opal, so that Opal could continue to hold court at her desk.

Eventually, it became clear to the staff that Opal was slowly dying; by this time she was 93 years old. When she would lie down in her bed she would roll out and crawl under her roommate's bed or out into the hall; she did not seem to want to be alone. Even bringing her bed out did not seem to satisfy her. She would be in the wheelchair and get very fatigued, then she would kind of ooze out of the wheelchair. One day she oozed out of her wheelchair and got into the little space underneath the desk at the nurses' station and immediately fell asleep. The evening shift was coming on and the day shift began apologizing for having a resident sleeping under the nurses' station, but the evening shift said, "No, No, No, she doesn't sleep very well anymore. If she's sleeping let her stay there." They got their heads together and realized that what Opal was trying to tell them was that she wanted to be near them, and she wanted to be in a covered, enclosed space to take some of her naps. So the staff got an egg crate, foam mattress, put a sheet over it, brought her pillow and afghan out, and used that as a napping/sleeping place for Opal.

It was rather peculiar to see a resident sleeping under the nurses' station, and some of the other residents and families were distressed by it. A medical records person suggested that staff put up a sign, so they made a sign that said, "Please don't be alarmed; this space has been established for the safety and comfort of this resident." As Opal grew weaker, the staff had to ease her into this space because she could not get down there by herself. At one point when a nurse was doing that, Opal raised her hand, looking as if she wanted to strike the nurse—which she had done in the past. The nurse pulled back but then she noticed that Opal's face did not look angry so she moved her head closer. Opal put her hand on the side of the nurse's face and caressed her. During the last week of Opal's life, she allowed the staff to hold her, cuddle her, and rock her when they were putting her down into that space, and she returned the hugs and the pats. Shortly before Opal died, she said to one of the nurses, "I can hear the angels coming." The nurse replied, "Yes, Opal the angels will be coming to take care of you, but until the angels come we'll be here to take care of you."

This work is sacred work in the most universal sense of the word, and those who have done the work for any length of time know its sacred value. Caregivers have a special responsibility to respect the autonomy of residents who depend on them to recognize and meet so many of their needs.

References

Rader, J., Semradek, J., McKenzie, D. & McMahon, M. (1992). *Restraint Strategies:* Reducing restraints in Oregon's long-term care facilities. *Journal of Gerontological Nursing, 18(11),* 49–56.

Zingmark, K., Norberg, A. & Sandman, P. O. (1993). Experience of at-homeness and homesickness in patients with Alzheimer's Disease. *The American Journal of Alzheimer's Care and Related Disorders and Research, 8* 10–16.

Chapter Fifteen

Prologue to the Future

Joyce Semradek and Lucia Gamroth

T he chapters in this book discuss obstacles to autonomy that are grounded in past ways of conceptualizing the needs of elderly persons for service, past ways of conceptualizing autonomy, and past ways of organizing, financing, and regulating care. The authors present challenges to the old ways of thinking about and delivering long-term-care services. And they offer specific alternatives to the old ways of doing things.

This final chapter revisits the major issues presented in the preceding chapters and outlines the changes in practice that can be derived from the various approaches discussed. It concludes with recommendations for innovations in long-term care that need testing and with questions for study to find ways to enhance autonomy and improve the quality of life for older persons in long-term-care institutions.

Concept of Autonomy in Long-Term Care

Three conceptual issues underlie the discussions of innovative solutions to institutional living for the elderly. The first issue involves the definition of autonomy, especially as it relates to independence and choice; the second has to do with individual autonomy and the rights of others; and the third is the link between power and autonomy.

Autonomy, narrowly defined, focuses on self-determination and is synonymous with independence. Defined thus, autonomy is beyond the reach of many elderly persons in nursing homes. Long-term care is by definition designed for those people whose needs or limitations are such that they are not independent. Further, the nature and degree of dependency vary considerably, even among those in nursing homes, and our conception of autonomy must allow for this variability.

Dependency may be imposed by cognitive and physical impairment. For example, many persons in long-term-care facilities are capable of making independent decisions but are dependent on others to execute them. Others may have cognitive limitations that interfere with decision making, though they are physically intact. Some residents have both cognitive and physical limitations that increase their dependency on others.

In addition, residents' ways of coping with the impairments, their past history of managing their affairs and their personal preferences influence their dependency. Low self-esteem, or a sense of powerlessness or hopelessness in response to altered capacity or lifestyle may make some residents reluctant to take responsibility for decisions. Further, a personal history of dependency may leave some residents unprepared to make decisions; to be expected to do so may pose an unacceptable burden. Still others may simply lack the information to make informed decisions. Isolation and disconnection are concomitants of dependency. The physical and cognitive impairments and the living arrangements of long-term-care facilities isolate residents from others and break their links to the past and hopes for the future. This disconnectedness and the emotional response to altered circumstances make it difficult to assess decision-making capacity and the authenticity of decisions.

The definition of autonomy for long-term care must consider the variability in residents' capacity and willingness to make decisions, communicate them, and carry them out. Further, it must be broadened to include personal identity, continuity, and meaning in life. The variability in residents' capabilities and backgrounds places a special burden on staff in long-term-care facilities to recognize and honor residents' preferences, and ensure that their rights are respected. The first step toward meeting this responsibility is conceptual clarity about autonomy in long-term care.

The second issue underlying the discussions in this book has to do with enhancing the autonomy of an individual in a group—with the notion that individuals who are self determining, have rights and responsibilities, and are "autonomous" nevertheless live in a facility with others who likewise have rights and preferences. The question then is when and how individual rights are given priority over the rights of the group or the common good, and when individual rights are subordinate.

In his discussion of the concept of autonomy in Chapter 1, Collopy makes clear that autonomy should not be viewed as a series of isolated decisions or acts but seen in the context of the individual's life (past history and future hopes), and the context in which the individual currently lives (in relationship to others in the community). However, in discussions about ways to enhance autonomy in long-term care there is little mention of the potential conflict between individual rights and preferences, and the rights of the community or majority. The good of the individual versus the common good has received little attention in long-term care because the individuals in question have had so little chance to exercise their rights that they have had few occasions to infringe on the rights of others. However, as we begin to focus on ways to enhance autonomy for residents in long-term-care facilities, this issue will become more important. For staff, who must consider the rights of all residents, it is already an issue.

Staff must not use other residents' rights as an excuse for imposing restrictions on an individual. Nevertheless, when staff members consider the good of all residents, they may find themselves in the position of denying one person's autonomy in the interest of others' rights. Some people will say that this not the staff's role; that residents should be making the rules governing their living situation. But staff inevitably will be expected to enforce the rules, and when residents are cognitively impaired or wish to avoid confrontation, staff will also be expected to make them.

The third issue underlying discussions of autonomy relates to the political origin of our notion of autonomy and the importance of power in that conception, as Collopy reminds us. The link to the political and to power makes it clear that autonomy is not something an individual can possess in isolation—it is a relational concept. The reference to politics also reminds us that capacity to act is not the defining characteristic of the powerful: Decision makers, not those who execute their decisions hold the power. Thus it is not merely the physical capacity of the residents in long-term-care facilities that determines their power: It is the way in which these facilities and the services they provide are structured.

When we talk about enhancing autonomy for residents in long-term-care facilities, discussion usually focuses on providing choice for the residents. However, autonomy is more than choice. It is being able to direct others to provide the assistance we need or being able to influence the decisions and actions of others that affect our living situation. Further, to enhance autonomy, choice must be meaningful in the context of the resident's life and the decisions authentic given the resident's life experience.

The conception of autonomy in long-term-care should therefore include not only the ability to decide for oneself, but also the ability to command others to carry out the personal decisions that one is not able to carry out oneself, and to influence the decisions of others as well as their actions. Finally, the ability to exercise autonomy should not be limited to those who can communicate their preferences verbally: Nonverbal communications should be heeded so that even the cognitively impaired are not coerced into conformity with someone else's wishes.

Enhancing Autonomy in Long-Term Care

A common theme in the chapters in this book is that the environment in long-term-care facilities is dehumanizing and creates increased dependence and powerlessness. This is attributed to a variety of factors but one singled out for special attention is the dominance of the medical model in the design, organization and ambiance of nursing homes. Recommended changes in the organization of facilities to provide long-term care emphasize the provision of residential and personal care services in contrast to the current organization of facilities, which emphasizes medical or therapeutic services. Nursing homes were conceived as part of the health care system and designed to facilitate the delivery of medical and nursing care as opposed to personal care. The hierarchical structure of the medical model has been cited as interfering with resident autonomy. The professional care providers—nurses and physicians—have greater knowledge with respect to therapeutic decisions and the power that goes with it. In nursing homes this power has become generalized to all areas of life. The suggestion to separate the medical care dimension from other dimensions of the residents' life calls attention to the possibility that decision making and resident choice in those different areas may differ. That is, residents may wish to have more say in matters of everyday life but may prefer to have care and treatment decisions made by a physician or nurse.

Two recommendations flow from these perceptions of the problem: One is to separate the health care services in long-term care from personal care services and residential or housing arrangements, and restructure the way in which services are delivered. The second is to work within the existing structure but make the environment more home-like and staff members more aware of their responsibility to respect individual differences and preferences.

Restructuring Long-Term Care

Two alternative approaches to restructuring long-term care have been proposed. The first makes the nursing home more like a private residence in the larger community. The facility is viewed primarily as a home in which residents maintain as much of their past life as possible. The resident has an individual apartment (or locked room in assisted living facilities) and other services are available on request or provided on a contract basis. Medical professionals and other personnel are available, but use of their services remains under the resident's control. The community-based, comprehensive Danish model that Wagner describes and Wilson's assisted living model are variations of this approach. In both cases, the resident is viewed as a citizen of the larger community.

The other approach focuses on the creation of a community within the facility; both residents and providers play a citizen's role in the life of this community and in its governance. Kari and Barkan present variations of this approach, which differ in the nature of the involvement each describes. Kari sees the nursing home as a political community; Barkan sees it as a spiritual community. She talks of bringing political mechanisms into the facility to encourage participation in the public life and governance of the community; he talks about ways to encourage and recognize the individual's contributions to the social and spiritual life of the community.

As Kari focuses on governance in the nursing home, she talks about giving power and control to residents over decisions that affect the public life of the community. Barkan does not focus on governance, but on creating a communal spirit and a sense of individuals' responsibility for each other, a sense of belonging and importance to the group. He makes links not to the broader community, but to the residents' past history and to the future.

Though Kari does not explicitly address the link of the nursing home to the larger community or to the health care system, the perspective she takes holds that participation in governance at the unit level will change the larger political system. In contrast, Barkan believes that the success of the model he is proposing for the nursing home depends on changing the larger political system. Further, he specifically recommends that a similar approach be used to change the politics and regulatory system governing nursing homes.

The distinction between communal living as shared living arrangements and "community" as a group of people who are organized for some purposes but retain independent living arrangements will be useful as new plans are implemented to enhance living for those with long term care needs. People are often forced into communal living when they have been accustomed to and would prefer a different arrangement. Residents can be given choices in the extent to which they share or participate in the life of the facility.

Any change in the long-term-care system will not only involve the organization of services within a facility but also the links between facilities and the larger system. The importance of recognizing these links in planning change at the facility level was illustrated in the chapter by Rader and others.

Individualizing Care in Nursing Homes

Changes that enhance autonomy but do not require restructuring the facility may be intermediate steps toward achieving one or the other of the models. For example, Turremark converted a medical facility in Sweden into a more home-like environment in which residents have greater control over their lives. In this approach, change occurs primarily in the orientation of staff rather than in the organization or internal governance of the facility or the payment structure. Strategies for immediate use that do not require structural change or additional cost were suggested in five categories by participants at the conference on Enhancing Autonomy in Long Term Care Facilities.

1. *Ways staff can recognize and honor residents' wishes despite their cognitive or other disabilities.* Careful observation of the resident enables staff to notice resistance to care, or positive responses to activities that could be repeated another time, and other nonverbal clues to preferences, likes, and dislikes. Observation also provides clues to explain behavior or change in behavior. Other advice is not to assume that staff know what is best but to ask residents to express their preferences. Other suggestions in this category focused on ways to improve the staff's understanding of the residents. However, much more work is needed to produce explicit guidelines for assessing and understanding residents with difficulty in verbal communication.

2. *Ways to help residents maintain contact and honor commitments from the past.* Specific suggestions for assisting residents to maintain contacts with family and friends included helping them use the telephone, send cards and letters, and shop even if they cannot leave the facility (by having something available within the facility or brought in periodically by local merchants); and making it easier for family to become involved in activities at the facility. Suggested methods of encouraging remembrance of things past included displaying old photographs of the local area or family. Methods of helping staff know the resident included home visits before admission, and providing information about the resident in his room on a bioboard or biographical book.

3. *Ways to help residents meet responsibilities for their own care, the ongoing life of the nursing home, and fellow residents.* Suggestions included focusing care conferences on what people can do rather than what they cannot do; asking residents what they would like to do and encouraging them to do it, allowing residents to help others and even asking them to take some responsibility, and, finally, developing a greater sense of community.

4. *Environments to enhance or support autonomy.* Suggestions included making the common areas of the facility as well as residents' rooms more home-like by allowing residents to furnish their own rooms or select furnishings that are noninstitutional. Making the dining room more home-like, serving meals family style, and providing greater flexibility at mealtimes and access to snacks all are easily implemented.
5. *Ways to help staff and family accept residents' choices when those choices do not conform to their expectations or wishes.* Specific suggestions included encouraging observations of residents to understand the reasons for their behavior, helping staff and family recognize when residents' refusals may be indications of depression and when they reflect residents' *authentic* choices.

Most of the strategies suggested for individualizing care involve expanding the choices available to residents. Choices are limited by finances, physical condition, and by what people know—not just their cognitive ability, but what they understand about available options. Choices are also limited by context—considerations for the effects of one person's choice on other people. Thus, one way to "discover" strategies to enhance autonomy is to ask questions about what can be done to alter existing constraints on choice and what choices are available even within unchangeable limits.

In identifying strategies for improving autonomy and decision making, it may be helpful to think about them in these categories—medical care, housing, and personal care. The areas in which people have choices will vary with their dependency and needs for assistance with housing (the amount of choice they have in where they live is largely financial). They will also vary depending on where people get services, how much help they need with personal care, and how much help they need with health care. For example, people usually do not have the information necessary to make decisions about medical care and therefore put themselves into the hands of the physician. (This may of course change in end of life care, with refusal of medications, etc.)

To be creative in enhancing autonomy, staff and others need encouragement and support. The strategies suggested earlier may stimulate other creative solutions to specific clinical situations. Some innovations will need to be tried and evaluated in multiple situations before they are widely disseminated. Many nursing homes are trying new ways to improve the life of residents, but often the innovative ideas and interventions are not widely known. We need a way to identify innovations and get them into the public domain so they can be used and tested.

Testing the Proposed Strategies in Research and Practice

Strategies for enhancing autonomy vary in the extent to which they have been tested—some have been used in practice and have been systematically evaluated; some have been tried in one place and anecdotal reports of their efficacy are available from staff, residents and family members; others have not yet been tried but are innovative suggestions based on the experience of caregivers, residents, and family members. Still others are recommendations of researchers who have studied autonomy and have derived potential solutions from their data. It is our position that the effects of all strategies should be evaluated and the outcomes documented so that there is a basis for recommending the interventions beyond the immediate situation for which they were created.

We propose that the creative ideas of providers and caretakers of all types be systematically evaluated as a basis for expanding our repertoire of strategies that work. To develop our knowledge of these strategies, the characteristics of residents with whom they are effective, and the circumstances in which they work, the best place to begin is in the nursing home or other facility in which they are to be used.

Providers and staff within facilities need to be encouraged to get involved in demonstration projects and systematic evaluation of innovations that they believe enhance autonomy—whether these are changes in staff assignments, care planning, scheduling to meet individual preferences for meals, and so on, or structural changes that alter private and communal living space. Academic investigators can provide technical assistance so that evaluation is not a burden to facilities, whose main obligation is to residents. A partnership between academics and those whose job it is to produce results can make a difference in the choices offered to long-term-care residents and in their autonomy during time spent in long-term-care facilities. Collaboration is needed in designing studies that will make a difference, implementing the changes, and evaluating results. A similar argument can be made for collaboration between researchers and policy makers.

From the obstacles to autonomy discussed in preceding chapters and summarized in the consensus statement (see Appendix) and from the alternative models and other recommended strategies presented as solutions to the problem, we can identify needed research. Types of studies that are needed can be grouped into six categories:

1. Clinical studies that focus on interventions used by caregivers to improve resident autonomy including studies of the characteristics of residents with whom they are effective and situational factors that enhance or inhibit their effectiveness.
2. Management studies that focus on interventions available to nursing home administrators, including nursing administrators, to improve services. Examples are studies comparing or evaluating various quality monitoring and improvement strategies; studies of staffing, staff organization, and education related to specific changes in practice; and studies of alternative ways of care planning, reporting, documenting, and communicating among staff to enhance the autonomy of residents and the efficiency of staff.
3. Demonstration projects that evaluate alternative models for providing personal, medical, and nursing services in various living arrangements.
4. Studies of alternative ways of financing long-term care that emphasize outcomes, especially those related to quality of life and autonomy.
5. Studies that focus on the conceptualization and measurement of outcomes for long-term care.
6. Studies of the effectiveness of regulations in maintaining standards and producing change in long-term-care practice.

Summary

Collopy ended Chapter 1 by raising the question of who should conceptualize autonomy for long term care. Our answer to the question is that the conceptual work should be done by all parties involved in the long-term-care system, just as all should collaborate in defining the issues and crafting the solutions to the problems confronting us.

We would like to conclude by raising a similar question with respect to the research agenda. Who should set the research agenda for improving autonomy in long term care? Should it be the academics and researchers who typically set research agendas, or should it be the providers, at all levels, who will be making the changes in services to those older persons needing long-term care? Again, we believe that the best approach is a collaborative one. The most fruitful research will come about through collaboration among academic researchers, policy makers, practitioners, providers, regulators, and recipients of care. Such collaboration, begun at the conference and furthered in this book, can provide the impetus for continuing improvement in the quality of life for long-term-care residents.

Appendix

Consensus Statement

As the population in the United States ages, the use of formal long-term-care facilities is increasing. Each year four out of every 100 persons older than the age of 65 enter a nursing home and many others use facilities such as assisted living, foster care, board and care, and subacute care. Though only 5% of the elderly population is in a nursing home at any one time, the lifetime risk of institutionalization is approximately 52% for women at age 65 and 30% for men. Thus, time in a long term care setting may become an experience of most Americans. There are two major subpopulations in nursing homes: short stayers who are receiving hospice or rehabilitation care or convalescing from acute illnesses, and whose average length of stay is less than 90 days, and residents who stay 6 months or longer, usually because of severe chronic illnesses or dementia.

Since the publication of the Report of the President's Commission on Bioethics in 1976, autonomy has been viewed as a key principle in health care. However, the role of autonomy in long term care, especially for elders who have significant physical or cognitive impairments, has only recently been discussed.

Autonomy, the right to have control over one's life, is a significant value to most people and is supported by a long history of legal and ethical thinking. Clearly, this value is not limited to elders in nursing homes. The enhancement of autonomy is a worthwhile consideration in all areas where elders live. For example, autonomy is a central consideration in the concept of "aging in place." However, potential loss of autonomy is often the reason given for avoiding "institutionalization," which makes it particularly important to examine autonomy in institutions.

Prompted by advocacy groups, as well as innovative programs both in the United States and abroad, the Benedictine Institute for Long Term Care convened a consensus development conference on Enhancing Resident Autonomy in Long Term Care Facilities on September 9 to 11, 1993. After a day and a half of presentations by experts in the field, a consensus panel including residents, social workers, nurses, administrators, advocates, physicians, regulators, and the public considered the philosophical and scientific evidence about autonomy in light of the following questions:

1. What factors hinder the autonomy of residents in existing long term care facilities?
2. What factors facilitate autonomy and self-determination of residents in institutional settings?
3. What are the constraints to instituting a model of care that supports resident autonomy and self-determination?
4. What short- and long-term changes in policy and practice are required to enhance resident autonomy?
5. What are the priorities for future research to enhance resident autonomy and self-determination?

This consensus statement is addressed to those sites where autonomy is most likely to be restricted over long periods, that is, nursing homes, assisted living, residential care facilities, and subacute care facilities. These will be collectively referred to as "facilities." The ability to exercise the right of autonomy in long term care facilities can be significantly enhanced or compromised by the attitudes of staff, the physical environment, the organization in which caregiving occurs, the way care is financed and regulated and the view of elders held by society. This statement provides an overview of the factors that support and inhibit or constrain resident autonomy, required changes in practice and policy, and priorities for future research to enhance autonomy in long term care.

Definition of Autonomy

The concept of autonomy is broad and not subject to narrow definition. It may refer to individual liberty, privacy, free choice, self-governance, and moral independence. In the best of circumstances, autonomy refers to the freedom to make decisions (decisional autonomy) and to act on those decisions (autonomy of execution). Yet defining autonomy solely in terms of decisions neglects the broader view that having autonomy gives meaning to life.

Further, defining autonomy narrowly places autonomy beyond the reach of many elderly persons in nursing homes. Indeed, defined narrowly, the very notion of autonomy in long-term care is an oxymoron. Long-term care is by definition designed to care for and protect those people whose needs or limitations are such that they cannot live independently.

For example, many persons in long-term-care facilities may be quite capable of making independent decisions but they are physically unable to execute them. Other residents are limited in their choices by financial dependence. Still others are cognitively limited in the ability to make independent decisions, though they may still be able to function physically. Depression, low self-esteem in response to disease or disability, or a sense of powerlessness or hopelessness may make some residents reluctant to take responsibility for decisions. Further, a personal history of dependency may leave some residents unprepared to make decisions; they may choose not to act autonomously. Because residents are frail and dependent, family members may wish to participate in decision making and may have views inconsistent with resident's wishes. Finally, some residents may lack the information to make informed choices or the personal strengths and assertive skills to challenge persons in authority.

In addition to their limiting personal characteristics, isolation and disconnection are common among the elders in virtually all long-term-care environments. Not only are they isolated from one another, but their relationship to time is skewed as they grow disconnected from their past and their future. This lack of a meaningful life in real time weakens the will and the human spirit, which form the basis for autonomy.

Clearly, in long-term care the definition of autonomy must be modified to consider the realities of resident limitations and broadened to include personal identity, continuity, and meaning in life.

Factors That Inhibit Autonomy

In existing long-term-care facilities, autonomy of residents is inhibited by the attitudes of staff toward residents, the organization and environment of facilities, and the policies governing long-term care. All three levels—staff, facility and system—are affected by our society's negative views of aging and old age. In the United States we lack a positive philosophy about growth, development, and special capabilities in old age. High value is placed upon youth and the productive years; the later years of life are often viewed as a time to be endured, not a time of further growth and development. This ageism translates into care givers and care systems that are largely constrictive and inhibitory of autonomy.

Staff Issues

As noted earlier, residents in long-term care often have significant levels of disability, limiting their capacity to independently carry out activities of daily living. As the range of independent actions shrinks, the need for more autonomy of decisionmaking increases. However, staff often acts on the principle that if a resident cannot execute a decision, the resident cannot make a decision. That is, staff equate loss of physical capacity with loss of decisional autonomy. Equally important in restricting autonomy is staff's tendency to view the ability of persons to make decisions as an "all or nothing" phenomenon rather than as specific to a particular decision. In addition, staff tend to treat people who are cognitively impaired as if they do not have the right to say "no." Further, staff often assumes that a person who has problems with communication (e.g., as a result of a stroke) also is cognitively impaired. Though residents who can no longer indicate their decisions verbally may do so through actions or prior expressed wishes, staff often ignores these cues.

Working in an environment that places the greatest value on accomplishing tasks and routines, staff has no training in or support for individualized care that calls for knowing the resident as a unique human being. Staff often lacks information about the resident's history, values, and preferences, making it difficult to recognize authentic or unique choices. Furthermore, frequent staff turnover and low staff/resident ratios make it difficult to develop the knowledge necessary to promote individualized approaches. And staff members may bring limitations and a history to the caregiving situation that put them in direct conflict with what they are trying to foster.

Facility Issues

A significant concern in our society is whether those who stay in long-term-care facilities for long periods should be primarily treated as "patients" in a health care setting or as "residents" in a more home-like environment. Most nursing homes follow a hospital/medical model of care, which focuses on medical routines and tasks and not on the promotion of individual autonomy. In the narrow medical model, "good care" is generally defined by how well staff meet the medical care needs of a person and by the facility's level of sanitation. Nursing tasks and schedules take priority over individual needs, preferences, and independence.

The medical model tends to encourage a paternalistic, "we know best" approach by staff. Residents who are compliant and follow the medical regime prescribed by others are rewarded. Those who do not tend to be labeled as unreasonable or difficult, rather than being viewed as asserting their right of refusal; they may encounter subtle forms of retaliation for their autonomy. The staff-resident role is generally one in which staff believe they can determine what is in the resident's best interest better than the resident can. Residents are expected to defer to staff and cooperate with all recommendations; those who fail to cooperate tend to be devalued by staff. This orientation, in which staff are expected to define and solve problems, precludes opportunities to develop resident capabilities and facilitate their decision making or attempts to act on decisions.

Long-term-care facilities place low priority on the development of a context or community within the environment that nurtures autonomy, self-esteem, and meaning in life. Further, the design of facilities does not promote community. Instead, institutions reinforce limitations on the ability of residents to retain an identity, forge new relationships, learn how the facility works, and redefine their relationships to their new life and to the wider world.

Common features of long-term care facilities are regimentation and regulation—something not frequently encountered in people's own homes. For the resident, regimentation contributes to a pervasive sense of loss of control. Moreover, the hierarchical nature of organizations in which caregivers' work hinders autonomy. Caregivers who feel disempowered (i.e., who perceive that they lack the authority to make and carry out simple decisions without permission) or are not included as contributing members of the care team are less able to promote autonomy for the residents for whom they care. The routines and rigidity inherent in organizational structures have similar effects. Further, staff who are burdened by the tasks of caregiving seldom have time to facilitate choice and decision-making. (Enabling a person to do more for himself or herself can initially take more time.) Many nursing homes are understaffed, and direct care staff are paid shockingly low wages. Further, these staff are not rewarded for enhancing residents' autonomy or function.

Another barrier is an overriding philosophy of care that focuses on perceived "safety at all costs" rather than individual choices and reasonable risks. While the Nursing Home Reform provisions of OBRA of 1987 mandates a resident-centered approach to care, in actual practice the fear of being blamed or sued should an injury occur may prevent staff from being truly resident centered and respecting a resident's right to take risks. In addition, many facilities are geared to the needs of cognitively impaired residents and may neglect the needs of those with intact cognitive function.

The physical environment of long term care facilities can also limit autonomy. Limited space, sharing rooms, lack of personal possessions, and lack of privacy all encroach on the resident's autonomy.

System Issues

Many regulations geared at protecting vulnerable members of society and ensuring high standards of care may have the unintended effects of limiting individual residents' autonomy. For example, while OBRA 1987 provides opportunities for resident choice and self-determination, other existing regulations continue to restrict the autonomy of residents. Federal, state and local regulations sometimes conflict with each other. For example, local building and life safety codes may limit what can be done to create a more home-like environment, which is emphasized by OBRA. Regulations are often directed at the "lowest common denominator," leading to restrictions in choice for all in order to protect the few. Further, OBRA requirements for documentation may cause caregivers to choose between filling out forms or spending time with a resident.

Because of a lack of philosophy and conviction, providers are not proactive with the regulations. At times, interpretations of regulations also hinder resident autonomy. Further, adversarial relationships between providers, regulators, and consumers often create conflict. Surveyors approach facilities with the expectation that there is something wrong to be discovered rather than working collaboratively to create conditions whereby resident autonomy is enhanced. Such relationships limit the development of innovative approaches to meeting resident needs and preferences.

The system of payment for long-term care also inhibits autonomy. Most of the public funding for long term care comes from Medicaid, yet to be eligible for Medicaid, persons must relinquish all their resources. Thus they are in a dependent position with no resources that might enable them to return to independence and autonomy. Policies regarding the kinds of help deemed appropriate for persons receiving public funding can also reduce autonomy. For example, while having a private room is recognized as important to autonomy, persons receiving public funds generally do not have this choice under the current financing system. Reimbursement policies which limit coverage of types of assistive devices (e.g., the proper type of wheelchair that would make a resident more independent) also restrict autonomy.

Factors that Support Autonomy

Staff

Caregivers who know residents as unique human beings are more sensitive to issues of autonomy and personhood and are more likely to facilitate self-determination in others. They can significantly promote the residents' autonomy by being agents in carrying out choices of residents unable to do so for themselves and by supporting residents' problem-solving skills and acceptance of reciprocal responsibilities. A relationship of mutual interest and respect promotes autonomy in both the resident and the caregiver. This is important because staff who feel disempowered are less likely to promote and support resident autonomy. In facilities that promote resident autonomy, training to develop capabilities in problem solving and self-determination is provided to both staff and residents.

Certified nursing assistants participate in care planning, their ideas are sought and their contributions are recognized.

Facility

Several facilities in the United States and in other countries have developed models or strategies for increasing the autonomy of residents in long-term care. All are based on a well-thought-out and clearly articulated philosophy of care. These models show that it is possible for persons with long term care needs to exercise greater autonomy and self-direction without unduly compromising care and care outcomes. Indeed, not only is care not compromised, but well being is enhanced. Characteristics of care settings that facilitate autonomy are described subsequently.

Individualized care promotes and puts into practice the concepts of normalcy in daily life, privacy, self-determination, choice, personal dignity and a warm, home-like physical environment. The focus is on the abilities of a resident, not disabilities. The resident exercises primary control over his or her own life rather than the institution maintaining this control. This means that residents generally direct their own care, actively participate in decision making, problem solving, and control of their schedules, living space, and food intake. In other words, the needs of the person are given priority over facility routines.

Adequate information about choices, alternatives that are available, and a chance to discuss the options are all crucial to enabling residents to exercise an informed decision. The shift in values involves embracing the concepts of shared responsibility, bounded choice, and managed risk. These programs recognize that one cannot take away all real or perceived vulnerability without taking away individuality. Choosing from among risks is accepted as a part of normal life. Residents also need to be provided with reasonable time to make decisions.

Self-esteem and connection to others are fostered. For example, through daily meetings, creative writing and the establishment of the value of being an "elder," residents are provided opportunities to grow. Residents are encouraged and provided opportunities to maintain relationships and activities outside the facility.

The orientation of these models encourages the view that residents can take responsibility to help themselves and care about their peers. The range of diverse interests among residents is clearly recognized. Problems are defined and studied in a fuller, more complex way and solutions incorporate multiple inputs. Residents are involved in decision making about activities that affect their lives. In some cases, resident councils are an important vehicle for input into facility policy and organizational change.

Programs in which residents can direct their own care and help to solve problems affecting their care support autonomy. Moreover, programs that support a self-care model, focused on residents' abilities and strengths while offering support in areas in which residents' desire or need assistance, promote autonomy.

Privacy and control over one's environment (e.g., choice of single-occupancy rooms and safekeeping of possessions) are prerequisites for expressing autonomy. The ability to create a home environment with one's familiar furniture and cherished possessions is important. Control over room temperature, decorations, and dress contributes to a sense of worth, as does greater control over one's daily schedule of activities and care. Dining facilities are personalized. Public spaces foster community involvement and shared decision making.

System

Regulations can be useful in stimulating enhancement of autonomy in long-term care. The OBRA 1987 guidelines have been the stimulus for dramatic reduction or elimination of restraint use in long-term care, and they have had a positive effect in assisting residents to reach their full potential. Similarly, regulations may be used as baseline standards that support autonomy of the resident including regulations requiring disclosure of important information and the development of programs for involvement of residents in governance. Collaborative development of guidelines for practice, involving consumers, providers, and regulators, is a key in enhancing autonomy. Further, for change to occur in the way in which caregivers practice, training must involve all parties who have an impact on practice including regulators and families.

In models of care where residents have greatest autonomy, payment for long term care is not made directly to the facility. Rather, older persons receive pensions and purchase the services they wish from the facility. Their pensions are sufficient to cover the services and staff needed to help the residents remain independent. This system gives older people considerably more control over their care and their daily life.

Recommendations

Autonomy must be recognized and enhanced to the maximum extent possible for all persons who live in long-term care facilities. The enhancement of autonomous decision making and ability to act on those decisions should be an integral and essential aspect of caring for such persons.

These recommendations focus on changes in policy that will remove current barriers to autonomy, changes in philosophy, and practice that will incorporate the features of the models described here, and research in those areas where outcomes are not clear with current data in the United States.

Philosophy: The board, administrator, staff, residents, and families should all participate in developing the facility's philosophy statement, which includes principles of autonomy, and then examine on an ongoing basis how life in the home expresses that philosophy.

Policy Changes

Evaluate all regulations for the manner in which they restrict autonomy. We must identify and work to change state or federal policies that create barriers to autonomy. Regulations can also be used to enhance autonomy. Requirements for the provision of transportation, the use of personal furnishing and possessions, and information and disclosure requirements for residents about choices and implications of those choices are all amenable to sensitively crafted regulations.

Establish a formal structure to identify problems and develop solutions which are agreeable to all stakeholders—regulators, providers, residents, and families. Shared decision making can be used to foster respect and promote creative solutions. Through discussions, respect between regulators, providers, residents, and family members can be fostered.

Modify the reimbursement system to enhance autonomy. Autonomy as an outcome measure of care could be used to provide for rewards in reimbursements.

Look at alternative methods of funding long-term care that are more consistent with resident autonomy than the current system.

Practice Changes

Involve residents and staff in facility governance. Individuals need to be included in effective mechanisms for agenda setting, decision making and policy change. Use a variety of ways to get input (e.g., resident councils, focus groups, and regular community meetings). Input from these meetings needs to be made integral to the decision making operations of the facility, and result in actual outcomes. All participants can be trained to develop public skills, such as agenda setting and negotiation. Such meetings can be used to promote a sense of community where it is safe to share feelings or complaints.

Involve all individuals in decision making affecting their lives within the organization. Staff and residents should examine and critique the facility mission statement and how practice reflects that philosophy, to ensure concordance with what is "preached." The culture of the setting—what is and is "not done here"—should also be examined. The pattern of residents' daily life before admission should be identified with the goal of increasing facility flexibility to accommodate valued individual routines and activities.

Residents should be more involved in decisions about the risks they choose. Such decisions can be approached from the viewpoint of what would take place in their own homes.

Residents should be encouraged to be involved in *their* care and shaping of the environment. To make these changes, an organizational environment that is safe for change needs to be created and supported by administration.

Alter ways of assigning staff, planning care, and evaluating performance so that caregiver responsibility is promoted and un-

derstanding of resident preferences is improved. Permanent staff assignments are essential to this process. Facilities should begin the process of education to help staff feel responsibility for enhancing residents' decision-making opportunities. This can be done in several ways. Educational programs, reinforced by clinical consultation and follow-up, should emphasize person-centered care rather than task-oriented care. Attention to psychosocial issues can be modeled. An expectation that caregivers will consider the history of the person's former self, values, and preferences can be made a part of the culture of the facility. Relationships that are compassionate, rather than distanced professional ones, can be fostered, recognizing, expecting and encouraging the full range of residents' emotional expressions, including anger, jealousy, and fear. Staff development should focus on ways to increase receptive and expressive communication, both verbal and nonverbal, with residents.

Flexibility in the way things are done, e.g., scheduling and providing personal care, should be adopted.

Consistently seek expanded opportunities for resident choice. Everyone should have the option of a private room or, when a private room is not preferred, the choice of a roommate. We recognize that certain factors may influence the provision of private rooms (e.g., current Medicaid expectations and the resident's desire for a roommate or companionship). However, the essential determinant should be the resident's choice rather than an established rule or economic constraint. Physical environments should be individualized using personal furnishings and belongings. Common rooms should be made similar to the home setting—for example, turning day rooms into living rooms and providing access to a well-stocked refrigerator on a 24-hour basis will greatly contribute to a sense of normalcy. Residents should have a say about what they eat, when they sleep, rest and carry out other activities.

Priorities for Future Research

A wide variety of potential research projects is possible when considering ways to enhance autonomy for residents in long-term care facilities. The following should be given priority:

1. Evaluate the use of reimbursement incentives to reward improvements in function or autonomous actions.

2. Develop and test alternative models of organizing and delivering services to those needing long term care. Demonstrations could range from tests of community-based, comprehensive care delivery systems to comparisons of variations within one facility, such as use of special care units and use of heterogeneous units.

3. Develop and test alternative models of environments (physical, psychosocial, and organizational) that support autonomy and individual needs.

4. Develop and test methods and skills that caregivers can use in assessing the decision-making capacity of those with dementia or limited verbal communication and test strategies to enhance autonomy in functionally and cognitively impaired residents.

5. Develop quality care indicators that focus on positive outcomes, such as increased function rather than measures that focus on negative results or untoward events, such pressure ulcers.

Consensus Panel Members

Kenneth Brummel-Smith, MD
Section of Geriatrics
Portland Veterans Administration
Medical Center
Portland, Oregon

Jackie Coombs
Resident
Laurelwood Care Center
Belleview, Washington

Meredith Cote, JD
Director
Office of Long Term Care
Ombudsman
Salem, Oregon

Maggie Donius, RN, MN
Gerontological Clinical
Specialist
Benedictine Nursing Center
Mt. Angel, Oregon

Walt Friesen, MA, BD, MS
Licensed Professional
Counselor
Beaverton Family Counseling Center
Portland, Oregon

Steven D. Helgerson, MD, MPH
Associate Regional Administrator
Health Care Financing
Administration
Division of Health Standards
and Quality
Seattle, Washington

Lana Huiras, CNA
Colton, Oregon

Darlene A. McKenzie, RN, PhD
Associate Professor
Oregon Health Sciences University
School of Nursing
Portland, Oregon

Maurice Reece
Administrator
Marian Retirement Center
Sublimity, Oregon

Marion Sodergren, RN
Director of Nursing
Robison Jewish Home
Portland, Oregon

Carter Catlett Williams, MSW,
ACSW,
Social Work Consultant in Aging
Rochester, New York

James C. Wilson
Administrator
Senior and Disabled Services
Division
Salem, Oregon

Index